Ways of Meaning

Ways of Meaning

An Introduction to a Philosophy of Language

Mark de Bretton Platts

ROUTLEDGE & KEGAN PAUL
London, Henley and Boston

First published in 1979
by Routledge & Kegan Paul Ltd
39 Store Street
London WC1E 7DD,
Broadway House,
Newtown Road
Henley-on-Thames
Oxon RG9 1EN and
9 Park Street
Boston, Mass. 02108, USA.

Set in 10 on 11 Times Roman
and printed in Great Britain by
Ebenezer Baylis and Son Ltd
The Trinity Press, Worcester, and London.

British Library Cataloguing in Publication Data

Platts, Mark de Bretton

Ways of meaning.
1. Languages – Philosophy
I. Title
401   P106   78-40699

ISBN 0 7100 0000 6
ISBN 0 7100 0001 4   Pbk

For Hilary Putnam

Human language is like a cracked kettle on which we beat out tunes for bears to dance to, when all the time we are longing to move the stars to pity.

Flaubert

The system of sounds is the instrument on which we articulate the words of our language; if one of these elements is modified there can be diverse consequences, but the fact in itself does not concern words which are, as it were, the melodies of our repertoire.

Saussure

Reality is infinitely varied compared even with the subtlest workings of abstract thought and does not tolerate broad, clear-cut distinctions. Reality strives for infinite graduation.

Dostoyevsky

Contents

Contents

PART FOUR: LAW AND NO-BLAME

Preface

Evangelism, however worthy its cause, is distasteful; I have tried to write an unevangelical book, but it has not always proven easy. The idea for this book arose partly from difficulties I and many others have encountered in recent years in teaching the philosophy of language and many topics in philosophical logic. These difficulties are grounded in the *inaccessibility* to the average, or even to the good, student of much crucial recent work in these areas: this inaccessibility is in part material, many important contributions being published in expensive, and sometimes obscure, collections; but the much more important element is the great difficulty of much of the work published, a difficulty that places such work beyond the intellectual reach of all but the best students. In this book, therefore, I have tried to present and discuss what seem to me the most important recent contributions to the philosophy of language in a straightforward and accessible manner; in so doing, I have tried to avoid debasing or belittling those contributions. Needless to say, I think the importance of these recent developments transcends passing fashion; I also think that this is insufficiently grasped and appreciated even by many professional philosophers. Hence the recurrent danger of evangelism. The surest safeguards against this threat are as great a clarity of expression as possible and a persistence in drawing out the most general, and often unstated, assumptions built into the views expounded and defended; so I have tried, stumbling, to follow these safeguards.

I presuppose a fairly minimal knowledge of elementary, first-order logic; but I have not bothered to insert into the text various proofs relied upon (proofs, for example, of T-sentences) since the proofs concerned are elementary and tedious. There will be those who will see this as a snub to formal logic, but they will be wrong. The presentation of the views under consideration follows what some might consider an eccentric route; in the Introduction, I have tried to indicate the route I shall be following, and to give a passing defence of that route. I have attempted to present an introduction to one philosophy of language; I have not attempted to write *Summa Semantica*.

My most persistent intellectual debt is to John McDowell, who first taught me about the philosophy of language here expounded, and from whom I have never ceased to learn. He also read the penultimate version, and saved me from a thousand errors. Others to read that same version, or parts thereof, and to correct many mistakes and to make useful suggestions for improvements, were Samuel Guttenplan, Ted Honderich, Mary Mothersill, Paul Snowdon, Roger Scruton and Michael Woods. Nearly all of the final version was written while visiting, under the aegis of the British Council, the Instituto de Investigaciones Filosóficas of the Universidad Nacional Autónoma de México; the stimulation provided by that visit was matched only by the great hospitality of the people there. Somewhat unfairly, I must single out Hugo Margáin as having helped me greatly with the final version. During the completion of the work I profited greatly from discussions with Ian McFetridge who has helped and encouraged me at numerous points. My publisher, David Godwin, has assisted me way beyond the bounds of duty. I am also aware of somewhat more ancient, though no less substantial, debts to A. J. Ayer, David Charles, Dorothy Edgington, Gareth Evans, David Hamlyn, James Hopkins, Hans Kamp, J. L. Mackie, Colin McGinn, Christopher Peacocke, Hilary Putnam, P. F. Strawson, Barry Taylor, Frank Thompson, and, especially, David Wiggins, while my indebtedness to the writings of Donald Davidson should be obvious on more or less every page.

Such acknowledgments deserve a better outcome. It is no formality to stress that all responsibility for the errors remaining is mine.

Birkbeck College   M. de B. P.
London

Introduction

Language not having existed, man had to invent it. Not that the invention was planned: given that such planning would require a level of mental sophistication that only language makes possible, it could not have been. But the process of invention has not stopped; language continues to evolve, usually still, though now no longer of necessity, in an unplanned manner. So it is that the student of language is in constant danger of losing a part of his subject-matter. But the difficulties consequent upon linguistic evolution – those involved in extracting a synchronic view of a time-slice of a diachronic process – are far from being the greatest that such a student encounters.

Language is the product of linguistic behaviour; languages exist only as the abstracted media of linguistic exchange. The variety of such exchange, the diversity of that behaviour: these constitute the profoundest difficulty for any attempt systematically to theorise about language, the abstraction. The extra-linguistic contexts of both speaker and audience in which utterances are produced and heard; the intentions of the speaker, the response he intends to secure in his audience, and the responses, if any, that actually occur; the kind of action, if any, over and above that of saying something, which the speaker sees himself as performing (e.g. warning the audience of some danger); the kind of action, if any, over and above that of saying something, which the speaker actually performs (e.g. frightening his audience); the pattern of noises uttered, the intonations and inflexions; the gestures, if any, accompanying the emission of noise: all these factors are variable in seemingly countless ways, combining to produce a diversity and complexity of linguistic behaviour which threatens to defy comprehension.

But comprehension there is. As native speakers we find the

1

linguistic acts performed by members of our native speech-community comprehensible; we understand such actions readily, to the point of doing so quite unreflectively. As theorists of linguistic exchange our primary, and forbidding, task is to render that native comprehension itself comprehensible; to do so is to consider reflectively our usual unreflective comprehension. We have to consider quite what is involved in understanding a linguistic action; we have to determine quite which elements, in which manners of combination, are to be drawn upon in explanation of that understanding. We have to consider quite how it is that we identify the *language* in which a speaker performs a given action, shading down into the subtlest distinctions of idiolect; the discrete *sentence*, or sentences, used in that performance; the *mood* of the sentence – indicative, imperative, interrogative – so identified; the characteristics of the *sentential components* (e.g. which elements are subject expressions, which predicative, which demonstrative); the *literal meaning* of the sentence uttered; the manner in which that meaning is a function of the meaning of the sub-sentential elements.

The initial assumption of this book is that in rendering linguistic comprehension intelligible a central, ineliminable role will be played by a notion of *the strict and literal meaning of a sentence*. This assumption is subsequently given a partial defence by an exact specification of the role this notion is to play (Chapter II, Section 5); but ultimately, the defence of this assumption is merely that I cannot conceive of what a theory would be like that did not rest upon it.

This notion is, I think, a perfectly intuitive one; partial support for this is found in the ease with which intuition can distinguish the literal meaning of what is said from further shades of meaning (Chapter III, Sections 2, 3). But even if such intuition is taken on trust, it does not tell us how the notion is to be defined nor how it is to be applied. Ultimately, the notion can be defined only by consideration of the role it has to play (Chapter II, Sections 5–6); and the application of the notion so defined must be determined by quite general considerations of the methodology of linguistic study (Chapter II, Sections 5–6).

However, heuristic and historical considerations favour a less immediate route to these central matters, even though that route invites suspicion of sleight of hand once those matters are reached. A recurrent thought in the comparatively recent history of semantics is that the meaning of a sentence can be given by stating the conditions under which it is true.

But to all names properly formed from our primitive signs there belongs not only a reference but also a sense. Every such name of a truth-value expresses a sense, a thought.[1] It is determined by what we have laid down under what conditions every such name designates The True. The sense of this name, the thought, is the sense or thought that these conditions are fulfilled (Frege, *Grundgesetze*, I.32 in Steinberg and Jacobovits, p. 17).

To understand a proposition means to know what is the case if it is true (Wittgenstein, *Tractatus Logico-Philosophicus*, 4.024).

To know the meaning of a sentence is to know in which of the possible cases it would be true and in which not (Carnap, *Meaning and Necessity*, p. 10).

The definition works by giving necessary and sufficient conditions for the truth of every sentence, and to give truth-conditions is a way of giving the meaning of a sentence (Davidson, 'Truth and Meaning', p. 7).

You have given all the meanings when you have given the truth-conditions of all the sentences (W. V. Quine, 'Reply to Davidson', in *Words and Objections*, ed. Davidson and Hintikka, p. 333).

In part the appearance of unity here is illusory; for many of those cited understand the notion of the meaning of a sentence in distinctive ways. The expression 'the meaning of a sentence' is a term of art, to be understood, as just now said, by its theoretical role. But prior to consideration of that, the appearance of unity is striking; perhaps striking enough for the vague doctrine that the meaning of a sentence can be given by stating its truth-conditions to merit somewhat more detailed elaboration. Such elaboration must clearly begin with a consideration of the notion of truth on which the doctrine rests; thus a moderately, though far from fully, comprehensive account of the notion of truth is given (Chapter I) before the relevance of that account to the theory of meaning is brought out through a general examination of the aims and forms of such a theory (Chapter II, Sections 1–5). The conditions of application of the theory thus abstractly characterised can then be discussed (Chapter II, Sections 5–6) to produce a theory that should be applicable to any given language.

It would be foolish to suggest that the theory that this route issues in is the only developed, persistingly attractive theory of meaning there is. To defuse the attraction of other theories the most familiar, and the most persistent, is then examined (Chapter III, Section 3); the general result of that examination is the reinforcement

---

[1] For Frege, a *sentence* is a name of a truth-value.

of the initially developed theory of sentence-meaning through the revelation of the need in the alternative considered for some prior notion of sentence-meaning sharing the formal properties of that characterised by that initial theory. Thus this slight detour returns us close to our original resting place.

That resting place, however, is still left characterised in highly general terms; it receives more concrete, and detailed, realisation when the favoured theory is applied to various locutions and kinds of expression found within the English language (Part Two). The locutions and expressions considered are chosen by reference to three, non-exclusive, interests: their importance in the history of semantics; their capacity to raise central matters in logical theory; and their ability to force the detailed development of the favoured theory in central aspects. Thus while this middle part of the book is focused upon the exhibition or revelation of various structures of meaning found in English, the exercise is not quite as parochial as it might, at casual glance, appear.

Still, that casual appearance has a use, for it forces upon us the question of why the theory of language outlined and applied should be of much philosophical interest. And here it is easy to be too modest about the enterprise.

Doubtless, the human linguistic ability is a striking, almost magical, thing; perhaps it even encapsulates some distinctively human characteristics. But there is little in that, as yet, to oblige *philosophical* interest. Doubtless also many philosophical disputes have arisen solely because of equivocation upon the meanings of expressions, giving a recurrent point to the demand for clarification of meanings of terms employed. But that is no *more* true of philosophical disputes than of those in other areas. Nor has anyone yet presented a minimally compelling argument showing that philosophical disputes *only* arise because of erroneous usage of terms; so the aim of constructing a correct theory of meaning, and developing its application, cannot even represent a form of philosophical suicide.

Austin is sometimes presented as a subscriber to this self-destructive view of philosophy, with a proper sensitivity to matters of ordinary meaning being the weapon of destruction. But consider:

> Then, for the Last Word. Certainly ordinary language has no claim to be the last word, if there is such a thing, It embodies, indeed, something better than the metaphysics of the Stone Age, namely, as was said, the inherited experience and acumen of many generations of men. But then, that acumen has been concentrated primarily upon the practical business of life. If a distinction works well for practical purposes in ordinary life (no mean feat, for even ordinary life is full of hard cases),

then there is sure to be something in it, it will not mark
nothing: yet this is likely enough not to be the best way of
arranging things if our interests are more extensive or
intellectual than the ordinary. And again, that experience has
been derived only from the sources available to ordinary men
throughout most of civilised history: it has not been fed from
the resources of the microscope and its successors. And it
must be added too, that superstition and error and fantasy of
all kinds do become incorporated in ordinary language and
even sometimes stand up to the survival test (only, when they do,
why should we not detect it?). Certainly, then, ordinary
language is *not* the last word: in principle it can everywhere be
supplemented and improved upon and superseded. Only
remember, it *is* the *first* word (Austin, *Philosophical Papers*,
p. 133).

Here Austin offers us an explanation of why it is that philosophy
has taken the common linguistic turn, of why it is that philosophers
are, or should be, usually concerned with usual meanings; for these
meanings embody the commonplace metaphysics of the Contemporary Age. And even when we move beyond the First Word and
its accompanying metaphysic, when we attempt to revise that metaphysical view, we shall generally rely upon a fair part of the ordinary
language which, in total, encapsulates that view. If the ship is
successfully to be rebuilt while at sea, it is as well to know the make-
up of the unmodified ship in fine detail.

In Austin's own hands, this initial examination was often under-
taken without any views upon the general form of a theory of
meaning, let alone any specific theory, being stated or defended.
(But see Austin, *How To Do Things With Words*, where theory
explicitly begins.) Such a consciously unsystematic and apparently
untheoretical procedure is unlikely to induce much confidence. Thus
an interest in the proper form of a theory of meaning could be seen
as the essential theoretical prelude to the First Word – as the Zeroth
Word, perhaps. But this is still too modest.

It is not our customary language alone which has built into it a
view of the world; the most general view is incorporated, quite
inevitably, within the account of the proper form of a theory of
meaning. Such an account must presume upon the relation between
language and the world; in so doing, it will presume upon the world.
There can be no neutral general form of the theory of meaning. The
account developed in this book is reasonably labelled *realistic*. It
assumes that sentences can be true (or false) independently of our
capacity, or incapacity, to recognise them as true or false; it assumes
that we can know what it is for a sentence to be true or false, that

we can know the truth-conditions of a particular sentence, even if it is beyond our capacities to recognise whether those truth-conditions obtain or not. The account assumes the independent existence of objects and of natural kinds of objects, whether or not we have yet recognised or identified them, whether or not we even as yet have the capacity so to recognise them. It assumes that we can understand the names of such objects and of such kinds of objects even if we lack the capacity to recognise or to identify them. These are matters upon which no theory of meaning, incorporating as it must a view of the relation between language and reality, can be disinterested. The view taken upon these matters within the task of constructing a theory of meaning will transcend any passing changes in the languages to which the theory is applied; and at each point in the evolution of a language, that view will *determine* the commonplace metaphysic the language is then seen to encapsulate.

It is essential, then, that any theorist of meaning show that these most general consequences of his favoured theory are defensible. This defence will be largely focused upon the coherence of the account the theory issues in of the competent speaker's *understanding* of his language, for the notion of meaning is ultimately anchored by that of understanding (Chapter II, Sections 1, 5, 6). The defence of the favoured version of the truth-conditions theory of meaning is touched upon at various points in the earlier parts of this book, but the full defence is reserved for the final part, through an examination of various arguments purporting to show that the realistic consequences of the theory are indefensible (Chapter IX). Finally, the question of the scope of this realistic view, and so of the original theory of meaning, is touched upon through an examination of one kind of realism about moral discourse, one way of straightforwardly extending the favoured theory of meaning to sentences of a moral character (Chapter X). I do not know whether, and if so how, this extension can be made; but if the result of the detailed development of this view of the theory of meaning is to sharpen the issues in that area, that will be justification enough of the whole enterprise.

Part One

The Elements of Meaning

Chapter 1

Truth: Conditions, Predicates, and Definitions

1 Theories of Truth

Satisfaction is relative to an interest; this is as true of philosophical theories as of dinner companions. Before we can assess the adequacy of a theory, we need to be clear quite what interest that theory is meant to satisfy, quite what its point is. It need not be a failing in a theory that it does not resolve a problem that it does not set out to resolve; although it would be, for example, if the neglected problem was one that it was reasonable to require any theory of the relevant kind to meet.

The present relevance of this is simple: the term 'theory of truth' has been applied to quite disparate exercises (cf. Ayer, *The Concept of a Person*, pp. 162–87). One such exercise might be called the *descriptive analysis* of truth; this is the attempt to describe the meaning of the term 'truth', and cognates like 'That's true', 'It's true that . . .', and '. . . is true', as they are customarily used.

Another enterprise is the attempt to provide a test, or set of tests, by which can be determined the truth-values of given sentences. The phrasing of this is deliberately vague. Different kinds of subject-matter – mathematical, moral, geographical, etc. – might require different kinds of test. Further, very different results will be arrived at depending upon the constraints imposed on the tests available. Should the tests be ones that I alone, without assistance from others, can apply to sentences? Can an acceptable test rely upon memory? Or upon practical success? All these possibilities are readily discerned in the history of the subject. Also discernible in that history is a third, somewhat obscure, enterprise, that of specifying the metaphysical ground of truth. In virtue of what is a belief true or false? Correspondence to the empirical world, to a supersensible reality, coherence with other beliefs, even merely the act of belief itself? This third enterprise can readily collapse into the second or

9

even the first; to the extent that it does not it is as obscure as all metaphysical questions. Still, it has seemed to many that there might be a further, independent question here: for example, the same philosopher could hold, apparently consistently, both that the metaphysical ground of truth is correspondence with a supersensible reality, and also that this is useless as a test for truth; perhaps the best test of truth is some version of pragmatism, the use of practical success as a guide to truth. When we add to this the possibility that the notion of truth usually employed is revealed by the first enterprise to be, say, that of internal coherence, the ways in which the three specified tasks can pull apart becomes clear. Indeed, they can pull apart yet further: for each of the enterprises can be pursued in either a descriptive or a revisionary manner, in terms of what is the case or of what ought to be the case. So we have at least six things that have been called a 'theory of truth'.

Which kind of theory of truth are we interested in? Our starting point is the claim that the meaning of a sentence can be given by stating its truth-conditions. What we want, initially, is some *descriptive* account of the notion of *truth* that figures in this claim. But we need not concern ourselves with the abstract noun 'truth', 'a camel . . . of a logical construction, which cannot get past the eye even of a grammarian' (Austin, *Philosophical Papers*, p. 85). Our interest is, specifically, in what it means to say that various conditions are jointly sufficient and individually necessary for the truth of a sentence; nothing, except the risk of blindness, is lost if we present such conditions for a given sentence in the form

'. . . ' is true if and only if. . . .

Thus we escape from the camel of an abstract noun to the more modest, and manageable, predicate '. . . is true'; and that modesty is reinforced by the concern solely with the descriptive analysis of that predicate.

However, in the present context the appearance of modesty is misleading. Treatment of the truth-predicate, like any other expression in the language, will be affected by the favoured theory of meaning; yet our interest in that predicate is prompted by the search for a theory of meaning. In such a quandary, the most rational strategy is to proceed in a modest, piecemeal manner, to stick with the innocuous; at this point, our account of the truth-predicate *must* be a series of truisms. Anything else would beg the question of the desired theory of meaning.

2 Ramsey's Theory of Truth

One truism about the truth-predicate, familiar from Ramsey, is this:

to say that '*p*' is true is to say exactly the same as to say that *p*.[1] Wherever one can be said, so can the other; their difference is stylistic or rhetorical. The precise equivalence being claimed here need not concern us; again, lacking a theory of meaning, we could not hope to elucidate this equivalence. It is enough for the moment if we take the claim to be that ' "*p*" is true' and '*p*' are extensionally equivalent, they have the same truth-value. We thus have the Ramsey formula (R) as the embodiment of one truism about truth:

(R) '*p*' is true if and only if *p*.

This truism has not been universally accepted; but, more important, we should note four matters arising from it.

(i) However (R) is construed, it is not the whole truth about truth. Truth terminology is used in contexts other than that illustrated by (R): 'It is true that . . .'; 'Truth is stranger than fiction'; 'I shall be true to you forever'. (R) does not even tell us about all occurrences of the truth-predicate: 'That's true'; 'Everything the Pope says is true'. Much could be said about these other occurrences and constructions, and about their connections with that in (R); still, (R) tells us all we need to know about the truth-predicate, since all we want for the discussion of the truth-conditions theory of meaning is the truth-predicate as it occurs in the form exemplified by (R). At least (R) tells us all the uncontroversial things about such usages of the predicate. Maybe the construction in (R) is ultimately derived from another truth-construction; but without assuming a theory of meaning we could not explore this possibility, so we might as well ignore it.

(ii) It seems to be assumed in the Ramsey formula that sentences are truth-bearers, the bearers of the truth-predicate; and I have talked all along as if they are. This is an obscure issue, and ultimately, I think, a comparatively unimportant one. I shall, however, return to it briefly a little later.

(iii) Consider an unproblematic instance of the Ramsey formula – say

'Grass is green' is true if and only if grass is green.

Such an instance of (R), and hence (R) itself, has been interpreted in two radically distinct ways; these two readings are perfectly compatible, although different philosophers have emphasised the one or the other. I shall label these the *redundancy reading* and the *realist reading*. Ramsey appeared to emphasise the redundancy reading; such sentences were meant to show that the truth-predicate is

[1] This is not historically accurate, since Ramsey discussed sentences, not of the form ' "*p*" is true', but of the form 'It is true that *p*' (Pitcher, *Truth*, pp. 16–17). This misrepresentation is not trivial, but its heuristic point in leading us quickly to Tarski's theory is clear.

eliminable and so redundant, at least in sentences of this form. Ramsey's reading could be put like this: whenever you want to say that 'Grass is green' is true, you might just as well say that grass is green; so the truth-predicate in the first of these sayings is redundant. *If* all other truth-constructions were then shown to be derivative from that in (R)-sentences, we would have something deserving the title 'Redundancy Theory of Truth'. We might wish to keep truth-talk in the language for reasons of rhetoric or convenience (cf. Putnam, *Meaning and the Moral Sciences*, pp. 15–16), or perhaps even for engaging in certain kinds of highly general, quasi-philosophical discourse (see Quine, *From a Logical Point of View*, pp. 1–19); but aside from such considerations, truth-talk is redundant, with (R)-sentences as the recipes for avoiding it. It is, however, a mistake to think, as many seem to have done, that these redundancy theses imply either that there is *no* philosophical problem about the nature of truth or that *no* interesting explication of truth-talk can be given. This will emerge during the later development of Ramsey's theory; but it should be clear from the outset because of the compatibility of the redundancy with the realist reading of (R)-sentences. Taking our instance of (R), we might ask: what makes it the case that 'Grass is green' is true? This seems an obscure question, but there is a surprisingly simple answer to it: what makes it the case is the obtaining of the state of affairs specified by the right-hand side (RHS) of the appropriate (R)-sentence – that is, grass's being green. And that is a matter settled, not by language, but by the world, by an extra-linguistic reality. Thus does our instance of (R) differ, at least until we go on to apply the Ramsey truism, from

'Grass is green' is true if and only if 'Grass is green' is true.

On the realist view, (R)-sentences, while they may also be guides to the avoidance of truth-talk, are guides as to what makes a sentence true. Whether the guide is a practical one is another matter.

Three points should now be noted. First, it may not be possible, let alone necessary, to extend this realistic reading to all kinds of occurrences of the truth-predicate. It may be implausible to do so, for example, when the sentence of which truth is being predicated is an ethical sentence. Second, the apparent triviality of the realistic reading – the apparent triviality of saying that what makes it the case that 'Grass is green' is true is that grass is green – is much reduced when the sentence of which truth is predicated contains indexical expressions like 'I', 'now', and 'this'; in such cases, the sentence used to say what makes the indexical-containing sentence true is not exactly the same as that sentence (see pp. 39–42). But third, the triviality is always mere appearance. To see this, consider first the case where the sentence of which truth is predicated is in a different language from that in which we state what makes it the case that that sentence is true. For example, using English, we try to produce an (R)-sentence for a given French sentence. On the left-hand side (LHS) of the (R)-sentence occurs the French sentence in quotes; this is an English expression designating the French sentence. But the sentence occurring on the right-hand side (RHS) of the (R)-sentence is not quoted, is not designated, but is used; it must there-fore be an English sentence if franglais is to be avoided. Which English sentence do we use on the RHS? The obvious answer is: the *translation* of the French sentence designated on the LHS.[2] In such a case, then, the general format of an (R)-sentence is that the sentence named on the LHS is translated and the translation is then used on the RHS. Now, however, we can see that this same format can be read into the simpler case where only English sentences are involved. An (R)-sentence, even when we are using English to say what makes it the case that an English sentence is true, can only reasonably be expected to be true if the sentence used on the RHS has the same sense in that occurrence as it does in its quoted occur-rence on the LHS. What initially blinds us to this is the unobvious-ness of homophonic translation; but such translation occurs, and avoids triviality in (R)-sentences even in the one-language case. What counts in any of these cases as *translation*, as *correct translation*, is another matter, and one we need a theory of meaning to settle; but at this point we can perhaps help ourselves to this yet-to-be-explicated notion of translation in saying that (R)-sentences are to be con-strained by this condition of translation. Still, homophonic transla-tion might appear trivial, being merely an application of the identity function, so that invocation of this condition of translation does not free (R)-sentences of triviality in the homophonic case; it is therefore important to recognise that the *manner* in which (R)-sentences rest upon this condition of translation eliminates any vestige of triviality. Precisely because, in the one-language case, the sentence named on the LHS is *used* on the RHS, (R)-sentences are informative com-ments in a language about sentences of that language. The sentence

'Grass is green' is true if and only if grass is green.

expresses a contingent truth about the English language; it could very well not have been the case that it was grass's being green which made it the case that the English sentence 'Grass is green' is true. The contingent truth so expressed is both learnable and forgettable. (R)-sentences are never trivial.

I shall assume, without argument, that both the redundancy and the realist readings of the Ramsey formula are correct; I shall also

---

[2] This obvious answer is not quite right, however, when the sentence designated on the LHS contains indexical expressions.

understand instances of that formula as being constrained by the condition of translation.

(iv) The fourth point about the Ramsey formula is crucial; it constitutes the starting point for Tarski's celebrated theory of truth. The formula is this:

(R) '*p*' is true if and only if *p*.

As it stands, this is gibberish: the LHS attributes truth to the sixteenth letter of the alphabet, while the RHS is merely an inscription of that letter. This was passed over before by the tacit understanding of (R) as being generalised: the occurrences of '*p*' were understood to be bound by a universal quantifier, or else (R) was read as a schema, producing true sentences when '*p*' is replaced in both its occurrences by the same sentence. Indeed, the Ramsey formula must be generalised if it is even to begin to tell us the whole truth about such occurrences of the truth-predicate.

What, then, is the generalisation of (R)? Suppose generality is to be obtained by universal quantification; then we shall have

(*p*) ('*p*' is true if and only if *p*).

Everything now hangs upon the interpretation of the quantifier. First, it might be read objectually, so that '(*p*)' is tantamount to 'for each and every object *p*'; but with this reading, the generalisation is ill-formed. First, because the unquoted occurrence of '*p*' on the RHS of the biconditional, where '*p*' is used, not mentioned, will require that we make sense of sentences being names; but it is not clear that there is *any* kind of object that sentences can plausibly be treated as naming.

Second, even if we can overcome this first worry – say, by making sense of the idea that a used sentence names a state of affairs, or, perhaps, a truth-value – we shall then encounter the problem of handling the *mentioned* occurrence of '*p*'. If the formula is to be well formed, there must be one *kind* of object that *both* occurrences of '*p*' in the generalised, bound formula can be treated as naming. Given the (supposed) way of handling the first worry, this would require that quotation marks be treated as expressing functions from states of affairs (or truth-values) to sentences, the items of which truth is predicated; that is, they must be seen as operating upon an expression that names a state of affairs (or a truth-value) to produce an expression that names a sentence. But this seems of very doubtful coherence. The quantifier in the generalised formula, then, cannot be objectual. But suppose we try the alternative, substitutional reading. It is not clear that this will keep the logic clean, but it will not work anyway. We are attempting to define the truth-predicate as part of the enterprise of defining truth. Yet consider the interpretation of the

14

substitutional quantifier. The interpretation of the existential quantification '$(\exists x)(Fx)$' is this: there is a name which, when concatenated with the predicate 'F', produces a *true* sentence. The interpretation of the universal quantification '$(x)(Fx)$' is this: all names, when concatenated with the predicate 'F', produce a *true* sentence. The problem is clear: substitutional quantification is defined in terms of truth, and so cannot itself be used to define truth. What of the residual possibility of treating (R) as a schema? Again, this can be of no help in the enterprise of defining truth, for the appropriate notion of a schema cannot be explained except in terms of truth. The claim would have to be that the result of replacing 'p' in both its occurrences by one and the same sentence is a *true* sentence of English.

Our truism seems to be fast deserting us: as it stands it is gibberish, and we have not been able to find a suitable generalised version. Were there only a finite number of sentences in the language, we could avoid these difficulties by the somewhat tedious task of simply compiling a list of the (R)-sentences, giving one such sentence for each sentence in the language under study. But this would give us no insight into the ways, if any, that the truth-conditions of a sentence are determined by its component expressions and their structural combinations; nor, of course, would such insight come from the methods of generalising (R) just revealed to be inadequate. Anyway, for a language containing an infinity of sentences the option of listing all the (R)-sentences is not open to us.

We might attempt, however, to capture the point of the Ramsey truism in a more roundabout manner. The truth-predicate, in the constructions that concern us, is the predicate that satisfies the following schema, where 's' is replaced by the designation of a sentence and 'p' by a translation of that sentence:

s is true if and only if p.

The thought now is that we can define this predicate, not by directly generalising this formula, but by the method of axiomatisation. That is, we attempt to construct a set of axioms and rules (a finite set so that *we* can write them down) which suffice logically to imply a sentence of this form for any randomly chosen sentence in the language we are studying, the object-language, the language of the sentence designated on the LHS; the sentences so implied are stated in our language, the meta-language, the language of the whole final sentence. We thus use the Ramsey formula to state our target, not to achieve it. It will thus be a sufficient condition of an axiomatisation of a predicate 'is X' being an axiomatisation of a truth-predicate that it logically imply all T-sentences, that is, all sentences of the form

(T) *s* is X if and only if *p*

where '*s*' is replaced by the designation of any arbitrarily chosen sentence in the language under study, and '*p*' by that same sentence or its translation, depending on whether or not the object-language is contained in the meta-language. In this sufficiency condition we see the distinctive role of the truth-predicate as a device of dis-quotation, the Quinean variant of the Ramsey redundancy thesis: this predicate enables us to move from talk about language (the named sentence on the LHS) to talk about the world (the used sentence on the RHS) (Quine, *The Ways of Paradox*, pp. 308–21). The truth-predicate sweeps away, so to speak, the quotation marks, producing a sentence suitable for saying the same thing as a sentence (that on the RHS) in which quotation does not occur. This result is only forthcoming when we supplement the condition that the sentences on the LHS and RHS of the biconditional in the Ramsey formula (R) have the same truth-value, be extensionally equivalent, with the additional translation constraint just now introduced.

The sufficiency condition (T) is in essence Tarski's Convention T for testing the adequacy of a proposed definition of truth (Tarski, *Logic, Semantics, Metamathematics*, pp. 152–278, esp. pp. 187–8). My concern has simply been to show how naturally it arises from the truistic considerations in Ramsey's theory. Now we have to illustrate the working of Convention T, its use in the characterisation of a truth-predicate. This will be done for a number of artificial languages of increasing degrees of complexity; its application to natural languages is exemplified in the second part of this book.

3 Simple Truth-Definitions

I begin with an Unstructured Feature Placing Language, UFPL. This consists of a finite number of sentences, and does not admit of their combination into more complex sentences. The axiomatisation is therefore simple and dull.

A *Syntax*

(1) '*p*', '*q*', '*r*' are sentences.
(2) Nothing else is a sentence.

The truth-definition proceeds straightforwardly. Given the un-structured nature of the sentences, along with their finite number, we can treat the sentences as primitive, listing their truth-conditions as follows:

B *Truth-Definition*

(1) (i) '*p*' is true iff it is raining.
(ii) '*q*' is true iff it is snowing.
(iii) '*r*' is true iff it is freezing.

How the translations on the RHS are obtained is not our present concern. Nor, obviously, should we linger over this language. Of rather more interest is the Propositional Calculus Language PCL. This, again, has a finite stock of unstructured sentences, but, unlike the UFPL, it does admit of their combination into more complex sentences by means of a finite stock of sentential connectives. We have, then, the following:

A *Syntax*

(1) '*p*', '*q*', '*r*' are sentences.
(2) If A is any sentence and B is any sentence, then
'($^\frown$A$^\frown$ & '$^\frown$B$^\frown$)' is a sentence.³
(3) If A is any sentence and B is any sentence, then
'($^\frown$A$^\frown$ v '$^\frown$B$^\frown$)' is a sentence.
(4) If A is any sentence, then '$\sim$'$^\frown$A is a sentence.
(5) . . . (for the other connectives).
(6) Nothing else is a sentence.

There are two quite distinct PCLs, depending on whether or not compound sentences, previously formed out of simple sentences and sentential connectives, are themselves admissible as elements in yet more complex sentences. If not, there will be a finite number of sentences in the language – the Strictly Finite PCL, SFPCL. By contrast, if previously formed compound sentences are themselves subsequently admissible as components in yet more complex sentences, then the language has a potential infinity of sentences in it. Call this the unbound PCL, UPCL. The language specified by the syntax above is the UPCL.

When we consider the truth-definition for the UPCL, it is evident that we cannot proceed as we did with the UFPL, we cannot list a T-sentence for each sentence in the language – for we cannot compile an infinite list. What we have to do is to specify a way of generating a T-sentence for any sentence of arbitrary complexity. This we do by treating as primitive the unstructured sentences of the language, listing for each of this finite number its T-sentence; and by showing how the T-sentences of more complex sentences are determined by the T-sentences of the component simple sentences.

³ '$^\frown$' is a *concatenation* marker. Thus 'A$^\frown$B' means: the result of concatenating A and B.

B *Truth-Definition*

(1) (i) '*p*' is true iff it is raining.
    (ii) '*q*' is true iff it is snowing.
    (iii) '*r*' is true iff it is freezing.
(2) If A is any sentence and B is any sentence, then
    '('⌒A⌒' & '⌒B⌒')' is true iff A is true and B is true.
(3) If A is any sentence and B is any sentence, then
    '('⌒A⌒' v '⌒B⌒')' is true iff A is true or B is true.
(4) If A is any sentence, then '∼'⌒A is true iff A is not true.
(5) . . . . (for other connectives).

This truth-definition enables us to determine the T-sentence of any of the infinite number of sentences in the language. Take a simple case, the sentence '*p* & *r*'. First, we use B(2) to obtain this:

(1) '*p* & *r*' is true iff '*p*' is true and '*r*' is true.

Then we use the appropriate clauses of B(1) to reach the following:

(2) '*p* & *r*' is true iff it is raining and it is freezing.

Nothing could be simpler. The strategy is the same for all sentences; use B(2)–(5) to disquote the sentential connectives, and then use B(1) to disquote the primitives. This strategy implies this: on the RHS of the biconditional in the final T-sentence (i.e. (2) above) no predicate like 'is true' figures; but we do have such predicates on the RHS of the biconditional at the earlier stages of the derivation. This pattern, described more generally, will be seen to repeat itself throughout derivations of T-sentences of greater complexity: truth-determining notions figure on the RHS of the biconditional at all points in the derivation of the T-sentence other than the T-sentence itself.

Strictly speaking, none of this apparatus is necessary for the truth-definition in the SFPCL: that language contains a finite number of sentences, and it is therefore possible to list the corresponding T-sentences. For the moment we need merely note that by helping ourselves to a slight modification of the axiomatisation given for the UPCL in the case of the SFPCL, we both avoid the tedium of compiling the appropriate list and also connect our truth-definition much more tightly with the syntactic specification of the language.

4 Predicates and Satisfaction

What is achieved by this axiomatisation of the UPCL is a demonstration of the ways in which the T-sentences of compound sentences are determined by the T-sentences of their components. Suppose, now, that we tried to apply the same technique to the following sentence of English:

'Someone cuts my lawn and prunes my roses.'

This is a compound sentence: for example, it implies, but is not implied by, 'Someone cuts my lawn'. What, then, are its components? It is not *just* equivalent to this:

'Someone cuts my lawn *and* someone prunes my roses.'

For this omits the element, asserted by the original, that the *same* person does both. We might then try this:

'Someone cuts my lawn *and* someone prunes my roses *and* someone (*that* someone) does both.'

This indeed makes the original sentence a complex conjunction; but but look at the last conjunct! If asked to explain the meaning of that conjunct, we could but gesture back to the original sentence.

What this shows is that in English there are compound sentences whose components are not themselves sentences. The obvious way to represent the example is something like this:

'There is someone such that: (a) he cuts my lawn;
                and   (b) he prunes my roses.'

This is still not very satisfactory, but it draws attention to the fact that this complex English sentence is built up out of a quantifier ('There is someone such that'); a variable bound by the quantifier ('he' in both occurrences); predicates ('cuts my lawn', 'prunes my roses'); and a connective occurring between predicates ('and'). Since the components of this sentence are not sentences, they will not themselves have T-sentences; for only sentences can have a truth-value.

That is just one problem encountered by any attempt to define a truth-predicate for English. Fortunately, it is now readily resolved through consideration of an artificial language of a higher degree of complexity than the Propositional Calculus languages, the Predicate Calculus Language or the Quantificational Language QL. In this language there is a finite stock of names, 'a', 'b', 'c', . . . , 'n', along with a finite stock of predicates, 'F', 'G', 'H', . . . , 'N'. The language admits of the coupling of a name and a predicate to form a simple sentence. There will be a finite number of these: 'Fa', 'Fb', . . . 'Fn'; 'Ga', 'Gb', . . . , 'Gn'; . . . , 'Na', 'Nb', . . . , 'Nn'. Further, like the Propositional Calculus languages, this language admits of the formation of compound sentences out of these simple sentences using members of the finite stock of sentential connectives: for example, '$Fa \mathbin{\&} Gb$'. But unlike these previous languages, QL also admits of quantification, using both the existential quantifier '$(\exists x)\,(\ldots x \ldots)$' and the universal quantifier '$(x)\,(\ldots x \ldots)$'. With this admission

19

there comes the addition of a stock of variables, '*x*', '*x''*', '*x'''*',. . . . A variable concatenated with a predicate forms a simple open sentence: e.g. '*Fx''*'. Sentential connectives can occur between open sentences as well as closed: thus '*Fx'* & *Gx'''*'. Finally, such sentences can be closed by quantification: e.g. '(*x*) (∃*x'*) (*Fx* & *Gx'*)'.

The syntax of QL, although a matter of some complexity, raises no significant problems. We begin by listing the primitives of each category of expression; we then provide some definition of sentence-hood such as that given of 'well-formed formula' in the standard treatment of the predicate calculus. But whatever the details of the syntax of QL, as soon as we attempt to give a truth-definition for it along the same lines as those for the other languages we have considered, we encounter a problem – the problem we have seen English to pose. The general strategy was to demonstrate the way in which the T-sentence of a compound sentence is determined by the T-sentence(s) of its component(s). We cannot do this for QL because the components of a compound sentence need not themselves be sentences (i.e. closed sentences), and so need not have T-sentences. Our English sentence 'Someone cuts my lawn and prunes my roses' would be standardly translated into QL like this: '(∃*x*) (*Fx* & *Gx*)'. But that compound sentence is not built up out of closed sentences but out of sentential functions, open sentences.

Tarski made us appreciate this problem, and devised a beautifully simple solution. I shall quickly run through that solution, and the truth-definition for QL it produces; I shall then ruminate on it in hope of clarification.

Tarski's central idea comes in this passage:

> The possibility suggests itself, however, of introducing a more general concept which is applicable to any sentential function, can be recursively defined, and, when applied to sentences, leads us directly to the concept of truth. These requirements are met by the notion of the *satisfaction of a given sentential function by given objects*[4] (Tarski, *Logic, Semantics, Metamathematics,* p. 189).

The idea, then, is this: we axiomatically define a notion, satisfaction, that stands, roughly, to open sentences, sentential functions, or predicates, as truth stands to closed sentences. We then use that axiomatisation to define the truth-predicate. One such axiomatisation runs as follows (we need not now decide upon the final form of the axiomatisation):

---

[4] In my subsequent development of this idea, satisfiers are *sequences* of objects, not just objects; the reason for this emerges in a moment.

Truth-Definition for QL

(1) Names
    (i) '*a*' refers to *a*.
    (ii) '*b*' refers to *b*.
    (iii) ......
(2) Predicates
    (i) An object α satisfies '*F*' iff α is *F*.
    (ii) An object α satisfies '*G*' iff α is *G*.
    (iii) ......

We now specify the conditions under which the atomic formulae of the language are satisfied.

(3) A sequence *S* satisfies a predicate ϕ concatenated with a name *n* if and only if the object to which the name refers satisfies ϕ.
(4) A sequence *S* satisfies a predicate ϕ concatenated with the *k*-th variable (v_k) if and only if the *k*-th member of the sequence (s_k) satisfies ϕ.
(5) A sequence *S* satisfies the formula '($^\frown \phi ^\frown$ & '$^\frown \psi ^\frown$)' if and only if it satisfies ϕ and it satisfies ψ.
(6) A sequence *S* satisfies the existential quantification of a formula *A* with respect to v_k if and only if *A* is satisfied by some sequence *S'* which is like *S* except perhaps in the *k*-th term.[5]
(7) A sequence *S* satisfies the universal quantification of a formula *A* with respect to v_k if and only if *A* is satisfied by all sequences *S'* which are like *S* except perhaps in their *k*-th term.
(8) A sentence is true iff it is satisfied by all sequences.

None of this is likely to be immediately pellucid, so I shall attempt to clarify some of the matters involved.

Satisfaction is a relation between expressions and sequences of objects, with a limiting case of a sequence with one member. It is defined for closed, non-quantified sentences, as in clause (3) above, but the interest of the definition resides in the clauses dealing with open sentences, and the consequent treatment of quantified sentences. The precise relation of satisfaction is simply that defined by the rules just listed.

Anxiety about satisfaction is wont to remain. It could be put like this: the only way we can understand the notion of satisfaction is by reference to truth – satisfaction is to open sentences and sequences as truth is to closed sentences and the world. But if that is so, nothing is gained by defining truth in terms of satisfaction; satisfaction is neither independently nor antecedently understood. It is no good saying that the definition of truth in terms of satisfaction works; of

[5] Note the *perhaps*; this means that *S* counts as an *S'*-variant of itself.

course it does – the definition of satisfaction is fixed precisely by the need to obtain the correct definition of truth using it. But to present that definition as anything but a formal manoeuvre is misleading at best.

These vaguenesses deserve more respect than they are usually given. I think the anxieties can at least be eased by the following three sets of reflections.

(i) In what sense does the definition of satisfaction given presuppose the notion of truth? Suppose somebody independently hit upon the definition of satisfaction just given; would it then be improper for him to define truth in terms of it? Presumably not; but then the objection seems founded upon a contingent fact of human intellectual history, which has no relevance to the acceptability of a definition. Or maybe the objection is an application of some principle like this: one notion can be satisfactorily defined in terms of another only if the latter is more familiar than the former. But science multiplies counter-examples to such a principle.

One precise way in which a definition of something *like* satisfaction could presuppose the notion of truth would be if, as it were, a 'substitutional' definition of the term were given. Suppose, for example, that this clause of the original definition

(2) (i) An object α satisfies 'F' if and only if α is F

were replaced by this

(2) (i)* An object α satisfies 'F' if and only if concatenation of a name of α with the predicate 'F' produces a true sentence.

Here the definition of satisfaction clearly would presuppose the notion of truth. But the difference between (2) (i) and (2) (i)* suggests that the same is not true of our original definition of satisfaction.

(ii) The notion of satisfaction is not merely a term of art employed by philosophers of language. The notion is effectively employed by all those who do algebra (cf. Tarski, *Introduction to Logic*, pp. 4–7). Take, for example, the following algebraic formula:

$$x^2 = 4$$

All are told at school that this is satisfied by $+2$ or -2. They are also told that this pair of formulae

$$x^2 = 4$$
$$x^3 = 8$$

is satisfied only by $+2$. When told this, and accepting it, they are employing a notion which our definition generalises. Of course, you could gloss any of these occurrences of satisfaction in terms of truth; you could say, for example, that '$x^2 = 4$' is true *of* $+2$ and -2. But first, why should we so gloss it? Second, *is true of* is not the same as *is true*, which is what we are defining. 'Is true of' 'is satisfied by', is a two-place relation, while 'is true', the truth-predicate, is a one-place predicate. Third, not all occurrences of satisfaction are so readily glossed: we can talk, by the definition, of closed sentences being satisfied, but it is not clear that we can talk of what they are true of. So the relation of satisfaction is quite distinct from truth-talk; and the evidence of algebra suggests that there may be more of an independently understood notion of satisfaction than initial intuition might suggest.

(iii) The crucial rejoinder to the anxieties remains. We have seen that if we wish to characterise recursively a truth-predicate for languages of at least the degree of complexity of the predicate calculus we cannot do it by showing how the T-sentences of compound sentences are determined by the T-sentences of their components. The components are not closed sentences, do not admit of truth or falsehood, and do not have T-sentences. We have to find a truth-relevant property of these constituents, and that property is satisfaction. But there is another, connected truth to be noted: a basic structural component of these sentences is the predicate, the open sentence, the sentential function. Sentences in the predicate calculus are *built up* from predicate structures, as is evident from any of the standard accounts of the syntax of such languages. Now, the claim that satisfaction is an arbitrary formal device would carry with it the claim that the detection of predicate structure is an arbitrary formal manoeuvre. This claim is mistaken. (Note that it is quite different to maintain that the detection of a *particular* predicate structure is in some sense arbitrary.) The only reason for accepting this mistaken claim would be a crude acceptance of the much discussed doctrine that the primary unit of meaning is the sentence, not the word. On *that* dispute, it should suffice to call two witnesses, whose remarks should have put this tired dispute to rest:

> It has been maintained by Ryle and others that words have sense in an only derivative manner, that they are *abstractions* rather than *extractions* from sentence-sense. There is something we must acknowledge and something we must reject in this doctrine. What we must concede is that when we specify the contribution of words we specify what they contribute as verbs or predicates or names or whatever, i.e., as sentence-parts, to a whole sentence-sense. Neither their status as this or that part of speech nor the very idea of words having a sense can exist in isolation from the possibility of words' occurrence in sentences. But this is not yet to accept that words do not have sense as it were *autonomously*. And they must. If our *entire*

23

understanding of word-senses were derived by abstraction from the senses of sentences and if (as is obviously the case) we could only get to know a finite number of sentence-senses directly, there would be an infinite number of different ways of extrapolating to the senses of sentences whose meanings we have to work out. But we do in fact have an agreed way of working them out. This is because word-meanings are autonomous items, for which we can write dictionary entries. Quine has put the point in dispute so elegantly and concisely that it is enough to quote him:

The unit of communication is the sentence and not the word. This point of semantical theory was long obscured by the undeniable primacy, in one respect, of words. Sentences being limitless in number and words limited, we necessarily understand most sentences by construction from antecedently familiar words. Actually there is no conflict here. We can allow the sentences a full monopoly of 'meaning' in some sense, without denying that the meaning must be worked out. Then we can say that knowing words is knowing how to work out the meanings of sentences containing them. Dictionary definitions are mere clauses in a recursive definition of the meanings of sentences (Wiggins in Steinberg and Jacobovits, *Semantics*, pp. 24–5; the Quine passage is from Schoenman (ed.), *Bertrand Russell*, p. 306).

So: the sentence is primary as the unit of communication and the first unit of learning. Correspondingly, truth is primary as the dimension of assessment of the first unit of learning and of communication. But sentence-components, like predicates, are genuine components of sentences, components we are bound to rely upon in determining the meanings of novel sentences. Comparably, therefore, satisfaction is the property of those genuine predicate-components from which we determine the T-sentences of novel sentences containing these components. The only explicit, reflective way we can determine the T-sentences of novel sentences is by reference to the satisfaction-conditions for the predicate components – *just as* the only way we can understand the sense of novel sentences is by reference to the senses of the predicate-components of those sentences. The primacy of sentence-sense explains the unease that the definition of truth in terms of satisfaction induces; the inevitable independence of the sense of sentence-parts shows that unease to be unnecessary.

5 Sequences as Satisfiers

Having tried to ease anxieties about the relation of satisfaction, let me now say a little more about one of its *relata,* the satisfiers. In the treatment given, satisfiers are sequences of objects. (Technically, these are functions from natural numbers to objects.) Sequences, marked thus $\langle \ldots \rangle$, differ from sets of objects, marked thus $\{ \ldots \}$, in being *ordered.* The set consisting of the numbers one and two, $\{1, 2\}$, is identical to the set consisting of the numbers two and one, $\{2, 1\}$, for sets are identical if and only if they have the same members. But the sequence $\langle 1, 2 \rangle$ is not identical to the sequence $\langle 2, 1 \rangle$, for in sequences order matters. In general, $\langle x, y \rangle = \langle y, x \rangle$ only if $x = y$. We can, however, define ordered pairs, two-place sequences, in terms of unordered pairs like this:

$$\langle x, y \rangle = \{ \{x, x\}, \{x, y\} \}.$$

Ordered pairs are, so to speak, pairs of pairs. (This is only *one* way amongst several possibilities of defining one kind of sequence. There is no fact of the matter here, merely considerations of convenience and simplicity.)

The reason for the ordering is simple. To obtain the definition of satisfaction given, we need a one-to-one correspondence between each variable occurring in a sentence and members occupying distinct places of the sequence concerned. We assume the variables to be indexed from one to a potential infinity; we order the objects in the sequence; then to the first variable we assign the object in the first place, to the second the second, and so forth. Ordering the items is a formal device to ensure that one and only one member is assigned to each distinct variable in a sentence, although the same object can occur at more than one place in a sequence. Thus the indexing only matters when more than one variable occurs in a sentence; but for simplicity we specify the indexing even when handling a sentence with one variable.

The number of distinct quantifiers and variables occurring in distinct sentences in the language is potentially infinite. If that is so, truth-definition is facilitated if we consider only sequences with no clear limit to the number of their members. I shall therefore work with sequences with a denumerable infinity of members. (The number must be denumerable since counting is effectively required for the ordering of the members of the sequence.) In practice, of course, we shall rarely need to consider more than the first few members of the sequence.

All this may make sequences appear peculiar entities. Maybe they are; but we should note two crucial, connected matters about them. First, they are sequences of objects, not of names of objects, although, of course, names can figure *as* objects. Second, sequences exist independently of our specification of them. When we specify a particular sequence, we do not in so doing bring that sequence into

25

being; we merely describe what was in existence all along. There really are sequences with a denumerably infinite number of places. What is more, there is a non-denumerable infinity of them. This last point is a consequence of the following principles of the ontology of sequences, all of which are needed for the definition of satisfaction to work:

    (i) There is at least one denumerable sequence.

    (ii) For every sequence S, for every natural number i, and for every individual y, there is a sequence S' which differs from S in at most the i-th place, and whose i-th member is y.

    (iii) For any finite sequence S there is an infinite sequence which results from iterating the last term of S.

Note, finally, that there need be no natural rationale for the grouping together of the items in the sequence. The sequence of natural numbers

$$\langle 1, 2, 3, 4, 5, 6, \ldots \rangle$$

has no greater claim to existence than the sequence

$$\langle 1, \text{Moscow, Mark Platts, Dr Crippen, the dog at the bottom of the garden}, \ldots \rangle$$

Both exist: the only difference is that we have some idea of how to continue the one but not the other. But that is of no importance. Incidentally, I shall adopt the following (simplifying) convention: if the principle governing the continuation of the sequence is not obvious or specified, repeat the last member *ad infinitum*.

6 The Workings of Satisfaction

We may now be in a position to see more clearly how the definition of satisfaction works. In particular, it can be shown that for closed sentences, satisfaction is an all or nothing matter; closed sentences are satisfied by all sequences or by none. This is required by the definition if all closed sentences are to have a determinate truth-value. Let us look, then, at each of the rules stipulating satisfaction conditions for atomic formulae as given earlier.

    (3) A sequence S satisfies a predicate ϕ concatenated with a name n iff the object to which the name refers satisfies ϕ.

The sentences covered by this clause, resulting from the concatenation of name and predicate, are closed, non-quantified sentences, sentences containing no variables, bound or unbound. Now, it should be evident from the preceding discussion that whether or not a given sequence satisfies a given sentence depends upon the variables

26

in the sentence; so if a sentence contains no variables, the actual sequence given is irrelevant, its members and their order matter not at all. So if a sentence is satisfied by one sequence, it will be satisfied by all. Satisfaction here will be, quite trivially, an all or nothing matter. This leaves it open whether we hold the sentence satisfied by all or by none in the case where the atomic sentence is true – that is, where the object does satisfy the predicate. The decision here is determined by the later elements of the definition of satisfaction, together with the desire to have a uniform definition of truth. The other clauses, as we shall see, clearly require the equation of truth with satisfaction by all sequences; so to apply this definition to this case, we equate the satisfaction of, say, '*Fa*' by one (and therefore every) sequence with the circumstance of its truth – that is, with the object referred to by '*a*' satisfying '*F*'. The air of manoeuvre here does not matter, since this clause matters little.

(4) A sequence S satisfies a predicate ϕ concatenated with the k-th variable (v_k) iff the k-th member of the sequence (s_k) satisfies ϕ.

This clause applies to sentences containing unbound variables, and there is therefore no necessity that it ensure all or none satisfaction conditions. Consider the formula 'Fx''', with the index indicating that this is the second variable. Suppose '*F*' is the predicate *is a philosopher*. Then the formula is satisfied by this sequence

$$\langle \text{Hitler, Quine, the moon, } \ldots \rangle$$

but is not satisfied by this sequence

$$\langle \text{Hitler, the moon, Quine, } \ldots \rangle$$

for while Quine is a philosopher, the moon is not. The rules for sequence specification allow us to put the name of any object in any position in the specification of a sequence. So the only way an open sentence could be satisfied by all sequences would be if every object in the world satisfied the predicate concerned. If there is one object that does not, consider a sequence with that object in the appropriate place; that sequence will not satisfy the formula.

The satisfaction condition for conjunction (5), as for the other sentential connectives, is straightforward, so let us move on to the quantifiers.

(6) A sequence S satisfies the existential quantification of a formula A with respect to v_k iff A is satisfied by some sequence S' which is like S except perhaps in the k-th term.

To see how this produces all or nothing conditions, consider the

27

problematic sentence that led us to consider the predicate calculus language:

'Someone cuts my lawn and prunes my roses.'

This could be represented as follows, indexing the variable:

$(\exists x'') \, (Fx'' \, \& \, Gx'')$.

Suppose the sentence is true, that someone does both cut my lawn and prune my roses – say, Tom Brown. Now consider any sequence you like, for example,

$S \, \langle$ Cicero, the moon, 7, Quine, . . . $\rangle$

Does S satisfy the sentence? The variable is indexed as the second, so we need to consider the second object in the sequence. This is the moon; I take it that this satisfies neither of the predicates concerned. But consider this sequence:

$S' \, \langle$ Cicero, Tom Brown, 7, Quine, . . . $\rangle$

Suppose it to continue exactly as S continues. Then S' differs from S in at most the second place, since it differs from S in only the second place. But then the original definition (6) tells us that in virtue of this and of S''s satisfying the open sentence '$Fx'' \, \& \, Gx''$' S itself satisfies the complete quantified sentence. Note, crucially, that the requirement is that S', the satisfactory sequence, differs from S in *at most* the k-th place; it *need* not do so, in which case $S = S'$. It will prove useful to have an abbreviation of 'S' differs from S in at most the k-th place'; I shall write it like this: '$S' \, \underset{k}{\approx} \, S$'.

The preceding shows that the sequence S satisfies the sentence. But it is easy to see that if that is so, then all sequences satisfy the sentence. Suppose, *per impossibile*, that there were a sequence that did not. Then, by (6), it would be the case both that the k-th member of the sequence did not satisfy the predicates concerned, and also that there is no other sequence, like that sequence in all but the k-th place, whose k-th member satisfies the predicates. But there must be such a sequence: all we need to consider is the sequence obtained by taking the offending sequence and putting in its k-th place the item which does satisfy the predicates – viz. Tom Brown. If there is no such object to be substituted, then no sequence satisfies the sentence. Sentences of this form are satisfied by all sequences or by none; and as the details of the discussion show, they are satisfied by all when they are true.

It should also be clear that nothing hangs in this case on the particular index assigned to the variable in the predicate calculus representation of the English sentence concerned. I assigned it the index *two*; but a moment's reflection suggests that if the sequence satisfies the formula under *that* representation, it will satisfy it whatever index is given to the variable. The only problems that could arise would come in only if there were a rule forbidding the repetition of an object in a sequence; but there is no such rule, partly for this very reason. Indexing only matters when there is more than one variable involved; but even then nothing of substance hangs on which index is assigned to which variable, as long as distinct indices are assigned to distinct variables.

Note, finally, two points about this discussion of the existential quantifier. First, the all or nothing character of satisfaction means that when considering the circumstances under which a sentence of this form is true or false we do not have to consider explicitly the circumstances under which it is satisfied by all sequences, in a painstaking, sequence by sequence, manner. Since there's a non-denumerable infinity of sequences this is just as well! All we have to consider is one sequence. (This will be true of all closed sentences, as we shall see.) How this helps will emerge shortly. Second, in giving the satisfaction conditions of the existential quantifier in clause (6), the term 'some' is used; likewise, in giving the satisfaction conditions for the universal quantifier in (7), the term 'all' is used. Some might think this destroys the interest of the exercise; later we shall see why this thought is mistaken.

(7) A sequence S satisfies the universal quantification of a formula A with respect to v_k iff A is satisfied by all sequences S' which are like S except perhaps in their k-th term.

To see the working of this clause, consider the following English sentence:

'All aardvarks are flea-ridden.'

Orthodoxly (an orthodoxy we shall question later), this would be represented in predicate logic like this:

$(x'') (Fx'' \rightarrow Gx'')$

This, elementarily, is equivalent to:

$(x'') (\sim Fx'' \vee Gx'')$

Consider now a particular sequence, say,

S ⟨Cicero, Quine, the moon, . . .⟩

What is required for satisfaction is both that the second member of this sequence satisfies $\overline{\sim Fx'' \vee Gx''}$ (overlining *names* the expression overlined[6]), and also that the second member of all sequences S'

---

[6] I use two conventions (quotation and overlining) to represent designation of expressions in order to pay (inadequate) acknowledgment to the difficulties associated with designation. See Tarski: *Logic, Semantics, Metamathematics.*

such that $S' \underset{2}{\approx} S$, satisfy this formula. A member will satisfy this sequence if *either* it is not an aardvark or it is flea-ridden; the only way it can fail to satisfy it is by being both an aardvark and not flea-ridden. Thus, for example, the second member of S, Quine, satisfies the formula in virtue of his not being an aardvark. Suppose it true that there are no aardvarks that are not flea-ridden; then there is no object we can put in the second place of S, producing an S' which will not satisfy $\overline{\sim Fx'' \text{ v } Gx''}$. If there is such an object, then by clause (7) even S does not satisfy the sentence; for the definition requires that S and all S' such that $S' \underset{2}{\approx} S$ (that is, all S' *such that* S' differs from S in at most the second place) satisfy the formula if S is to satisfy the sentence.

Suppose S does satisfy the sentence; that is, S and every $S' \underset{2}{\approx} S$ satisfy $\overline{\sim Fx'' \text{ v } Gx''}$. Then it again follows that all sequences satisfy the sentence. Suppose there is a sequence $[S]$ which *per impossibile* does not. This must be either because the second member of $[S]$ does not satisfy $\overline{\sim Fx'' \text{ v } Gx''}$ or because the second member of some $S' \underset{2}{\approx} [S]$ does not satisfy the formula. But this means there is at least one aardvark that is not flea-ridden. But in that case, our original sequence S cannot have satisfied the sentence either: all we need to do is to consider the S'-variant of S in which this flea-free aardvark is the second member. Universally quantified sentences, therefore, are satisfied by all sequences or by none.

Loosely, we can see the difference between the satisfaction clauses for existentially and universally quantified sentences in terms of the difference between disjunction and conjunction. Consider the following tables, headed by a sentence of each kind and a sequence, and composed of the S'-variants of that sequence.

$(\exists x'')\ (Fx''\ \&\ Gx'')$	$(x'')\ (\sim Fx''\ \text{v}\ Gx'')$
S	
$\langle$Cicero, Quine, the moon, 7, . . .$\rangle$	$\langle$Cicero, Quine, the moon, 7, . . .$\rangle$
$S's$	
$\langle$Cicero, the moon, the moon, . . .$\rangle$	$\langle$Cicero, the moon, the moon, . . .$\rangle$
$\langle$Cicero, Napoleon, the moon, . . .$\rangle$	$\langle$Cicero, Napoleon, the moon, . . .$\rangle$
$\langle$Cicero, Platts, the moon, . . .$\rangle$	$\langle$Cicero, Platts, the moon, . . .$\rangle$
$\langle$Cicero, 37, the moon, . . .$\rangle$	$\langle$Cicero, 37, the moon, . . .$\rangle$
$\langle$Cicero, Moscow, the moon, . . .$\rangle$	$\langle$Cicero, Moscow, the moon, . . .$\rangle$
$\langle$Cicero, Tom Brown, the moon, . . .$\rangle$	$\langle$Cicero, Tom Brown, the moon, . . .$\rangle$

The S'-variants will continue as long as there are distinct objects to put in the second place. Now, the definition of satisfaction for the existential quantifier requires that *one* of the objects listed in the second place satisfy $\overline{Fx''\ \&\ Gx''}$; the definition of satisfaction for the universal quantifier requires that *each* object in the second place satisfy the formula $\overline{Fx'' \vee Gx''}$. Still, if there is an infinity of objects, these disjunctions and conjunctions of the S'-variants will be infinite in length; and when we turn to the definition of truth in terms of satisfaction by all sequences, remembering there to be a non-denumerable infinity of sequences, there will be a non-denumerable infinity of conjuncts and disjuncts – unless repetitions in the appropriate place are eliminated. The point is that in infinite domains – as, for example, that of the natural numbers – there will still be infinite disjunctions and conjunctions of S'-variants, so there is no hope in the analysis of the quantifiers in terms of disjunctions and conjunctions. Still, the analogy is there, and it may aid understanding a little.

The general conclusion is that, for closed sentences, satisfaction is an all or nothing matter. I want now to show how using the definition given we can obtain T-sentences for sentences of the predicate calculus – for that, you may remember, was the point of all this. We shall see, *en route*, how helpful the all or nothing nature of satisfaction can be.

Let's take the problem sentence that started this excursion going,

'Someone cuts my lawn and prunes my roses.'

We translate this as before:

$(\exists x'') (Fx'' \; \& \; Gx'')$.

By clause (8) of our definition of truth for this language (p. 21) we have this:

'$(\exists x'') (Fx'' \; \& \; Gx'')$' is true iff it is satisfied by all sequences.

The all or nothing character of satisfaction enables us to move to this claim:

'$(\exists x'') (Fx'' \; \& \; Gx'')$' is true iff it is satisfied by at least one sequence, S.

By clause (6), we now have this:

'$(\exists x'') (Fx'' \; \& \; Gx'')$' is true iff $\overline{Fx'' \; \& \; Gx''}$ is satisfied by some S', where $S' \underset{2}{\approx} S$.

Then by clause (5) we obtain:

'$(\exists x'') (Fx'' \; \& \; Gx'')$' is true iff some S', where $S' \underset{2}{\approx} S$, satisfies $\overline{Fx''}$ and satisfies $\overline{Gx''}$.

We now introduce a star function, $S^*(\;)$, which is a function from terms to members of sequences. For present purposes the following definition will suffice: if 'a' is a name of object a, $S^*(\overline{a}) = a$; if 'x'''' is

31

a variable, $S*\overline{(x'')}$ is the appropriate (i.e. the second) member of sequence S. (Cf. Mendelson, *Introduction to Mathematical Logic*, p. 50.) Using this device, we can now move to this:

'$(\exists x'')(Fx'' \& Gx'')$' is true iff for some S', $S'*\overline{(x'')}$ satisfies $\overline{Fx''}$ and satisfies $\overline{Gx''}$.

Using the appropriate predicate satisfaction clauses, (2) (i) and (2) (ii), we obtain:

'$(\exists x'')(Fx'' \& Gx'')$' is true iff for some S', $S'*\overline{(x'')}$ is F and is G.

A moment's reflection suggests that 'for some S', $S'*\overline{(x'')}$' is equivalent to 'some object'.[7] So we have:

'$(\exists x'')(Fx'' \& Gx'')$' is true iff some object is F and is G.

Translating back into English, and rephrasing the RHS, we have:

(T) 'Someone cuts my lawn and prunes my roses' is true iff someone cuts my lawn and prunes my roses.

Remember that the apparent triviality of the result does not matter – if anything, it is a virtue; what matters is being able systematically to derive such apparent trivialities from the rules of satisfaction. I have not presented a rigorous derivation (nor a rigorous truth-definition); but then, as said before, satisfaction is relative to an interest.

Let us consider one other example, this time using the universal quantifier. Consider the sentence

'All aardvarks are flea-ridden.'

Accepting for present purposes the standard representation in predicate logic, we have this:

$(x'')(Fx'' \to Gx'')$.

This is equivalent to:

$(x'')(\sim Fx'' \vee Gx'')$.

By clause (8) of the truth-definition, we have:

'$(x'')(\sim Fx'' \vee Gx'')$' is true iff it is satisfied by all sequences.

The all or nothing character of satisfaction enables us to move to this claim:

'$(x'')(\sim Fx'' \vee Gx'')$' is true iff it is satisfied by at least one sequence S.

[7] This intuitive point is formally tricky; the treatment of quantification proposed in Chapter IV helps here.

Using clause (7), we then have:

'$(x'')(\sim Fx'' \vee Gx'')$' is true iff $\overline{\sim Fx'' \vee Gx''}$ is satisfied by all S's, such that $S' \underset{2}{\approx} S$.

Rewriting, we have

'$(x'')(\sim Fx'' \vee Gx'')$' is true if every S' such that $S' \underset{2}{\approx} S$ satisfies $\overline{\sim Fx'' \vee Gx''}$.

Using the star-function, we move to this:

'$(x'')(\sim Fx'' \vee Gx'')$' is true iff for every S', $S'^{*}\overline{(x'')}$ satisfies $\overline{\sim Fx'' \vee Gx''}$.

Using the obvious clause for disjunction, we have:

'$(x'')(\sim Fx'' \vee Gx'')$' is true iff for every S', $S'^{*}\overline{(x'')}$ satisfies $\overline{\sim Fx''}$ or $S'^{*}\overline{(x'')}$ satisfies $\overline{Gx''}$.

Then, using (2) (i) and (2) (ii), we obtain:

'$(x'')(\sim Fx'' \vee Gx'')$' is true iff for every S', $S'^{*}\overline{(x'')}$ is $\sim F$ or is G.

Eliminating 'for all S', $S'^{*}\overline{(x'')}$' in the obvious way, and translating back into English, we obtain the appropriate T-sentence. Note finally that in both these derivations we find the pattern noted in proving T-sentences in the propositional calculus: on the RHS of the biconditional, semantic terms – like satisfaction, truth, and the star-function – occur at each stage except the final one.

7 Realism and Correspondence

The technicalities just sketched are not mere technicalities; they represent the framework within which a precise study of semantics is possible. Nearly all the remainder of this book will assume an understanding of these technicalities. But I want to continue this discussion of truth by considering two traditional questions that figure large in disputes about truth: the matter of correspondence theories and the problem of truth-bearers. I shall be comparatively brief with both of them.

When discussing Ramsey's treatment of R-sentences, I considered the realistic reading of such sentences alongside the redundancy reading; I also, without argument, declared myself for the realistic reading as well as the redundancy reading. The hallmark of realism as the term is used here is this: the applicability of the truth-predicate to a sentence is determined by extra-linguistic reality – except of course for sentences about language. Thus the R-sentence

'Snow is white' is true iff snow is white

tells us that the truth-predicate is correctly applicable to the sentence 'Snow is white', if and only if, the state of affairs described on the RHS obtains. Many, including Tarski, have held that any realistic theory is also a correspondence theory. I suggest, however, that it is useful to apply these labels separately: while all correspondence theories will be realistic theories, the reverse need not be true. Historically, most exponents of what have been called correspondence theories have gone beyond realistic theories, as characterised, in attempting to give a detailed, supposedly conventional correlation of parts of the truth-bearer with parts of some real entity that makes the truth-bearer true or false, be that entity a fact, state of affairs, or whatever. The hallmark of correspondence theories, as I shall understand the expression, is the construction of detailed structural conventional correspondence relations between the parts of the truth-bearer and parts of the truth-determining entities in the world.

Is the Tarskian theory sketched a correspondence theory in this sense? One line of thought suggests not, another suggests that it is. The negative line of thought is this: the recursive characterisation of a truth-predicate for propositional calculus languages, while perhaps realistic, falls well short of describing the requisite detailed structures. Indeed, the whole point is that there is no need to describe the structure within sentences. Maybe there is structure revealed within compound sentences, but there is none within the atomic sentences. Yet Tarski's theory is merely an application of the same approach to languages of greater complexity; but surely the greater complexity of a language cannot lead to a distinctive kind of truth-theory? The positive line of thought is this: in Tarski's theory, truth is defined in terms of satisfaction. A theory invoking satisfaction meets most of the characterisation of correspondence theories. It is a relation between truth-bearers and real entities, and is a structural relation of the desired kind: it concerns parts of the truth-bearers, sentential functions, and elements of reality, namely, sequences of objects. The role of sequences is the reason for 'most' in the sentence before last: for it is possible to hold to Tarski's theory without accepting an ontology of facts, states of affairs, or whatever, and perhaps further possible to accept such an ontology without accepting that sequences of objects are properly called *parts* of these entities. So the structural element in the world-end *relatum* can be disputed; hence the caution. Also, of course, sequences of objects are radically different entities from those traditionally employed in correspondence theories; but this hardly matters, and may anyway prove to the advantage of Tarski's theory. The more serious challenge would be that aimed at the other *relatum*, the truth-bearer. If the discernment of predicate structure within sentences were an arbitrary matter – as opposed to the discernment of *particular* predicate structures being an under-determined matter – perhaps the claim to correspondence would appear uninteresting. But this point has been dealt with earlier (pp. 23–4), and the arguments need not now be rehearsed. There is genuine predicate structure within, say, English; the detection of such structure is not mere whim. The structure revealed within a sentence by Tarski's theory is *there*, is central to our understanding of those sentences. This puts us in a position to see one error of the negative line of thought. Since there is genuine additional structural complexity, there is no reason to believe that a truth-theory for such a language cannot introduce new notions, like that of correspondence, that are not involved in truth-definition for simpler languages. The negative line of thought only has force if the invocation of predicate structure is an arbitrary formal manoeuvre; it is not, so the thought has no force.

We are saddled, then, with a correspondence theory of truth. It is another question whether this is desirable. Such a theory must characterise adequately both *relata* and the relation of correspondence. Subject to later discussion, on our theory sentences are truth-bearers, with sentential functions as the items satisfied; satisfaction as recursively defined is the relation; sequences of objects are satisfiers. Propositions, statements, facts, states of affairs, and other assorted relations of correspondence figure not at all. Most traditional discussion of correspondence theories has centred upon the adequacy of the definition of the relation or the adequacy of the requisite identity and individuation conditions of the *relata*. We avoid most of these worries since the relation is precisely defined and the *relata* are either clearly specified (sequences) or items any theory must acknowledge (sentences and sentential functions). What do need to be considered are two interesting general arguments which might be construed as objections to the theory.

Austin, in *How To Do Things With Words* (pp. 139–48), seems to present a general sketch of an argument designed to show the pointlessness of traditional discussions of truth – including, perhaps, his own earlier contributions.[8] His point is this: the phenomenon of vagueness, both of particular terms and of complete sentences, makes the notion of the truth of a sentence itself vague. So it cannot be precisely defined. For example, is it true that France is hexagonal? Well, it is and it isn't; it all depends upon the level of precision we

---

[8] Interestingly, Austin comes close at one point to assimilating *facts* to *objects*. The move to sequences of objects would then be unobjectionable to account for relational sentences. He says: 'Suppose we confront "France is hexagonal" with the facts; in this case, I suppose, with France . . .' (p. 142). Still, on Tarski's theory, France is not, so to speak, especially important: truth is satisfaction by *all* sequences.

take to be required. As Austin says 'the interests and purposes of the utterance and its context are all important' (p. 142). This worry need not delay us long. First, there are many sentences and many predicates that are not vague: those about precise spatial position, predicates involving numbers and so forth. More importantly, the phenomenon of vagueness is readily incorporated within our theory. On the RHS of a T-sentence, we have the same sentence used as is named on the LHS, or a translation thereof; if it is the same sentence, the vagueness is carried over; if not, we merely stipulate that the vagueness be carried over. We match vagueness with vagueness. This same vagueness can be assumed in the axioms governing sentential components. There is no unacceptable sharpening up of vagueness involved.[9]

The second argument is more important. It is implicit, I think, in Strawson's original response to Austin's attempted defence of a correspondence theory, particularly in his treatment of demonstrative and descriptive conventions. (See the first papers by Austin and Strawson in Pitcher, *Truth*.) Whether it is Strawson's or not, the argument is this. Correspondence theories of truth attempt a detailed account of conventional correlations between parts of sentences and elements of the world, in virtue of which correlations obtaining a sentence is true if it is true. Prior to the question of truth or falsity, however, is the question of the meaning of the sentence; the sentence has the same meaning be it true or false, and we can know its meaning without knowing whether it be true or false. But how is this meaning determined? Crudely, by conventional correlations between parts of sentences and elements or aspects of the world. For example the meaning of 'Paris has a cathedral' is determined by the *demonstrative conventions* linking the term 'Paris' with a particular object, and by *descriptive conventions* linking 'has a cathedral' with a general aspect that may or may not be instantiated in the world. These conventions – call them meaning conventions – give the sentence the meaning it has. Suppose we now go on to ask if the sentence is true? A correspondence theory of truth invites us to look for some *further* conventional correlations between parts of the sentence and aspects of the world, correlations over and above those embodied in the conventions that give the sentence its meaning. But it is clear that there are, and there can be, no such further conventional correlations: the only relevant correlations are those that determine the meaning of the sentence, it then being a matter for the world to determine whether the sentence

[9] Austin might have had the deeper thought in mind that the phenomenon of vagueness requires the rejection of the standard logic on which Tarski's theory is based, together with the thought that the replacing logic threatens Convention T. On this see Putnam, *Meaning and the Moral Sciences*, (pp. 18–33), and Haack, *Deviant Logic*, ch. VI.

is true or false. But that is not, and cannot be, determined by some further conventional correlation. There is neither need of, nor room for, distinctively *truth*-determining conventional correlations. Correspondence theories of truth mislocate the structural correlations: they take them from their proper resting place, the theory of meaning, and place them where they cannot fit, the theory of truth.

This is a sophisticated argument: and it is quite compatible with a realistic theory of truth. But it fails. First, a couple of fairly trivial points. The claim to priority of questions of meaning over questions of truth-value is unclear. Listening to a brilliant, utterly honest and reliable mathematician, I might realise that he holds a certain sentence true. Because of his reliability, I take the sentence to be true. But I do not understand it. Second, the argument is founded upon a sharp contrast between questions of meaning and questions of truth or fact; this is a contrast that Quine has given us reason to view with scepticism (Quine, *From a Logical Point of View*, pp. 20–46). But the important failing in this argument, connecting with the previous points, is this: it assumes a contrast between theories of meaning and theories of truth. Of course, there is a contrast between the meaning of a sentence and its *truth-value*, and so between knowing the meaning of a sentence and knowing its truth-value. It does not follow that there is a contrast between the meaning of a sentence and its truth-conditions, nor one between knowing the meaning of a sentence and knowing its truth-conditions. Correspondence theories of the Tarskian kind have been presented as theories as to how the truth-*conditions* of sentences are determined; the question of specific truth-value is a further one, and one the theory does not consider. And, as we have seen, it has not seemed clear to all philosophers that a theory about how the truth-conditions of a sentence are determined is distinct from a theory about how its meaning is determined; if they can be identified, questions of priority do not arise. This possible identification of theories of meaning and theories of truth-conditions will be discussed and developed in the next chapter; all we need note now is that this argument against correspondence theories rests upon the assumption that they cannot be identified. As such, the argument is important: for it can be taken as showing that a defender of a correspondence theory of truth must accept the identification of the theory of meaning with the theory of truth-conditions. And that is no small result, given that we have found in Tarski's work an argument for a correspondence theory of truth.

8 Truth-Bearers

I turn now, with a measure of reluctance, to an issue that figures large in standard discussions of truth, that of the bearers of truth. My reluctance stems from my failure to discern a well-defined, substantial problem here. I can see the point in claims that various entities posited as truth-bearers – statements, propositions – do not have adequately specified identity and individuation conditions. That issue is founded upon a truism: before we can posit particulars of a given kind – say, ϕs, – we need to have a grasp of the notion of a ϕ; and to have a grasp of the notion of a ϕ is to have a grasp of the notion of *a ϕ*. Coherent explanation of the notion of a particular of a kind is given only if adequate identity and individuation conditions for particulars of that kind are given; that is what *particularity* is. So whatever entities we posit as truth-bearers, identity and individuation conditions for them must be given. But beyond this negative matter, I am unclear how the issue of truth-bearers is to be settled; for I am unclear what the issue is. An indication of the muddle here is the ability of many philosophers to attribute to Strawson both a 'no property' theory of truth, the obscure claim that truth is not a property, and a theory about what the bearers of this (non) property are.[10]

Occasionally, the issue is presented as turning on ordinary language, on what is ordinarily spoken of as a bearer of truth. Usually, those presenting the issue in these terms claim that statements or propositions are truth-bearers. This is madness. Ordinary people do not make statements; this is the prerogative of hospital spokesmen and a certain species of ageing academic. Nor do they make propositions: that is the primary pastime of only a small part of the population, not entirely different in extension from that just mentioned. Ordinary discourse suggests that people *say things*, and attribute truth to *what was said*. But that is hardly a clear empirical base on which to build a theory. Here, more than anywhere else, the impoverished and fraudulent character of that passing phenomenon – 'ordinary language philosophy' – is revealed.

So the terms 'statement' and 'proposition' are terms of art, and should not be presented as anything else. Even as terms of art, they have been used in a multitude of ways. Loosely, I shall use the term *statement* to refer to an *act* of uttering a sentence, a dated event, and shall use the term *proposition* to refer to the content of the saying, to what was said. This bland explanation does not commit me to the coherence of these notions. Note, incidentally, that the positing of propositions as *what was said*, the bearer of truth, is a positing with a quite distinct motivation, and *perhaps* with a quite distinct resultant ontology, from the positing of propositions as either the meanings of sentences or the objects of mental states of the propositional attitude variety.

Propositions, as Quine has taught us, are dubious things at best.

[10] But see again the note on p. 11.

So why not rest with sentences or statements as truth-bearers? Statements are events, and have the same kinds of identity conditions as events in general. Those conditions are not unproblematic, and nor are those of sentences. But any theory of language will have to tackle these problems anyway, so why saddle ourselves with extra anxieties about propositions? There are a number of reasons that have been adduced for incurring this extra burden, of varying degrees of inadequacy. One is that we do not ordinarily talk of sentences or statements (in my sense) as truth-bearers; but that, as said, is beside the point. Another objection is that the same sentence can for one utterance be true and for another false. My saying 'My hair is falling out' is true, for the reader it may not be. To meet this we can either relativise the ascription of truth to sentences, utterances, persons, places, and times, or ascribe truth to utterances of sentences (statements), by persons at places and times. That is, we have either:

(T_1) *s* as uttered by person *u* at time *t* in place *w* is true iff *p*;

or

(T_2) The utterance of *s* by person *u* at time *t* in place *w* is true iff *p*.

Where indexicals occur in the designated sentence on the LHS, as far as possible we can replace them on the RHS using the variables. One example should convey the general idea:

'I am now cold' as uttered by person *u* at time *t* in place *w* is true iff *u* is cold at *t*.

I can see little to choose between (T_1) and (T_2) as the general schema; for no particular reason, I shall work with (T_1).[11] Since we do not wish to restrict attention to sentences that have been uttered, we need the following slight amendment:

(T'_1) *s* as potentially uttered by person *u* at time *t* in place *w* is true iff *p*.

Maybe there are sentences which require further variables to be introduced; but the general procedure is clear.

Finally, it might be objected that the same sentence, identified typographically and phonetically, can be true in one language but false in another; if the speaker *u* in (T'_1) is bilingual for the languages, the problem is clear. Here we can do one of two things. The first is

[11] Davidson ('True to the Facts') favours T_2. The reason, I assume, is his desire to have as simple a connection as possible between ' "*p*" is true' and 'It is true that *p*', together with the idea of handling the latter idiom in a similar manner to the treatment he proposes for indirect discourse (Davidson 'On Saying That'; see also Chapter V). This matter need not be pursued now.

further to relativise the truth-predicate to the language *L* concerned. We thus end up with

(T''₁)   *s* as potentially uttered by person *u* at time *t* in place *w* is true in *L* iff *p*.[12]

This might encounter further problems because of the apparent need now to say something about what true in *L*, true in L_1, true in L_2, and, generally, true in variable *L* have in common. (Cf. C. A. B. Peacocke in Evans and McDowell, *Truth and Meaning*, pp. 162–88.) Lest this worry proves insurmountable, we should note another way of handling this worry suggested by Putnam (*Mind, Language and Reality*, pp. 70–84). This is to hold that two typographically and phonetically identical units in different languages are *not* the same sentence. Different languages cannot share sentences. There are interesting problems here, but I shall not now pursue them. I shall tentatively conclude that (T''₁) will be adequate for our task, and hence that sentences, with the appropriate relativisations, are truth-bearers. But I do not hold this to be a claim of much interest.

9 Some Refinements[13]

Earlier, I introduced the distinction between the language of the sentences designated on the LHS of (R)-sentences, the object language, and the language of the rest of each (R)-sentence, including the sentence used on the RHS, the meta-language. This distinction is evident in cases of heterophonic translation – say, where we are giving in English the (R)-sentences for various French sentences – but might seem problematic in the case of homophonic translation, which I have earlier (misleadingly) called the one-language case.

It is often claimed that Tarski proved that the object-language and the meta-language will always differ, that the object-language can never be identical to the meta-language. In a famous theorem to-wards the end of his classic paper on truth, Tarski is *supposed* to have shown that a definition of truth for language *L* can only be developed in a language that goes beyond *L* either in terms of primitive symbol-ism or in terms of axiomatisation. But this is not strictly an accurate representation of what Tarski did. He in fact proved that if *L* is a consistent language capable of expressing arithmetic, then there is no sentential function in one free variable formulated in the primitive

---

[12] This language relativisation also sidesteps various threats of paradox; see Quine, *The Ways of Paradox*, pp. 1–18.

[13] Since this section was written, Kripke has published an important and novel paper on truth 'Outline of a Theory of Truth'. Rather than delaying this book for the (not inconsiderable) time I would need to understand and assess that paper, and rather than present a mass of ill-digested misunderstandings, I have decided to leave this section as it is.

symbolism of *L* and true of precisely the true sentences of *L*. But given our way of handling the truth-predicate, the relevance of this result is not clear. The notion of the satisfaction of a formula of *L* by infinite sequences of objects is defined by recursion on the length of the syntactical description of the formula; truth is then defined in terms of satisfaction. Now, predicates introduced into the language by recursive definitions – as is our truth-predicate – are not always eliminable in favour of expressions involving only the primitive symbolism of the language – the kind of expression Tarski's proof is concerned with. Still, if a predicate is introduced recursively into a language *L*, and *if* the proof theory of that language suffices to prove the existence of some class satisfying the clauses of the recursive definition, then there is a familiar method, deriving from Frege, for replacing the recursive definition by a direct one, an explicit definition in terms of the primitive symbolism of the language.[14] The conclusion to be drawn is that we can define truth for a language *L* recursively within *L* only if the proof theory for *L* does not suffice to prove the existence of some class satisfying the recursion clauses of the truth-definition. Under these circumstances, the object-language and the meta-language can apparently coincide.

More modestly, however, the need to avoid some of the family of semantic paradoxes suggests that this coincidence will not obtain. I shall not go into the detail of these paradoxes here (see Quine, *The Ways of Paradox,* pp. 1–18); suffice it to say that one method (I think the best) of avoiding these paradoxes is to deal only with language-relativised truth-predicates (which we have seen anyway to be a likely consequence of treating sentences as truth-bearers), and to hold in addition that the predicate *is true in L* cannot be part of *L*. This way the paradox-raising sentences cannot even be formulated. The predicate *is true in L'* cannot be part of *L'*, but can be part of the meta-meta-language *L''*. Thus object-language and meta-language will differ to that extent.

The sufficiency condition so far applied to definitions of truth is that they satisfy Convention T; that is, that the definition has as logical consequences all sentences of the form

(T) *s* is true if and only if *p*

where '*s*' is replaced by a canonical description of a sentence of the language *L*, and '*p*' replaced by that sentence, if the object-language is part of the meta-language, or its translation if not. But we have just now seen that the truth-predicate must be relativised to potential utterances, speakers, times, places and languages. These amendments

---

[14] An *explicit* definition enables the elimination of the defined term from any occurrence. On the relation between recursive and explicit definitions, see Tarski, *Logic, Semantics, Metamathematics.*

imply that the ideal of a definition of truth in *L* for natural language *L* satisfying Convention T is unattainable, for the presence of the variables required by indexical phenomena can prevent the generation of T-sentences. The response to this is to abandon hope of attaining this ideal of sufficiency, while still aiming as close as possible to it.

Even if we were to attempt to produce an explicit definition of truth in *L* in the meta-language *L'*, we should need *some* Tarski-like condition of adequacy. And we have anyway abandoned the project of *recursively* characterising *truth in L* in L in spite of our attempts to weaken the force of Tarski's proof. Why, then, should we continue to favour recursive definition in the meta-language over explicit definition in the meta-language? The advantage of the recursive approach is that it minimises, without eliminating, the differences between the meta-language and the object-language. On the recursive approach, those languages will carry the same *ontology*, and the increase in *ideology* is just the semantic concepts (cf. Davidson, 'In Defence of Convention T'). Whereas if we try to convert this into an explicit definition, both the ontology and the ideology of the meta-language vastly exceed that of the object-language – the excess that Tarski's proof points to. The, perhaps indecisive, motivation for minimising these differences between object- and meta-languages is not the simple desire to minimise the (intuitively artificial) contrast between object- and meta-languages, but is, rather, this: if the characterisation of a truth-predicate for a language is to play some yet to be determined role in the theory of meaning, then that characterisation will also play some yet to be determined role in the final account of speakers' understanding. The greater the contrast between object- and meta-languages, the greater is the danger (subject to articulation of the roles just mentioned) that our *explanation* of native speakers' understanding will involve the attribution to such speakers of some *grasp* of notions (those distinctive of the meta-language) which there is nothing in their explicitly manifestable verbal repertoire to suggest that they have any grasp of. Such an attribution would be a (needless) theoretical posit; it would lack any direct empirical content.

Chapter II

Theories of Truth and
Theories of Meaning

1 Novelty and Boundlessness in Language Use

The philosophy of language cannot be considered in isolation from the philosophy of mind. Any philosophy of language must exhibit the central role of meaning, and that notion critically interacts with that of *understanding*. The meaning of an expression in a language is what a competent speaker of the language understands by that expression. In this simple connection resides both interest and danger – the danger that false accounts of understanding may issue in the rejection of correct accounts of meaning. In spite of that danger, any theory of meaning must be assessed for the plausibility of the account it issues in of speakers' understanding.

Nowhere are the complexities of the interrelations between language and mind, and especially between meaning and understanding, more clearly or more generally exemplified than in the aspect of linguistic behaviour that Chomsky has labelled the *creativity of language use*. This phenomenon represents three distinct, though related, elements of the competent speaker's linguistic behaviour: the first is his ability to generate and understand an indefinitely large number of novel utterances; the second is the 'stimulus free' character of his language use; and the third is his ability to produce utterances which are 'apt to the situation'.

For present purposes we need only concern ourselves with the first of these elements, the fact that a language speaker, on acquiring mastery of a language with a finite vocabulary and a finite grammatical base, can then produce and understand any of an indefinitely large number of novel sentences in the language. Here we have two pictures, first, that of each language having a finite base, a picture suggested by the utter unclarity of a natural language having anything other than such a foundation (cf. Davidson, 'Theories of Meaning'); and second, the picture of this base somehow generating sentences without limit, to the point, for example, where most of the sentences in the language will never be uttered. But we have to remember that languages are abstractions from linguistic behaviour; so these pictures must *somehow* be realised in the competent speaker, must *somehow* be exhibited in his understanding. The realisation of the first picture is a tendentious matter, but the second, the unbounded character of natural languages, is straightforwardly realised in two 'creativities', or recognitional capacities: a semantic creativity, whereby the speaker is so constituted that he is capable, for an indefinite range of sentences, of understanding them, of recognising them *as* meaning such-and-such or so-and-so; and a syntactic creativity, whereby the speaker is so constituted that he is capable, for an indefinite range of strings of noises or symbols, of classifying them as grammatical or ungrammatical, of recognising them *as* grammatical or not. Thus when describing this competent speaker's capacities, we describe his semantic 'creativity', his understanding, in terms of his grasp of, his recognition of, the meanings of a boundless set of sentences.

Now, we encounter connected difficulties of description and explanation. Any full description of the competent speaker's capacities will include a description of what he has a grasp of; that is, it must include a description, in our language, of the meanings of the sentences that he understands, a description of *what* he recognises the sentences *as* meaning. But the limitless number of those sentences, the boundless nature of that grasp, precludes the only simple option, that of *listing*, for each sentence of his language that he understands, a sentence of our language that gives its meaning. We cannot compile an infinite list, neither of the sentences of his language he understands nor of the sentences in our language giving their meaning. There is also a problem of explanation, of reconciling the realisations in the speaker of the two pictures just mentioned: of explaining how it is that, starting from a finite syntactic and semantic base, the speaker has the boundless recognitional capacities outlined.

The moral is fairly clear. Both the descriptive and explanatory puzzles will be resolved if we construct a theory of meaning in our language for his language; this theory will have to show how the meaning of each sentence in his language depends upon its structure, how the meaning is determined by the semantic properties of its components, together with the semantic import of their syntactic combination, its syntactic structure. That is, the theory must imply a sentence of the form

(M) *s* means that *p*

for each sentence of his language, where '*s*' is replaced by a name of that sentence of the language and '*p*' by a sentence that, in some sense, gives the meaning of *s*; and it must do so through some general semantic treatment of the constituents of *s* and syntactic structures of *s*, which constituents and structures are but part of the finite stock of semantic and syntactic components found in the language. But the obviousness of this moral testifies to its comparative useless- ness – pending explication of the terms 'meaning', 'semantic proper- ties', 'components', and 'syntactic structures' as they figure in it. Also, until much more has been said about the relation between any such theory developed and the speaker's *actual* recognitional capacities and processes, the descriptive and explanatory tasks will remain: what makes the theory a description of *his* linguistic capaci- ties? What makes it an explanation of his *actual* competence?

This first element of the creativity of language use, then, presents a general and important, albeit vague, constraint upon semantic theories. It might reasonably be thought, therefore, that a rather more precise and perspicuous characterisation of it should be given. If one turns to Chomsky's writings in search of clarification, one is likely to be disappointed. This is unsurprising since his interests are not the same as ours. In *Cartesian Linguistics,* Chomsky's concern lies with the historical development of ideas, which requires that the characterisation of the relevant notions be somewhat incomplete; while in *Language and Mind,* his concern is with the implications of a whole network of linguistic phenomena for the philosophy of mind, and ultimately for the concept of a person, so he makes no attempt to isolate those elements within the network that are immediately relevant to semantic analysis. Still, I think Chomsky can be criticised, in a slight way, for coining the expression 'creativity' for this set of phenomena; for this suggests that this set is even more mysterious and obscure than it is, and so invites the worst kind of pseudo- explanation. He even comes close to the assimilation of linguistic 'creativity' to artistic creativity:

> A concern for the creative aspect of language use persists
> through the romantic period, in relation to the general problem
> of true creativity, in the full sense of this term. . . . From this
> conception of language, it is only a short step to the association
> of the creative aspect of language use with true artistic
> creativity. . . . The 'poetical' quality of ordinary language
> derives from its independence of immediate stimulation . . . and
> its freedom from practical ends. These characteristics, along
> with the boundlessness of language as an instrument of free
> self-expression, are essentially those emphasised by Descartes
> and his followers (*Cartesian Linguistics,* pp. 16–17).

Now it is not clear whether Chomsky here is merely concerned with the historically conceived connections of language creativity or whether he is indeed sanctioning the assimilation of linguistic creativity to artistic creativity, or creativity 'in the full sense of this term'. But if he is doing the latter – which would, I suppose, explain his coining of the phrase 'the creative aspect of language use' – then he is surely mistaken. It may be that we can provide no other explication of the phenomenon of linguistic creativity than that provided by its assimilation to 'true creativity, in the full sense of this term'; but if so, let us admit we can provide no explication of the phenomenon at all. At least as regards the element of 'creativity' that concerns us – the boundless, novel aspect of language use – the term sets us off on completely the wrong track. The whole aim of the kind of theory of meaning just broadly sketched is to reveal that first element as tantamount to our ability to put two and two together; this is an important ability, but it is the opposite of creativity (ordinarily so-called).

I shall therefore talk of the boundless, or the novel, aspect of language use. I shall attempt to illuminate this aspect a little more by consideration of two criticisms that have recently been made of the emphasis placed by linguists and philosophers alike upon this aspect of language use, and more generally, upon the complete set of Chomskian 'creativity' phenomena. The first criticism is Gilbert Harman's, and is primarily concerned with the general phenomenon of linguistic creativity ('Three Levels of Meaning'). Harman suggests that this phenomenon ceases to be puzzling when seen as a natural consequence of two facts: first, that we usually speak and communicate in the language in which we think; and second, that we have the power for creative thought. Now, the second of these facts is surely desperately obscure: as Chomsky remarks, the question of how creative thought is possible is 'a complete mystery'. But anyway, when considering the boundless and novel aspects of language use, Harman's suggestion merely serves to postpone the problem. If we accept the conception of thinking tacit in Harman's remarks, we are still left with the problem of how we have the ability to create and understand a limitless number of novel, grammatical thoughts; and any explanation of that appears likely to invoke precisely the kind of Chomskian consideration which Harman wishes to render superfluous. This could only be avoided if one's recognitional relation to one's own thoughts was different from one's relation to one's own publicly uttered sentences; but if our picture of thought, like Harman's, is that of 'speaking' to oneself in sentences in one's own mind's ear, then there seems no guarantee that in that thought only grammatical, intelligible 'sentences' will occur – any more than there is for *talking* to oneself. So we can say that we *understand* the sentences 'heard', that we exercise our syntactic and semantic recognitional capacities upon them; the explanation of these capacities is therefore still needed, and will not differ in form from the explanation of those capacities in relation to public utterances.

The second criticism comes from Hilary Putnam, and is directed primarily at the emphasis upon the boundless aspect of language use (*Mind, Language and Reality*, pp. 139–52). Putnam describes the problem posed by this as 'relatively straightforward' on the grounds that it is easy to describe how logical words can be used to build up complex sentences out of simple ones, and that it is also easy to say how the truth-conditions of those complex sentences are related to the truth-conditions of the simpler sentences from which they are derived.

All of this is correct; and it may be that Putnam's main concern is to dispel the air of mystery surrounding talk of 'creativity' by pointing out that the way to explain our limitless capacities is the construction of a theory of meaning which reveals those capacities as comparable to that of seeing that two and two is four. Still, Putnam misleads about the scope and ease of doing this. The problem of boundlessness does not originate with, and is not restricted to, what are traditionally viewed as *logical* words. Consider reported speech: even with this one idiom, which does not figure in any of the customary inventories of 'logical words', it seems that the boundless element can be present. We can generate and understand any of an indefinitely large number of sentences of the form '*X* said that *p*' in accordance with the following simple series: '*A* said that *p*'; '*B* said that *A* said that *p*'; '*A* said that *B* said that *A* said that *p*'; and so on. Each of the sentences in this indefinitely extendable series has a quite distinct meaning; we believe we can understand each such sentence; yet we have no clear idea of the 'contribution' that the embedded sentence ('*p*' in the simplest case) makes to the meaning of the whole sentence; or, in Putnam's terms, we have no account of how the truth-conditions of the whole sentence are related to the truth-conditions of the embedded sentence. Or consider the puzzles that arise in connection with complex singular terms, as exemplified in the following, indefinitely extendable, series of sentences: 'Pegasus is bald'; 'The horse behind Pegasus is bald'; 'The horse behind the horse behind Pegasus is bald'; and so on. Each of these sentences has a quite distinct meaning (has quite different conditions of truth); yet this difference of meaning cannot be explained in terms of the difference in the truth-conditions of the components and the consequent difference in the truth-conditions of the whole, for singular terms ('the horse behind Pegasus', etc.) do not have truth-conditions. So the problem of how we come to understand any of the indefinitely large number of such sentences is simply not touched by talk of the relations between the truth-conditions of complex sentences and the truth-conditions of simple sentences.

Nor are these minor and isolated irritations. We have, for example, little or no idea of the contribution to the meanings of complex sentences made by the components in the case of counterfactuals, causal statements, and statements about belief, perception, and intention. Even this list is by no means exhaustive. To say that the problems posed by the unbounded aspect of language use are 'relatively straightforward' while these problems remain unsolved is optimistic at best. However, it might be more useful to treat Putnam's criticism as a demand for a systematic clarification of the unbounded aspect of language use. Such a clarification is partly to be found in our discussion in the last chapter of languages of increasing degrees of complexity. We need not rehearse that discussion now. What we should do is acknowledge that complexity can increase way beyond the levels considered there; which level or levels natural languages figure on is an open question.

It is not the boundless character of natural languages that should occasion surprise; what would occasion reasonable surprise would be a finitely bounded natural language. To see this is in part to remove the air of mystery here. Consider the possibility that empirical investigation reveals there to be an upper limit – say, forty words – on the length of sentences we can understand. Then it would appear that the class of sentences that we can effectively understand is finite; so it would seem tiresomely myopic for grammarians and philosophers alike to continue to handle natural languages as if they were boundless. There is a bound: namely, that provided by our retentive capacities.

Before accepting this censure, we should pause a little. Consider the following pairs of sentences:

[A1]   John believes that *p*.
[A2]   Paul believes that John believes that *p*.
[B1]   John believes that Paul believes that John believes that *p*.
[B2]   Paul believes that John believes that Paul believes that John believes that *p*.

Intuitively, one wants to say this of these pairs of sentences: the rule of language governing the application of the expression '. . . believes that . . .' serves to license as semantically admissible both the 'move' from [A1] to [A2] and the 'move' from [B1] to [B2]; if either move is legitimate, results in a semantically acceptable sentence, then so is the other. Unless, of course, there is a restriction built into the rule governing the application of '. . . believes that . . .' concerning the lengths of sentences to which it can apply, or the number of times that the same component can be repeated (the same linguistic operation performed) within any one sentence. But now it can be seen quite how strange it would be were there to be any such restriction built into

48

the rule governing the use of an expression – a restriction, say, to sentences with thirty-eight or fewer words, or a restriction upon the number of times any sentence can be embedded within another sentence of, say, thirteen times. *That* is what would be odd, and the absence of such a restriction is correspondingly unpuzzling; so the boundless character of natural languages, which follows from the absence of any such restriction, is similarly unproblematic in kind.

Even if there is an empirical limit upon the number of sentences in the language we can understand, this need not now concern us. The same rules that govern the meanings of those complex sentences that we are able to understand will also govern the meanings of those complex sentences which are too complex for us as a matter of empirical fact to understand; but if our retentive capacities were greater we should be able to understand this latter class of sentences, and so there is a point to saying that, in abstraction, they are syntactically and semantically well formed. It is simpler at this point to idealise away limitations arising from retentive limitations; they will be readily enough inserted at the end of the day. But it is not just a matter of simplicity and idealisation: there are also the elements of novelty and understanding. Even if we could compile a list of the supposedly finite number of sentences in the language comprehensible to us, giving the meaning of each as if it were, so to speak, a primitive sentence, this would ignore our *understanding* of these sentences, and would leave quite without explanation our capacity to understand them at first hearing. By revealing structure within each of this finite set of sentences, we at least edge towards an explanation of this capacity; the need to reveal such structure will be forced upon us if we abstract away from retentive limitations, and treat the language, and our linguistic capabilities, as boundless.

2 Some Possible Constraints on Theories of Meaning: Holism and Monism

The descriptive and explanatory puzzles posed by the boundless and novel character of language use could be resolved by the construction of an adequate theory of meaning for the language used. What form should such a theory take? And what would constitute its adequacy?

As said earlier, we might require of such a theory that it imply a sentence of the form

(*M*) *s* means that *p*

for each sentence *s* of the language under study, where '*s*' is replaced by a name of a sentence and '*p*' by a sentence that, in a sense partly determined by the theory, 'gives the meaning' of *s*. The notion of *giving the meaning* of a sentence is a technical notion, the role of

49

which we shall examine shortly; but we have held all along that it must connect, crucially, with the language speaker's *understanding* of the sentence *s*, with his semantic recognitional capacity.

It is a trivial requirement on the adequacy of such a theory that it tell us what *all* meaningful sentences mean; this requirement of *completeness* can hardly be controversial. A quite distinct, and much more controversial, adequacy condition is that of *holism*, which has been vividly expressed in the following words: '(W)e can give the meaning of any sentence (or word) only by giving the meaning of every sentence (and word) in the language' (Davidson, 'Truth and Meaning', p. 5).

To understand this holistic claim we have to understand its rationale; that rationale draws attention to two possible prior adequacy conditions on theories of meaning. First, there is a condition that might be called that of semantic monism. This is that the rules that determine the meaning of each and every sentence in the language should all be of the same general kind. When we give an explanation of the meaning of any word or sentence, whatever the surface characteristics of that sentence (e.g. be it indicative, imperative, or interrogative), the explanation of that meaning has always to be of the same general type, has always to refer to the same kinds of considerations about that sentence. In Michael Dummett's terminology, the point is that there must be some *key concept* in the theory of meaning, some notion that figures in the explanation of the meaning of any sentence. Suppose we were to adopt this monistic condition, along with a second condition, that of *complete extensional access*: this is the condition that the key concept can be and only can be fully defined by its role within the theory; there is no more to an understanding of the key concept than an understanding of its role within the theory of meaning. Then we can begin to see how the holistic condition might follow. Suppose we have developed a theory of meaning that applies, as yet, to only part of the language under study, which purports, against the holistic condition, to give the meanings of only some of the expressions in the language. By semantic monism, the key concept that figures in the explanation of those given meanings must also figure in the explanation of the yet to be given meanings; but by the condition of complete extensional access, that notion is fully understood only by a grasp of its role in the theory of meaning for the complete language. Then, trivially, at the pre-holistic stage envisaged we have an incomplete understanding of that key concept; we therefore have an incomplete grasp of the meaning-claims presented at that stage; we therefore cannot reasonably have full confidence in the meaning-claims given by the partial, non-holistic theory.

We have, therefore, three possible constraints upon a theory of meaning, together with a sketch of their interrelations. Should we adopt these three constraints? The argument for adopting the monistic constraint is this: without a key concept, word meanings will be incapable of unification. Earlier, we discussed the primacy of the sentence as the unit of meaning. Words have meaning through their contribution to sentence meaning, that contribution being determined by the theory of meaning. Now suppose that one 'key' concept applied, say, to indicative sentences, another to imperatives. Consider a word that figures in both an indicative and an imperative sentence. Its meaning is determined by its contribution to the meanings of both these sentences (though not only these sentences, of course); but, then, its contribution to each must be different since, *ex hypothesi*, it is a quite distinct *kind* of contribution, a contribution whose character is determined by a quite distinct key concept in each case. The primacy of sentence meaning combines with the evident possibility of giving unified word meanings to imply monism, to imply that there be one key concept.

The rationale for holism is the argument sketched from monism and complete extensional access. Whatever one thinks of that argument, holism encounters a formidable difficulty. This is not just the blank assertion that it is possible to give the meanings of some expressions in the language without giving, or being able to give, them all; it is rather the stronger thought that this must be possible if the language is to be learnable. Our understanding of novel sentences is explicable only by reference to the meanings of sentences and words already learnt; but this implies that it is possible to learn the meanings of those words and sentences in isolation from the rest of the language. Much could be said about the kinds of words and sentences that form this independently learnable base, but it is quite clear that there is such a base if facts about learning and agreement on meanings of new sentences are to be explained.

If this argument against holism is found as compelling as that for monism, the consequence is clear: we have to reject the condition of complete extensional access. The essential key concept is not definable solely by its role within the theory of meaning. If this is correct, it is a matter of some importance; but I am not sure that it is correct because I am uncertain whether the argument against holism is decisive. That argument begins with the fact that knowledge of meanings can get going by encounter with only part of the language, as exemplified in language acquisition. But the holistic theorist might hold that this encounter with the 'independently learnable base' merely suggests *hypotheses* which we adopt *pro tem*, but whose obtaining is not actually independent of consideration of the rest of the language. And thus our subsequent encounters with the (holistic) non-base might alter our understanding of that base itself. Thus while to account for language acquisition there must be, say, some 'relatively' observational discourse (whose 'topic', say, is approximately determined by basic stimulus-meaning factors), this will still only be an *approximation*; subsequent experience might lead us to *modify* that approximation.

At this point, I cannot see how this question can be settled. I shall therefore suspend judgment both on the holistic condition and on that of complete extensional access. Only the constraint of semantic monism will be carried over.

3 The Elimination of '. . . means that . . .'

Our initial thought was that we should require that our theory of meaning prove a sentence of the form

(*M*) *s* means that *p*

for each sentence *s* in the language under study; that is, our theory should yield what Dummett calls *direct* statements of meaning ('What is a Theory of Meaning?', p. 99). *Meaning* is the key concept in the theory of meaning! So we should set out to define '. . . means that . . .' as it occurs in ordinary language.

However obvious this thought might seem, it faces grave difficulties. The first is simply a doubt as to the usefulness of axiomatising the expression '. . . means that . . .' as it occurs in ordinary language. That locution is too broad for our present purposes. It can be employed in cases where there is no linguistic element: 'That spot means that he has a most nasty disease'. Even if there is a linguistic element, it may not figure in its desired role: 'His babbling means that he is frightened', 'His muttering means that part of his brain is being stimulated by Dr X's electrodes', 'His telling you his life-history just means that he is very nervous today'. Further, even when we edge nearer sentence-meaning, we still have irrelevant cases. The colloquial employment of '. . . means that . . .' usually relates, not to sameness of literal meaning, but to sameness of communicative import: 'His saying that your English is grammatical means that he considers you a hopeless philosopher', 'His telling you his life-story means that he desires you'. What is required is a notion of *strict and literal meaning*; the extraction of this from our customary talk of meaning will not prove easy. Nor is it clear that such an idiom need antecedently exist in either the object-language or the meta-language; it may be a term of art answering directly to nothing in the language we are employing (i.e. the meta-language).

But even if there is such a notion present in the meta-language, or even if there is a set of phenomena present in the community under study that adequately constrains the definition of such a notion in the meta-language, a second difficulty remains. The notion of *strictly and literally means that* is an intensional one, it creates intensional contexts: that is, contexts in which substitution of co-extensive expressions need not preserve truth-value. From

'Snow is white' strictly and literally means that snow is white

and

'Snow is white' and 'Grass is green' have the same truth-value

we cannot deduce

'Snow is white' strictly and literally means that grass is green.

The idiom produces intensional contexts. The difficulty now is that the only systematic account of intensional contexts that survives even the most cursory glance explains the intensionality by reference to the notion of *meaning*. This is why, for example, the following inference is valid:

'Jane is a harlot' strictly and literally means that Jane is a harlot.
'Jane is a harlot' and 'Jane is a whore' have the same meaning.
So 'Jane is a harlot' strictly and literally means that Jane is a whore.

The general explanation of intensional contexts requires reference to meanings; and explanation of the properties of any given intensional construction requires reference to the meanings of the particular expressions occurring in it. If this is correct, there is no point to the employment of intensional idioms within the systematic, axiomatic component of a theory of meaning.

Finally, and most importantly, the logical machinery involved in proving sentences giving the meaning of each sentence in the language under study will certainly prove vastly more complex, and might ultimately prove unobtainable, if the sentences giving the meanings of object-language sentences contain intensional constructions like '. . . means that . . .'. Such constructions must therefore be eliminated from the theory of meaning. But how is this to be done? In particular, how could it be done given that '. . . means that . . .' does create an intensional context?

4 Meaning and Truth-Conditions

One of the most persistent thoughts in discussion of semantics is encapsulated in Quine's remark: 'You have given all the meanings when you have given the truth-conditions of all the sentences' (Quine in Davidson and Hintikka, *Words and Objections,* p. 333). Quine continues as follows: 'Davidson took the connection to heart and drew this conclusion: the way to develop a systematic account of

C

meanings for a language is to develop Tarski's recursive definition of
truth for that language.' This passage invites a number of questions.

(1) What, if any, is the *argument* for identifying the meaning of a
sentence with the conditions for its truth?
(2) What is the *argument* for holding that the way to do this is by
the construction of a Tarski-style truth-predicate for the
language under study?
(3) Quite how is this to be done? What are the constraints on the
exercise?

To begin with, consider a passage in which Donald Davidson
appears to present the arguments referred to in questions (1) and (2).
Starting from the (unsatisfactory) thought that a theory of meaning
should prove a sentence of the form

(M) *s* means that *p*

for each sentence in the object-language, Davidson goes on to say
this:

The theory will have done its work if it provides, for every
sentence *s* in the language under study, a matching sentence (to
replace '*p*') that, in some way yet to be made clear, 'gives the
meaning' of *s*. One obvious candidate for the matching sentence
is just *s* itself, if the object language is contained in the meta-
language; otherwise a translation of *s* in the metalanguage.
As a final bold step, let us try treating the position occupied
by '*p*' extensionally: to implement this, sweep away the obscure
'means that', provide the sentence that replaces '*p*' with a
proper sentential connective, and supply the description that
replaces '*s*' with its own predicate. The plausible result is

(*T*) *s* is *T* if and only if *p* (Davidson, 'Truth and Meaning', p. 6).

The conclusion of this passage is that we require that the theory of
meaning place restrictions on the predicate 'is T' such that all
sentences of the form of (T) meeting the substantive restrictions on
relations between '*s*' and '*p*' replacements be logically implied by the
theory. But now, Davidson holds, we have arrived at 'the point of
discovery'; for this requirement on theories of meaning is precisely
the same as the convention proposed by Tarski for testing the
adequacy of any formal semantical definition of truth. So the
predicate 'is T' mentioned in the constraint on theories of meaning
will be coextensive with the truth-predicate; it will apply to all and
only the true sentences of the language under study. Hence 'a theory
of meaning for a language L shows "how the meanings of sentences
depend upon the meanings of words" if it contains a (recursive)
definition of truth-in-L' (Davidson, 'Truth and Meaning', p. 7). The

task of semantic analysis of any natural language is that of constructing a recursive definition of truth for that language; we have to show,
for any given sentence, how its truth-conditions are determined by
the semantic properties of its components together with the semantic
import of their structural combination.

It is not, perhaps, clear that this is indeed meant by Davidson as
an argument for his theory. No matter; it is instructive to see anyway
the extent to which it works when so construed. The argument can
be spelt out as follows:

(1) We require of a theory of meaning that it match each sentence *s* in
the language under study with some sentence in the meta-language
that 'gives its meaning'.
(2) It is no use stating this requirement as being that the theory imply
for each sentence *s* an M-sentence of the form

   (M) *s* means that *p*

for we must eliminate the intensional '. . . means that . . .' in favour
of an extensional connective.
(3) We could try 'if . . . then . . .' or 'only if . . .'; but since we are
aiming at equivalence of meaning, the biconditional is the obvious
candidate. This would produce

   $s \equiv p$.

(4) But this is not well formed. The expression on the LHS of the
biconditional is a name; the whole sentence is thus comparable to

   Tim if and only if it is snowing.

Given that the biconditional is a sentential connective, we have to
make the name on the LHS into a sentence. The obvious way to do
this is to attach a predicate to it, so obtaining

   (X) *s* is $X \equiv p$.

(5) But now, given that *p* gives the meaning of *s*, we see that the
predicate 'is *X*' will at least be coextensive with a Tarskian truth-
predicate. Since no alternative interpretation of 'is *X*' is evident, we
might as well take that interpretation.

How do these steps stand up when thus spelt out? (1) is simply the
specification of the need for completeness in the theory of meaning
and can therefore be passed over. (2) is the further requirement of
extensionality, rejecting the attempt to work with an intensional
construction. The arguments sketched just now are presumably the
considerations motivating Davidson at this point. (3) is acceptable
once we recognise the need for equivalence of meaning in the
analysis. (4) is certainly correct in its claim about well-formedness; it

55

would not be right if it claimed that the only way to make a name into a sentence was to attach a one-place predicate to it. Still, that is one way of doing so, and it is perhaps the simplest. Finally, (5) seems correct if it does not deny that there could be other, coextensive predicates that could do the job.

It thus seems that while Davidson has not presented a strict deductive argument for the identification of a theory of meaning with a definition of the truth-predicate, he has presented a plausible, intuitive argument for this identification: an argument, as it were, of the 'inference to the simplest methodology' variety. Unfortunately, this argument does not work, even by these looser standards. While it was reasonable for Tarski when defining the truth-predicate to impose the condition of *translation* on *s* and *p*, we cannot help ourselves to this notion when engaged in constructing a theory of meaning. For translation here must mean *correct translation*; and *correct translation* must mean *meaning-preserving* translation. Tarski can impose on the schema

(T) *s* is T if and only if *p*

the requirement that *p* be a translation of *s*, with homophonic translation as the simplest case; theorists of meaning cannot, for this 'constraint' should be the result, the *yield*, of the theory, not its presumption. Some other constraint or set of constraints could be imposed which it is believed would yield this result, as it were, indirectly; but when engaged in the construction of a theory of meaning, we can hardly impose this constraint of translation or sameness of meaning as it stands. But then it is clear that without this constraint, there is no reason to identify the predicate required for the theory of meaning, 'is *X*', with a Tarskian truth-predicate.

We have, as yet, no argument for focusing upon *truth* at all. Still, if we presume that notion to be our focal point, a way of putting the preceding is this: Tarski was concerned with *defining* a truth-predicate, and so could help himself to the notion of translation; we are concerned with a theory of meaning, which should yield translational claims, and so obviously cannot so help ourselves. We need, not a *definition* of truth founded upon the notion of translation, but a *theory* of truth for the language that *settles* questions of translation.

Still, we lack reason for focusing upon *truth* at all, for identifying the meaning of a sentence with its truth-conditions. A very modest case, inviting at least indulgence, might be made from the following considerations. First, even critics of the theory tend to accept that the theory is literally true. Strawson describes it as 'a generally harmless and salutary thing to say' (*Logico-Linguistic Papers,* p. 188). Grice, when analysing particular locutions, presents his results by listing the truth-conditions of the locutions. (For example, Grice,

56

'The Causal Theory of Perception'.) What critics dispute is whether the theory says enough. This is already in contrast to other theories, where even the claim to dull truth is disputed, forgetting matters of fine detail or complete adequacy. Second – a point we shall return to in detail – the truth-conditions theory is, at least at first glance, the most readily *empiricisable* theory of meaning. The securest data upon which to found an empirical theory of meaning, because the least theoretically loaded, are assent and dissent behaviour; the connection with truth is obvious. What is novel in Davidson's work is not the subscription to the truth-conditions theory; rather, it is the perception (or misperception) of the connections between such a theory and empirical methods of investigation.

Until we return to this second point, the considerations adduced are too vague to induce more than interest in the truth-conditions theory of meaning. Matters become a little more precise when we turn to the second of our initial questions, that concerning the further argument for holding that the way to implement this vague doctrine is the construction of a Tarski-style truth-predicate for the language under study. In this invocation of Tarski, we see Davidson's other major contribution here; although we have seen that his explicit argument for that invocation fails. First, we should note that something more has to be involved if the truth-conditions theory is to be of interest: the simple claim that the meaning of a sentence is given by its truth-conditions is just too vague to be of any use as it stands. But it is unclear that there is any alternative way of developing this vague doctrine that is of anything like comparable precision and merit. Tarski's theory promises such precision where previously there was only vagueness. It provides us with a paradigm of analysis, the formal semantical treatment of quantificational language sketched in the last chapter. That treatment shows precisely how the truth-conditions of complex sentences are determined by the truth-import of their components. The vague doctrine that the meaning of such a sentence must be a function of the meaning of its components is replaced by an exact demonstration of how this function operates. Maybe some questions about the meanings of such sentences are not answered; but only perversity could prompt the claim that none are. Second, by invoking Tarski's programme we gain not just precision but system: the very systematic element in an account of truth that *must* be present if the notion of truth is to be the key notion in an extensional theory of meaning for a language containing a potential infinity of sentences.

Giving the truth-conditions of a statement in the Tarskian manner determines its meaning by incorporating that statement, or the sentence used in making it, within a systematic account of the language as a whole, such that that sentence can be seen as but one

57

of the indefinitely large number of sentences in the language. Less abstractly, the simple statement of the truth-conditions in the form of a T-sentence is indeed of little (though not of no) value, a 'snow-bound triviality' as Davidson has it; where the value is realised is in the construction of a device that serves to generate, to prove, all the near trivial T-sentences. The journey, not the destination, matters. The journey that issues in the near-trivial destination shows *how* that destination is reached: it shows not just *what* the truth-conditions are but *how* the truth-conditions are determined. Finally, we have already seen reason to prefer Tarski's recursive, finite approach to truth-definition to others.

5 The Role of the Theory of Meaning

The considerations just adduced are piecemeal; if they are to gain substantial coherence they must be fed into more general, and ambitious considerations. The term *meaning*, like that of *giving the meaning*, is a term of art. The content of this technical notion is fixed by its role within an overall theory of linguistic behaviour; that role determines, and is determined by, the *point* of the notion. Appreciation of this is largely due to a line of argument recently developed by John McDowell (McDowell in Evans and McDowell, *Truth and Meaning*, pp. 42–66).

McDowell's argument formally mirrors Davidson's strategy in holding that we do not, so to speak, *start* from the bald doctrine that the meaning of a sentence can be specified by stating its truth-conditions; rather we *begin* from more general considerations. Davidson's argument, as we saw, began from reflection upon the aim, role and function of a theory of meaning, focusing in particular upon the need to handle all of the infinity of sentences in the language. McDowell's starting point is slightly different: it is the need to see the role of a theory of meaning *within* a general theory explaining behaviour. Both hold that we subsequently *discover* the connection with truth; we have seen, however, that Davidson's attempt to build this bridge fails.

The reason for the shared strategy is this. If we begin with the truth-conditions theory, we are readily led to the view that the form of a theory of meaning will be a (finite) set of rules and axioms that prove, for any sentence of the language under study, a theorem of the form '*s* is true iff *p*', where '*s*' is replaced by a 'suitable designation' of the sentence and '*p*' by a sentence. The strategic trouble with this approach is not just that it gives us no reason to accept the starting point; rather, it *appears* to incur an obligation to explicate the notion of truth on which the theory *appears* to place such an explanatory burden. It seems inadequate at this point to rely upon the axiomatic definition of truth given, and more generally suspect to rely upon any language-relativised notion of truth. The critic requires, apparently reasonably, an explanation of the *true* in *true in L*, of *true in variable L*. To avoid this demand – which the threat of paradox suggests cannot be met – the obvious manoeuvre is to replace 'is true' by some unspecified predicate 'is *f*', and *then* to lay down conditions relating *s* and *p* which ensure that 'is *f*' could be acceptably replaced by 'is true'. In this oblique way, we would indeed give some *further* characterisation of truth: the truth-predicate is precisely that predicate (amongst others?) which satisfies the specified constraints on *s* and *p*. But within the context of a theory of meaning, this leads nowhere: for the obvious constraints – that *s* and *p* express the same thought, have the same sense, be correct translations of each other – all rely, covertly or explicitly, upon the notion of sameness of sentence-sense, the very notion we wish our theory of meaning to explicate.

An alternative strategy is therefore called for. McDowell's is to spell out 'the function of a theory of sense in a systematic description of what is involved in understanding a language'. As the first part of this, he makes the desired form of theorems of the theory yet more schematic: merely *something* of the form '*s . . . p*', just some pairing of object- and meta-language sentences. The filling, to echo Davidson, is not *yet* what matters.

The crucial point to see is that a theory of meaning, of strict and literal sense, will only be part of an overall theory of understanding. It will need supplementation by, and will interact with, what McDowell, following Dummett, calls a theory of *force*. This theory of force has at least two elements: it enables us to spot the mode of utterance of a sentence, the most general kind of speech-act being performed upon an occasion of utterance – assertion, question, command; and it will show us how to obtain for any utterance, however elliptical, whatever its mode of utterance and whatever its grammatical mood, a suitably related indicative sentence. We might add that a third part of the overall theory, the syntactic theory, will yield a way of detecting the grammatical mood of the sentence – indicative, interrogative, imperative.[1] For while, for example, indicatives are usually employed in the making of assertions, they need not be: commands can certainly be issued by utterance of indicatives. So this combined theory of force and syntax enables us to spot the mood and the mode of an utterance, and to obtain an indicative component from any utterance. This last point reflects an important matter: McDowell is motivated here by an acceptance of semantic monism, together with the thought that the way to combine monism with a

[1] It is, of course, unclear how a theory of force could perform its second task without performing this third (additional?) task.

plausible account of the varieties of mood and mode is to detect the same *kind* of unit within all sentences uttered, whatever their mood and mode. McDowell's belief that this common element will be indicative might seem to *presume* the truth-conditions theory of meaning, the very point at issue. But, first, nothing yet hangs on McDowell's labelling this common element 'indicative'; what matters is that there be some such common element. Second, assumption that the common element be indicative does not yet presume the truth-conditions theory. And third, there are independent reasons for treating the indicative as primary, reasons which explain the general emphasis which the indicative receives within nearly all theories of meaning. The indicative has a syntactic, semantic, and communicative completeness that the other moods lack: the absence of tense in imperatives; the eccentricity of a language with questions but no means of answering them; the dependence of commands upon the idea of their being satisfied; the crucial role of the indicative in language acquisition. All these invite the thought that the common element required by semantic monism will be indicative; and the second of our three points leaves this studiedly neutral upon the issue of the final form of a theory of meaning.

We start, then, from some native utterance, described, say, as: 'He uttered the noises such-and-such'. The theory of force, then, enables us to identify *modes* of utterance, and to extract an object-language indicative mood element from all utterances. The theory of sense, of meaning, now pairs this indicative element with a meta-language sentence, so enabling us, the speakers of the meta-language, to say, for example, 'He is asserting that p', 'He is asking whether q' and so on, as descriptions of acts of utterance by object-language speakers. But now we need to see that such deliverances of the combined theory of force and sense can be tested, in part, by whether they lead to the ascription of intelligible sets of propositional attitudes, centrally, beliefs (from assertions) and desires (from commands).[2] The intelligibility of such ascription is determined both by the translator's own beliefs and desires, his observations of the native speaker's actions (both verbal and non-verbal), and his observations of the general circumstances of the native speaker – e.g. the kinds of observations he can reasonably be held to have made. Thus we have various practical maxims: do not attribute lunatic beliefs to the object-language speaker unless you have good reason for doing so; do not attribute to him desires that it is within his own powers to satisfy but which he does nothing whatever to satisfy, unless you have good

---

[2] I would not wish to be taken, here or elsewhere, as suggesting that the move from linguistic action descriptions to propositional attitude ascriptions is straightforward. Here, there is much comparatively untheoretical analytical work still to be done.

reason for doing so; do not attribute to him knowledge of entities (say, sub-atomic particles) that he is in no position to observe. At *this* point, where there is as yet no filling between '*s*' and '*p*', the constraint upon the theory is that it licenses the ascription of plausible propositional attitudes. But this does *not* give any conceptual primacy to propositional attitudes, the kind of primacy found in the theory (see chapter III) of Grice, for the ascription of such attitudes is not just constrained by the kinds of consideration just mentioned, nor does it just constrain the combined theory, and so the theory of meaning; it is also constrained by that theory of meaning itself. The content of a propositional attitude ascribed is not just constrained by the considerations just mentioned: indeed, there would be a hopeless indeterminacy, at times approaching full extensionality, in attitudes solely so ascribed. The content of attitudes ascribed on the basis of the utterance of a sentence is also constrained – indeed, the requisite intensionality introduced – by the theory of sense, of meaning, which reveals that content as dependent upon the repeatable contribution of sentence constituents. Construction of a combined theory of force and sense, and so of a theory of sense, is part and parcel of the construction of a theory of propositional attitudes. What matters is to see how the pieces fit together: not to *reduce* one piece to another, nor to see one piece as *fixed* by another with no reciprocal interaction.

It is clear from this that the connection between *s* and *p* must include this: that '*p*' can be used to specify the *content* of propositional acts which would be performed by uttering '*s*'. That is what a theory of meaning must fix. But if we now consider the filling between *s* and *p*, we can see that any filling that meets this condition of acceptability can acceptably be replaced by 'is true if and only if'. For the effect of the disquotation device, the truth-predicate, is to produce a sentence which can be used to say the very same thing, to perform the very same propositional acts, as could the original sentence *s* prior to quotation or designation. That the truth-predicate is so insertable is a discovery: the general ruminations about the role of a theory of meaning within an explanation of behaviour can be appreciated *before* the adequacy of the truth-predicate is realised. That truth functions as a disquotation device – the anodyne Ramseyan theory – is *all* we need to appreciate, and all we need to say, to see that a theory of sense is a theory of truth, that 'truth is what a theory of sense is a theory of'. What *further* do we need to say about truth? It is not, as McDowell puts it, that 'sense is what a theory of truth is a theory of'; if it were, the demand for independent explication of the truth-predicate would be reasonable, and the thinness of the disquotational view of truth a drawback; rather, to repeat, it is that 'truth is what a theory of sense is a theory of', and it is an advantage that in reaching this result we need only presume the weak disquotational thesis. Quite general reflection upon the connection between *s* and *p* required by the broader framework of explanation of behaviour ensures, granted the thin disquotational thesis, that whatever the filling between *s* and *p*, it will either *be* the construction 'is true if and only if' or will be justifiably replaceable by it.

That is a compelling, albeit highly abstract, argument; with the preceding piecemeal considerations in mind, let us try to concretise it briefly by asking *why* we should, in fact, work with the truth-predicate filling; for McDowell's argument does *not* show that that predicate is the only admissible filling in view of the overall role of the theory of meaning. And at risk of inviting repetition, let us split this further development up monosyllabically.

(i) Why do we designate the sentence *s* but not the sentence *p*? We designate *s* because until we have an account of its sense we cannot *use* it, and, anyway, it is what we want to talk *about*! But if we also designated *p*, then in the homophonic case our theory would be trivial, and in the heterophonic case all we could do would be to construct translation manuals. Such an approach would literally divorce language from reality, and would render the theory useless in propositional attitude ascription: we could make *no* sense of the difference between 'A believes that *p*' and 'A believes that "*p*" expresses a truth'.

(ii) Why 'if and only if' rather than some *other* sentential connective? This extensional connective makes the proof theory unproblematic; and we are, after all, aiming at *equivalence*: either of sense, or, at an earlier stage, of possible propositional acts performed using *s* and *p*.

(iii) Why 'is *f*'? We need to make a sentence out of the name on the LHS of the biconditional, and the easiest way of doing so is to attach a predicate to that name.

(iv) Why 'is true'? (a) This does indeed give us the doctrine that the meaning of a sentence is given by stating its truth-conditions, a doctrine that, as we have seen, is accepted as literally true even by its critics. (b) We build a bridge with the least theoretically loaded evidential base, and so ease the route to an empirical theory of meaning. (c) We obtain a connection with Tarski's work on truth, a connection that replaces vagueness by precision, provides us with a paradigm of semantic theory (the treatment of quantificational language), and that promises the essential systematic structure within a theory of meaning.

McDowell's argument may also be concretised a little by dwelling upon the overall picture it presents of rendering linguistic behaviour intelligible. We start from the observation of an object-language speaker's utterance of a sentence s. We take this to be a piece of intentional linguistic behaviour, a linguistic action. The theory of force serves first to identify the general kind of speech-act performed by the speaker, the mode m of utterance. The second, syntactic element in the theory of force identifies the mood of the sentence s, a purely grammatical feature of the sentence. Then the third element of the theory of force pairs with this sentence s an indicative sentence s' of the object language; schematically, it is the function f which tells us that $f(s) = s'$. In the case where the original sentence s is indicative, the function is the identity-function: $f(s) = s$. Where s is non-indicative in mood, the function f will be more complex. A rough idea of its working will come from a couple of examples. If s is the imperative 'Shut the window', f will first operate to transform the sentence into something like: 'Make it true that the window is shut'; f will then extract 'the window is shut' as the indicative s'. Interrogatives are much more complicated, and may often involve the extraction of an *open* indicative sentence s'. Thus 'Who won the battle of Hastings?' first becomes: 'What object satisfies this: x won the battle of Hastings?'; then s' is extracted as the open sentence 'x won the battle of Hastings'. (Cf. McGinn, 'Semantics for Nonindicative Sentences'.) There is, of course, much scope for dispute as to quite *how* the indicative sentence is extracted; but however that is done, the indicative sentence so obtained is then fed into the theory of meaning, the theory of sense. On McDowell's view, this will be a Tarskian truth-theory which will yield a T-sentence (or a satisfaction sentence where s' is an open sentence) as its output:

(T) s' is true if and only if p.

We are then in a position to move from the description 'He uttered the sentence s' to 'He m-ed that p'. This redescription is crucial, because it licenses the ascription of propositional attitudes to the speaker: if he asserts that p, then standardly he believes that p; if he commands that q, then standardly he desires that q. There are good questions about when this standard implication fails – e.g. cases of sarcasm – but I shall pass over this now. The propositional attitudes so ascribed, as was said, can be intelligible or unintelligible: if they are unintelligible we must move back through the whole machinery of the theories of sense and force until we find an adjustment which issues in an ultimate plausible attitude ascription *without* rendering other attitudes, attributed on the basis of other utterances, unintelligible. Where the initial error is to be located cannot be settled in advance: thus there is no question of having the theory of force or the theory of sense *right* prior to the assessment of propositional attitude ascriptions; all parts of the theory interact.

63

6 A Definition of Sentence-Meaning

What is it for a sentence s in language L to mean that p? We are now surprisingly close to being able to define this. Suppose that we have a truth-theory θ for L, located as the theory of sense in the picture of understanding linguistic behaviour just outlined. Then one condition of s meaning that p is this:

(i) It is a theorem of θ that s is true if and only if p.

This is clearly not enough: θ might be a lousy truth-theory. What we want is that θ be a *true* truth-theory, and part of what this involves arises from the thought that it is a necessary condition of s meaning that p that s and p have the same truth-value. So we might add the following clause to the definition:

(ii) The truth-theory θ only proves true biconditionals, only proves true T-sentences.

But this raises an obvious problem. T-sentences are of the form

(T) s is true if and only if p.

Such a sentence is true if and only if the sentences flanking the biconditional have the same truth-value. That on the RHS is unproblematic: it is in our own language, and we can straightforwardly determine (or form rational beliefs about) its truth-value. But that on the LHS says of a sentence of the object-language that it is true: how could we know whether that is correct or not without first knowing the meaning of the named sentence there occurring?

Here we might be tempted to search for some behavioural access to the truth-value of the sentence on the LHS of the biconditional. We might, for example, follow Davidson in looking for some behaviourally definable relation or some psychological relation identifiable prior to interpretation between object-language speakers and object-language sentences as uttered – say, that of *holding true*.[3] Assuming we succeed in identifying and defining such a relation, we might then adopt the following principle of charity: members of the community standing in this relation towards a particular utterance of a sentence is *prima facie* evidence that the sentence so uttered is true. That is, if they hold it true, it is likely that it is true. They are unlikely to be consistently mistaken about the truth-values of sentences; more to the point, the thought is, if they were so mistaken we could never detect this since this principle of charity is unavoidable in the construction of the behaviourally based theory of meaning

[3] The proper interpretation of Davidson's notion of *holding true* is somewhat unclear; see especially his 'Radical Interpretation', p. 322 and 'Belief and the Basis of Meaning', pp. 311–12.

that is needed *before* error can be detected. Thus it is not even clear that the assumption of wholesale error makes any sense. Now, using this principle of charity and observing native speakers' behavioural responses to utterances of sentences, we make tentative assignments of truth-values to native sentences and hence tentative assignments of truth-values to sentences in our language saying that various native sentences are true, the LHS of the (T)-sentences. Thus we tentatively assign truth-values to the (T)-sentences themselves. What we require of the final theory is that all the (T)-sentences be true: but we do not just pursue the wild-goose chase for such a theory. Native speakers can, of course, be mistaken: the connection between their holding a sentence true and its being true is only a *prima facie* one. So considerations of simplicity and plausibility in the final truth-theory occur, and such considerations can lead us to overrule some of the *prima facie* connections between holding true and being true in order to profit in our final theory. The trade-off here is the usual one between theory and data, and is constrained in the same way that the trade-off is constrained in other areas of science. In particular we shall be more prepared to overrule holding true behaviour, to attribute error to the community, in various obvious cases: those where behavioural responses differ within the native community; those where there is difference about the truth-value of *p* within our community; those involving highly theoretical rather than simple observational sentences; those involving evaluative notions; those where we can understand *how* they might have been led to error. But the final constraint remains: all provable (T)-sentences must be true. It is just that we can juggle a little.

This approach faces a major difficulty: that of defining and establishing the existence of the appropriate relation, that of *holding true*. But we can sidestep discussion of this tortuous issue by seeing that conditions (i) and (ii), even if applicable in this way, are insufficient for the definition of sentence-meaning: for we shall then see that the addition needed renders this behavioural detour unnecessary, even if possible.

Are conditions (i) and (ii) sufficient for *s* to mean that *p*? Two points suggest that they clearly are not. First, given a truth-theory that serves up only true biconditionals, we can construct quite automatically any number of other truth-theories which also only serve up true biconditionals, yet which pair quite different meta-language sentences with each object-language sentence. For example, we can construct a theory that yields on the RHS of each T-sentence the conjunction of that served up by the previous theory with a truth, say, 'Snow is white'. A moment's reflection shows that '*p*' and '*p &* snow is white' will agree in truth-value; so if the original truth-theory satisfied clause (ii) of the definition, so will this new one.

That anxiety might appear a mere technicality; it is anyway not clear what is to be done with it. The second objection is more evidently substantial, and serves also to direct us to a solution. A theory of meaning, we have maintained throughout, must connect with speakers' understanding of their language. One concrete instance of this is that we should not credit them with an understanding that they do not have. Now consider a backward community who have a term for 'water', but, lacking a developed science, know nothing of its structure. Taking any sentence of theirs in which the term for water is used, we shall obtain a *true* T-sentence if on the RHS we replace 'water' by 'H_2O'; for 'water' and 'H_2O' are extensionally equivalent. But to use the H_2O sentence on the RHS is mistaken, since it credits the native speakers with an understanding, a knowledge, they lack. This is also the failing in the conjunctive truth-theory first mentioned: it, too, fails to match meaning with understanding.

The difficulty is clear; so also is the solution, especially in the light of McDowell's argument for the truth-conditions theory of meaning. Whatever theory of meaning, whichever truth-definition, we accept, it will combine with the theory of force and particular utterances made by speakers to license the ascription to those speakers of various propositional attitudes: centrally, beliefs from assertions and desires from commands. The attitudes so ascribed can be unintelligible in a variety of ways. One way is illustrated by the conjunctive truth-theory, which implies that they desire that snow be white whenever they issue an order and express their belief that it is so whenever they express any belief at all. It is not that one cannot imagine far-fetched circumstances in which these attitudes and expressions of attitudes would obtain; but one would need independent evidence that this was so. Another kind of unintelligibility is illustrated by the water-H_2O example: on that truth-definition, we attribute an understanding to native speakers of a scientific theory that there is nothing else in their practice – no laboratories, experiments, chemical notation – to support. We must rule out any truth-theory that leads to such absurdities: we have to recognise that attribution of a set of such attitudes to the speakers of the object-language cannot be part of a process of *understanding* them at all.

We therefore have to require of our theory of sense that it combine with the theory of force and the evidence of speakers' linguistic and non-linguistic behaviour to produce a plausible assignment of propositional attitudes to those speakers. But now it is a short step to seeing that the *Ersatz* of *holding true*, or whatever, is redundant: that the T-sentences of the truth-theory θ interact with the theory of force and the observed facts of speakers' behaviour to produce a plausible assignment of propositional attitudes to speakers itself requires that all those T-sentences be true, itself requires condition (ii). The propositional attitude condition is ineliminable; and it renders redundant any attempt to ground condition (ii) independently. We therefore have as our final definition of 'Sentence *s* in language *L* means that *p*' the following:

There is a truth-theory θ for *L* such that:
(a) It is a theorem of θ that *s* is true if and only if *p*; and
(b) the deliverances of that theory combine with an acceptable theory of force and with observed linguistic and non-linguistic behaviour to license the ascription of plausible propositional attitudes to speakers of *L*.

This approach enjoys the advantages of a fully extensional, structurally systematic truth-theory, of the same general form as Tarski's. It admits of the requisite empirical character of the theory of meaning through the observations that ground the notion of the plausible in (b). And it captures the distinctive *intensionality* of the notion of meaning through the connection forged in (b) with propositional attitude ascription. But, to reiterate, in so doing it gives no primacy to propositional attitude ascription: it merely exhibits the ways in which the pieces must ultimately fit together.

Chapter III

Shades of Meaning

1 Traditional Analysis

In the course of this century there is a particular enduring conception of philosophical analysis in the English-speaking world which it is possible to discern. (This is what I believe has been called a *loosely ruminative* and *comparative-historical* remark.) That conception has at least three, apparently independent, components. First, there is the view that analysis of meanings can be an *a priori* procedure: truths about meanings, at least in one's own language, can be known without recourse to empirical observation. Second, there is the belief that the meaning of some particular sentence or word can be determined in isolation from beliefs about the meanings of other sentences or words. And third, there is a doctrine, or set of doctrines, that might be labelled *consequentialist*. The meaning of a sentence (in the indicative mood) can be specified by listing all the consequences of that sentence, all that must be the case if the sentence is to be true; while the meaning of a word can be given by listing all the consequences of a sentence in which that word occurs, and which arise only because of the presence of that word. This third, consequentialist element receives a clear expression in Wittgenstein's *Prototractatus*:

> The analysis of signs must come to an end at some point,
> because if signs are to express anything at all, meaning must
> belong to them in a way which is once and for all complete . . .
> if a proposition is to have sense, the syntactical employment
> of each of its parts must have been established in advance. For
> example, it cannot occur to one only subsequently that a
> certain proposition follows from it. Before a proposition can
> have a sense it must be completely settled what propositions
> follow from it (3. 20102–3).

How much of this tradition is compatible with the conception of the theory of meaning developed in the first two chapters of this book? Consideration of the compatibility of that conception with the first, *a priori* component of traditional analysis must ultimately wait upon a discussion of the account that conception issues in of speakers' understanding of their natural language. But prior to that discussion, there is at least reason to doubt the obviousness of this first component. Language use is a practical skill, a manifestation at first sight of 'knowing how' not of 'knowing that'. The exercise of this practical skill is ordinarily quite unreflective: we just say things. As theorists of language we reflect upon this unreflective competence; in so doing, we attempt to secure for ourselves *propositional* knowledge of the language; in particular, propositional knowledge of the abstracted theory of sense, of truth-conditions. Ultimately, we need to consider whether an adequate account of speakers' understanding must reveal *them* as standing in some similar relation of propositional knowledge to the contents of that theory of sense. But the unreflective character of language use combined with the abstracted character of the theory of sense suggests that it is no *obvious* requirement that native speakers stand in such a relation to the contents of the theory.

We have many practical skills: in *accounting* for them, in equipping ourselves with theories that account for those skills, we do not just introspect: introspection yields wildly unlikely views of how it is that we ride bikes, eat, scratch the right spot. Rather, in such cases, we need empirical investigation of how the practical skill *works*, of what is involved and presupposed in it. Why should language be different in this respect? Why in this one area should the move from practical ability to propositional knowledge be attainable *a priori*? Why should not that move require empirical investigation? Because, I suppose, of the native speaker's understanding of his language. But, really, this claim is not so transparent, especially if the object of understanding is the abstraction, the theory of sense. For the only obvious manifestation of such an understanding is the speaker's ability, revealed by the combined operation of the theories of sense and force, to produce and comprehend intelligible utterances in identified modes. To suggest that such manifestations derive from the speaker's propositional knowledge of the theories of sense and force seems simply to falsify the unreflective character of language-use; and it seems further to involve the attribution of abstracted *discrete* portions of propositional knowledge that have, and could have, no discrete *manifestations*. Talk of 'implicit' propositional knowledge may sidestep the first of those anxieties; but it merely accentuates the second. It is not only behavioural dogmatism that issues in the rejection of this first component in traditional analytical methods.

This connects immediately with the second component of those methods. If, even as native competent speakers, we have no privileged access to the contents of the theory of sense, then we will always be in the position of the outsider, the radical interpreter, trying to secure such knowledge for himself (Davidson, 'Radical Interpretation'). In the preceding chapter, we discussed briefly Davidson's strong holistic thesis that 'we can give the meaning of any sentence (or word) only by giving the meaning of every sentence (and word) in the language' (Davidson, 'Truth and Meaning', p. 5). If such a thesis were made out for the radical interpreter, and if the competent native speaker is in no better position than such an interpreter *vis-à-vis* propositional knowledge of the contents of the theory of sense, then, clearly, the second element in traditional analysis must be rejected. But even if this extreme holism is false – say, because there must be some independently learnable, non-holistic base in the language – this will not necessarily save this second component. First, that component would be restricted in application to expressions occurring in that non-holistic base, which is hardly likely to include many expressions of philosophical interest. But more importantly, that base might well be *within itself* holistic to a high degree, such that the significance of, say, any one sentence occurring there can only be grasped if the significance of other sentences occurring in the base is grasped. It would be unsurprising if this were true for nearly all the sentences in the base: even for utterances of sentences in the base, we shall need, for comprehension, the abstraction of the theory of sense; that abstraction will reveal the senses of such sentences as generated by the senses of their constituents, together with the semantic import of their structural combination. It is consequently difficult to see how one could have reasonable confidence in one such generation *until* one has seen that the truth-theoretic axioms operative in that generation also work to generate intelligible senses for other sentences in that base.

The third, consequentialist, element looks more evidently compatible with the conception of the theory of meaning here employed. As I have characterised it, consequentialism is concerned with the *truth*-consequences of sentences (presumably, of indicative sentences as potentially uttered with the necessary relativisations); and what more natural and simple way is there of exhibiting the truth-consequences of a sentence – say, 'Snow is white' – than

(T) 'Snow is white' is true if and only if snow is white?

The consequence of 'Snow is white' being true is that snow is white!

A number of questions are raised by this. The primary question is: how are the truth-consequences of a sentence to be determined? We have outlined an answer in the preceding chapters: by the construction of an empirical truth-theory of sense in the style of Tarski. But, as just explained, this answer takes us well away from traditional analysis. So we might ask: how, for traditional analysis, are the truth-consequences of a sentence to be determined? We are told that this can be an *a priori* procedure, and that it can be done in a piece-meal, sentence-by-sentence, manner; but we are not told anything more. One thing I shall do now is to explore this in slightly more detail by consideration of Grice's recent work on conversational implication; for although that work is meant as a refinement on traditional analysis, it will be seen to have an important role to play within our own conception of the theory of meaning.

A second question is this: is it to be a quite inexplicable fact that a given sentence has the truth-consequences that it in fact has? Consideration of one attempt to fill this supposed lacuna will lead us to see the inadequacies in another recent influential theory of meaning, Grice's intentional theory.

Finally, a question might be raised about the apparent compatibility of consequentialism with the truth-conditions theory developed. Results of traditional consequentialist analysis were certainly not presented in the form of Tarskian T-sentences; rather, they exhibited on the RHS of such sentences the feature that Evans and McDowell have termed 'conceptual breakdown' (Evans and McDowell, *Truth and Meaning,* p. viii). The aim of such analysis was not just to pair a designated object-language sentence with a used meta-language sentence that 'gives its meaning'; it was rather to present an *analysis* of the object-language sentence by pairing it, say, with a conjunction of meta-language sentences, each conjunct being a necessary condition and the whole conjunction being a sufficient condition of the object-language sentence's being true. Thus instead of

(T) s is true if and only if p

the result is, say, of the form:

(C) s is true if and only if c_1 and c_2 and $c_3 \ldots$ and c_n.

Perhaps (C) was favoured as the form of output of semantic analyses because it was thought that T-sentences are trivial; or perhaps (C) was favoured because of adherence to a version of *atomism*, some doctrine to the effect that there are semantically primitive atoms out of which all other meaningful expressions are (semantically) built – so that T-sentences, or the comparable satisfaction sentences, would do for the atomic expressions, but only C-sentences would do for adequate analyses of compound expressions; or perhaps it was just thought obvious that our intuitive understanding of our native language enables us, *a priori*, semantically to decompose compound expressions.

All these thoughts are wrong. T-sentences are not trivial; if we once initiate semantic decomposition, the pursuit of atoms, the process so initiated will proceed without limit, so that the very possibility of a theory of meaning is destroyed; and our native understanding of sentences does not equip us for decompositional analyses of the language in either an *a priori* or an *a posteriori* manner. Such merit as there was within the desire for decompositional analyses comes out in our theory of meaning in an exact, unobjectionable manner: the *derivation* of the T-sentence for an object-language sentence (*not* the T-sentence itself) shows exactly how the meaning of that sentence is determined by the meanings of its constituent expressions together with the semantic import of their structural combination. There is thus every reason to favour T-sentences over sentences of the form of (C) as the deliverances of our theory of meaning.

General considerations suggest, moreover, that the class of sentence-constituents that must be treated as primitive – for which 'uninformative' axioms must be given – is very large indeed. Seeing that (as we shall later) will give us *one* reason for thinking that the central task for a semantic theory is not the *decompositional analysis* of expressions occurring within a sentence, but is, rather, the exhibition of the *logical form* of the sentence, the exhibition of the ways in which the sentence's primitive constituents *combine* to generate the meaning of the whole sentence. That exhibition occurs, to repeat, in the derivation of the T-sentence for that sentence within the theory of sense for the language.

2 Refining Traditional Analysis: Conversational Implicatures

To begin with, we need a crude acquaintance with three notions employed by traditional analysts. Suppose that *a* and *b* are sentences; then

a entails b if, and only if, '*a* & $\sim b$' is contradictory.

a presupposes b if, and only if, when *b* is false, *a* is neither true nor false.

a logically implies b if, and only if, '$a \rightarrow b$' remains true under all uniform substitutions for non-logical expressions.

These are only vague definitions, and none is unproblematic. That of entailment rests upon the unexplained notion of a contradiction; that of presupposition leaves unexplained how we determine that a sentence lacks a truth-value; that of logical truth assumes a class of logical particles without telling us how that class is determined. Still, the definitions given may give some *feel* for these notions of traditional analysis, and they can be supplemented by examples of each. Thus

(1) $2 + 2 = 4$ and $7 \times 9 = 63$

72

logically implies

(2) $2 + 2 = 4$.

This will also be an entailment since all logical implications are entailments, but not vice versa. However,

(3) They were married and they had children

does not logically imply

(4) They were married before they had children

since the structurally similar (1) produces no such implication.

(5) He has stopped beating his wife

presupposes

(6) He has been beating his wife;

and

(7) All his children are asleep

presupposes

(8) He has children.

(9) She was poor but she was honest

does not presuppose

(10) There is some contrast between poverty and honesty

since (9) could be false even were (10) false, say, in the event of her being rich and dishonest.

(11) Shut the door

trivially presupposes both

(12) The door is open

and

(13) The door is shut

and any other indicative sentence since commands do not have truth-values; they will lack truth-values whatever the truth-value of any other sentence. It is easy to modify the definition of presupposition to avoid this, but I shall not bother to do so.

(14) That's a bachelor

entails

(15) That's a man

but does not logically imply it.

That is no more than a rough exemplification of these notions; it is silent upon deep, theoretical anxieties, and says nothing about the many examples that do not fit so tidily into the scheme. Some of these examples will emerge shortly; but first we must consider various refinements that might be employed by the traditional consequentialist.

The major refinement needed is the notion of a *conversational implicature* developed by H. P. Grice.[1] Grice's starting point is this thought: suppose that we believe that entailments and at least some cases of presupposition (perhaps cases like (5)–(6) but not cases like (7)–(8)) are relevant to the meanings of sentences. Suppose further that we rely upon initial intuition in determining the entailments and meaning-relevant presuppositions of a sentence. Our intuition might tell us, for example, that the conjunction of a sentence with the negation of one of its putative consequents is *contradictory, incoherent, improper, something we would not say*. This might be thought to show that the putative consequence is indeed a semantic consequence of the sentence, and hence is part of the meaning of that original sentence. Grice tells us that this is unsatisfactory for a simple reason: our initial intuitions are insufficiently discriminatory. As the list just given of the output of our intuition suggests, intuition alone runs together diverse kinds of impropriety, and so diverse kinds of consequence. In particular, unaided intuition fails to distinguish meaning implications and conversational implicatures; for it fails to distinguish improprieties of meaning and conversational ones.

Grice gives three examples of this other, conversational, kind of implication. One is that by an utterance of

(16) His wife is in the bedroom or the bathroom

it is implied that

(17) The speaker does not know which of the rooms the wife is in.

A second is that from (9) to (10), the poverty-honesty pair; and the third is that from an utterance by Grice in a termly report, a college 'collection', on a philosophy pupil of

(18) Jones has beautiful handwriting

to

(19) Jones is no good at philosophy.

The studied irrelevance of the comment suggests a less than flattering opinion on the relevant subject.

[1] In Grice 'The Causal Theory of Perception'. I discuss Grice's view on the basis of this one readily obtainable source rather than relying, for example, on the great diversity of second-hand accounts of its subsequent development.

74

It is clear that there is something important in these cases; it is less clear that there is only one phenomenon or that there is an element common to all three cases. For example, the relation between the poverty-honesty pair (9) and (10) differs in an obvious, albeit vague, way from the other cases, in each of which the putative consequent makes reference to a person or to a subject-matter not explicitly mentioned in the original sentence. The consequence (17) makes reference to the utterer of (16), while the consequence (19) makes reference to Jones's competence at philosophy. The relation between (9) and (10), as presented by Grice, has no such distinguishing feature; as such, we should be wary of holding that relation to be a clear case of conversational implication.

How are conversational implications to be detected? Grice starts by giving four tests for them. Again, this invites the thought that we are concerned here with a plurality of phenomena – particularly if, as Grice seems to think, the tests can differ in their results in particular cases. The tests, anyway, are these:

(i) The first test is simply meant to establish whether or not the implication is presuppositional in character. We do this by trying to describe circumstances in which the falsehood of the consequence is compatible with the original sentence having a truth-value. On this test, Grice tells us, the wife-location pair (16)–(17) and (18)–(19), the collections pair, are clearly not presuppositional while the poverty-honesty pair is arguably not because of the possibility, mentioned before, that (9) can be false even though (10) is false – viz. because of the woman's wealth and dishonesty. What puzzles about this test is this: why cannot it be extended to show whether or not the considered implication is entailment by a comparable stage-setting of truth-values? This would solve our problems about detecting meaning-determining relations immediately. I take it that the reason the test cannot be so extended is that, at least in many interesting cases, our intuitions about the truth-values assignable are as suspect as the initial intuitions about impropriety. Yet if that is so in the detection of entailments, it must surely also be so in the detection of meaning-relevant presuppositions. So while this test might work in some simple cases, it cannot be generally relied upon.

(ii) Grice's second test is to ask what the 'vehicle of implication' is, what it is that carries the implication. Four (non-exclusive) candidates are: (a) what the speaker said or asserted; (b) the speaker; (c) the words the speaker used; (d) his saying it. (b) and (d) are meant to be the vehicles in cases of conversational implication. I should not dispute the contention that there are *some* circumstances in which we can make *some* sense of these contrasting vehicles; what should be disputed is whether this is a generally useful test, whether it gives a *generally* useful characterisation of conversational implicatures. If our intuitions about implications are suspect, then surely our intuitions about 'vehicles of implication' are yet more so; for the notion of the vehicle of implication must be treated as a term of art. This does not preclude the possibility that the application of this term of art is occasionally determinable by intuition; but it does suggest that the test is not a generally employable one.

(iii) Is the presence of the implication 'a matter of the meaning of some particular word or phrase occurring in the sentence in question'? Again, this is vague and shaky. In entailment, presupposition, and the poverty-honesty pair (9)–(10) I take it that the answer is meant to be affirmative. But what of (16)–(17),

(16) His wife is in the bedroom or the bathroom
(17) The speaker does not know which of the rooms the wife is in?

Isn't the implication the result of the word 'or'? This does not fully explain the implication; but then nor does the meaning of 'and' *fully* explain the case of logical implication (1)–(2),

(1) $2 + 2 = 4$ and $7 \times 9 = 63$
(2) $2 + 2 = 4$.

The meaning of 'or' has something to do with the implication in (16)–(17); substitute 'and' and the implication does not arise. (Maybe the wife is straddling the two rooms – or maybe the two rooms are one and the same.) The obvious, though vague, difference between logical implications like (1)–(2) and cases like (16)–(17) is not mentioned by Grice, namely that in the latter kind of case the consequent makes reference to a subject-matter not explicitly mentioned in the original sentence. Yet the presence here of 'explicitly' shows that this will not yield a satisfactory test either. Does (14), 'That's a bachelor', explicitly mention masculinity? Yes, *if* all entailments are 'explicitly' mentioned; but our problem is precisely to separate off entailments.

(iv) Fortunately, Grice's fourth test promises rather more. There are two tests here, what Grice calls a 'twin idea'. The relationship between these twins might well concern us. The first twin is the test of *detachability*. The implication from p to q is detachable if and only if there is some other form of words which can be used to state or assert 'just' what p 'might be used to assert', but which does not carry the implication that q. Applying this to our three examples of conversational implicature, Grice claims that (9)–(10) is detachable, as in 'She was poor and she was honest', whereas our other two examples are not. The second test is *cancellability*. The implication from p to q is cancellable if and only if we can add a further clause 'withholding commitment from what would otherwise be implied', 'without annulling the original assertion'. Grice claims that the collections pair (18)–(19) is clearly cancellable, and argues persuasively that the wife location case (16)–(17) is as well. The poverty-honesty pair (9)–(10) is less clear. Consider 'She was poor but she was honest, though of course I do not mean to imply that there is any contrast between poverty and honesty'. Grice says of this:

> (T)his would seem a puzzling and eccentric thing to have said; but though we should wish to quarrel with the speaker, I do not think we should go so far as to say that his utterance was unintelligible; we should suppose that he had adopted a most peculiar way of conveying the news that she was poor *and* honest.

I find *this* a puzzling and eccentric thing to have said. I take it that Grice does not wish entailments to be cancellable. But why not hold, analogously, that when someone says 'That person is a bachelor, though I do not mean to suggest that that person is unmarried' he has merely adopted 'a most peculiar way of conveying the news that' that person is male? There are few cancelled formulae that we cannot make sense of in this way, and so few uncancellable implications: perhaps the only obvious candidate for non-cancellability is the implication from p to p! Of course, the cancelling clause must not 'annul the original assertion'; but when does this annulment occur? It is not enough to say that it does *not* occur if we can make the utterance intelligible, for most entailments then become cancellable. If intuition is still our guide (though now a refined, guided guide), then it is unclear that in the cancelled version of (9) *part* of the original assertion is not 'annulled'.

If we are thus unconvinced by Grice's arguments for the cancellability of the poverty-honesty case (9)–(10), we are left in this position: (9)–(10) is detachable but not cancellable, while the wife location case (16)–(17) and the collections example (18)–(19) are cancellable but not detachable. This reinforces the initial suspicion that the phenomenon involved in (9)–(10) is quite different from that involved in the other two cases. Further, in as much as I have any grasp on Grice's second and third tests, a similar disparity arises. For (9)–(10), as Grice remarks, the speaker's words could be said to imply the contrast, whereas he holds that the comparable claim is not true for the other two cases. While for (9)–(10) the implication clearly is the result of a particular word or phrase – 'but' – whereas it is not for (18)–(19), and arguably not for (16)–(17). All of which suggests that we should shelve (9)–(10) as a clear case of a conversational implicature for the time being. Which might further suggest that we should shelve the detachability test. (16)–(17) and (18)–(19)

then remain the clear cases of conversational implicatures, and cancellability is left as the test of such an implicature.

This might, however, be somewhat over-hasty. Grice calls these tests twin ideas. Could twins separate as readily as the preceding discussion, like Grice's, suggests?

If the tests are to pull apart, either there are detachable non-cancellable implications or there are cancellable non-detachable implications. Consider the former possibility first. The detachability of an implication means that there is another form of words which can be used to assert 'just' what the original asserts, but without the implication arising. If this is so, the implication cannot be the result of the meaning of the sentence, assuming that meaning to determine 'just' what the sentence asserts; it must rather be the result of some particular form of expression occurring in the sentence or of some more general contextual matter. Yet if that is so, the implication must be cancellable. Since the implication is not the result of the meaning of the original sentence – as shown by its detachability – it must be possible to cancel it without 'annulling' the original assertion through 'annulling' part of the meaning of the sentence used to make that assertion. The condition that detachability preserves meaning is essential since otherwise nearly all entailments would be detachable. But this condition precludes the possibility of detachable non-cancellable implications.

What of cancellable non-detachable implications? The cancelled formula must preserve the significance of the original assertion, it must not 'annul' it. It follows that if an implication is cancellable, it must be possible that it be detached. If it is not in fact detachable, this merely reflects the poverty of the language as regards vocabulary in the particular area concerned or the pervasiveness of the contextual factors that give rise to the implication. In other words, there is no guarantee that there is in the language a detached version or that there are contexts of linguistic exchange in which the detached version is reasonably employable *as* the detached version; but it will always be possible that we *introduce* an appropriate detached version or that we *imagine* a context in which the detached version be correctly employable *as* the detached version. So the non-detachability of a cancellable implication will reflect merely a contingent limitation upon vocabulary *or* a contingent limitation upon contexts of conversational exchange.

It might even be possible to maintain a stronger position whereby any cancellable implication will in fact be detachable: it will be detachable precisely by the use of the cancelled formula. Use of this cancelled formula will be a way of 'introducing' the detached version into the language; it will also be a way of modifying the context of linguistic exchange to make employment of that detached version correct *as* employment of the detached version. Thus 'His wife is in the bedroom or the bathroom, but I do not mean to suggest that I do not know which' will be the detached version of 'His wife is in the bedroom or the bathroom'. The requirement on the detached version is that it say 'just' what the original says. Cancellability shows, for example, that in this case the original sentence does not say that the speaker does not know which room his wife is in; our detached formula (the cancelled formula) merely makes explicit what is *not* said in the original sentence. Why should this make it the case that the detached formula (the cancelled formula) does not say 'just' what the original says? Intuitions about whether a sentence which says that *p* and does *not* say that *q* and a sentence which says that *p* and says that *q* is not being said say 'just' the same thing are utterly unclear. But this is just to point to the ineliminable indecisiveness accompanying Grice's reliance upon, as it were, educated intuition. For the moment, however, all that matters is the reasonable possibility of holding all cancellable implications to be detachable.

Cancellability is, then, the surest test of conversational implications, but it is indeed a twin idea with that of detachability. Either all cancellable implications are detachable by means of the cancelled formulae; or they could be detached by means of newly coined vocabulary or through imaginable modifications of the context of linguistic exchange.

We have maintained that all detachable implications are cancellable; yet we previously said, following Grice, that the implication in the poverty-honesty case (9)–(10) was detachable but not readily cancellable; indeed, we even rejected Grice's cautious claims about its cancellability. Consistency requires us, then, to question now its detachability. This is not an implausible thing to do. Grice's claim was that 'She was poor and she was honest' was the detached version. But does this say 'just' what the original said? It is unclear that this is so, *just as* it is unclear that Grice's argument for the cancellability of the implication from (9) to (10) works. Of course, we rely here upon intuition: but Grice has given us nothing else to rely upon. Detachability and cancellability go hand in hand, and neither term should be applied to the (9)–(10) implication.

Rejection of this case as a case of conversational implicature would doubtless be more comfortable if some alternative account of this implication were presented. I do not now have such an account, but I shall mention one reason for holding that the suggestion of contrast is at least as important as the conjunctive properties, namely, that there are cases where 'but' is used *without* conjunctive properties but *with* the suggestion of contrast. You present a complex argument concluding that philosophers should be kings. I might reply: 'But the premises of your argument are wrong'; or even, 'But your premisses are false and the argument invalid'. Here 'but' has no conjunctive properties, merely contrastive. Doubtless this might just be a different use of 'but': sometimes, it might be said, it *is* used as a conjunctive sentential connective, and sometimes, as it were, as a contrastive interjection. But, first, we should be wary of 'just a different use' rejoinders, since they ultimately make *any* analysis irrefutable. Second, the apparent cases of the conjunctive sentential connective usage might be misleading. Compare 'She was poor but she was honest' and 'She was poor. But she was honest'. There is no need to see the second example as involving a sentential connective: ordinary conventions of discourse conjoin, as it were, adjacent assertions, as in 'She came into the room, he went pale, she attacked him'. Why, then, see the first example as involving a sentential connective? Why not see it as roughly equivalent to 'She was poor. Rather surprisingly in view of that, she was honest'? Is 'rather surprisingly in view of that' a conjunctive sentential connective? Surely not: it expresses a related attitude on the speaker's part. Likewise with 'but': yet that is the element that Grice, at least on one reading, wishes to *discard* from the meaning analysis of 'but'. Third, even if there *are* two uses of 'but', and if in one it *is* a sentential connective, still, the other, interjectory usage expressive of an attitude together with the thought that 'but' is hardly a *pun*-word like 'bank' invites the thought that the common element is precisely the attitude-expressive component. If so, to relegate that component to conversational implicature, to irrelevance for the meaning-analysis of 'but', is mistaken.

To repeat, that is *not* to give an analysis of 'but' connecting it with expressions of a contrastive attitude. That connection is not readily seen as entailment or presupposition; but it should not therefore be relegated to conversational implicature. The connection could only be accounted for *via* an account of 'attitude'-words in general. That account I do not have; but it might be beneficial in developing such an account to start with as innocent a word as 'but'.

We have, then, the wife location case (16)–(17) and the collections case (18)–(19) as clear examples of conversational implicatures, with cancellability and detachability, subject to slight qualification, as equivalent tests for such implicatures. This is not yet the whole story, however. Suppose a certain word or phrase – say 'snark' – is used by all and only those raised in Devonshire; the rest of us use 'cow' with the same meaning. Tom says: 'The snarks are in the meadow.' Consider the implication that Tom was raised in Devonshire. This implication is detachable: meaning is preserved in 'The cows are in the meadow', assuming 'cows' to be common linguistic property between Devonians and the rest of us. The implication is also cancellable: there is nothing wrong with 'The snarks are in the meadow, though I don't mean to suggest that I was raised in Devonshire' even if nobody ever actually says it. This implication therefore meets our criteria for being conversational. Yet it seems quite different from our two previous clearest cases of conversational implicatures. While it is true that Grice's test (iii) – does the implication arise from a particular word or phrase? – serves to rule out the Devonian case as described, it would not handle a similar case involving a whole sentence any part of which could be used by a non-Devonian, but the whole combination of which would only be used by a Devonian, nor would it handle cases involving distinctive syntactic constructions. Further, while Grice's second test, the vehicle of implication test, will help in some of these cases, it will not do so, as formulated, with the syntactic construction example, and anyway is vague and shaky. It is much better, therefore, to separate off the Devonian case by considering Grice's account of how conversational implicatures come about, of how they are *generated*.

In the Devonian case, the drawing of the implication is mediated by some principle like this: all and only those raised in Devonshire use the term 'snark' in ordinary discourse. ('Ordinary discourse' is meant to block the field linguist's use of 'snark'; that 'use' will anyway be a *mention*.) This principle is not very general: there is a reference to a particular idiom, and also to a particular group of speakers. By contrast, conversational implications are meant to arise from much more general principles; and these principles are meant to be, not observed empirical regularities, but *rules* governing conversational exchange. Grice gives one example of such a rule: 'One should not make a weaker statement rather than a stronger one unless there is good reason for doing so'. For example, suppose I know the wife referred to in (16), 'His wife is in the bedroom or the bathroom', to be in the bedroom. If I say that this is so, my statement is stronger than the statement (16) in implying (16) but not being implied by it. But suppose all I in fact assert is (16); suppose further that Grice's general principle is operative and is known by both speaker and audience to be operative. In most contexts the only reason I shall have for making the weaker statement rather than the stronger is because I have no knowledge, or even beliefs, about the truth or falsity of the stronger statement; given Grice's principle and the absence of any further motivation for making the weaker statement rather than the stronger, an audience hearing my assertion of (16) will conclude that I am not in a position to make a stronger statement about the wife's whereabouts, and will therefore conclude that I do not know which of the two rooms the wife is in. Thus the conversational implication arises. Of course, there are many circumstances in which I have other reasons for making the weaker statement; if in such a case the audience knows of those reasons, this conversational implication will not arise. Think of a typical game in which I aim to give away as little as I can while saying the truth; or suppose I know you to lust after the wife referred to, and wish merely to give you a sporting chance of finding her right off, my wish being known to you. These are not frequent situations in discourse; which is why conversational implicatures usually do arise.

Any adequate elucidation of this Gricean principle requires a general characterisation of *strength*. Consider, for example, the kind of sentence with which Grice was primarily concerned in his first writing on this subject, sentences about perception. Compare, for example, 'Tom sees that the cat is on the mat' and 'It looks to Tom as if the cat is on the mat'. Neither implies nor is implied by the other: hallucinations preclude the move from the latter to the former, cases of eccentric lighting preclude the converse move, given Grice's austere, literally perceptual, reading of the latter statement. The first statement is stronger in implying a material-object statement – 'The cat is on the mat' – yet the second is stronger in implying a *specific* mental statement about Tom, namely, itself. Yet Grice holds the former to be stronger than the latter. Obviously, Grice must intend the notion of strength to be context-relative: we do not consider the logical relations between the sentences (for there are none in the perceptual case) nor just the number of logical consequences; rather, we consider the number, if any, of logical consequences of a specified kind (e.g. material-object statements). Much more needs to be said about how the context determines the *kind* of statement that counts for strength; but perhaps, it could be shown that in the context of epistemological discussion material-object statements *are* stronger than mental statements. This is, however, a little odd in view of Grice's desire to distinguish sharply between analytical and epistemological questions.

At first sight, the principle of strength does nothing to explain the other clear case of conversational implicatures, (18)–(19). There is no initially clear sense in which 'Jones is good at philosophy' is *stronger* than 'Jones has beautiful handwriting': there are, sadly, no logical relations between them, while counting the number and classifying the kinds of logical consequence of each would seem fruitless. The obvious manoeuvre is to introduce another principle of conversational exchange, that of relevance. It might read something like this: make only statements relevant to the conversational situation unless you have good reason for not doing so. The relevance that matters is determined either by the subject-matter of the preceding discussion or by more general conventions, as in Grice's collections case (18)–(19). One good reason for not obeying the principle would be the desire to change the topic of conversation; the dangers of misunderstanding involved in doing so testify to the usual operation of this principle.

But whatever the principle of relevance, it does not completely explain this case. Why should Grice's studied irrelevance imply a strongly negative view of Jones's philosophical ability, rather than a positive one, one of indifference, or no view at all? What further needs to be assumed – and explained – is that Grice would not hesitate to express any of these other opinions or lack of opinion. There must be some further contextual factor, perhaps partly conventional, but also concerned with the beliefs of the audience about the speaker's psychological characteristics. It is not easy to see how these considerations could tidily be bundled together into a precise form. Likewise, while it *might* be possible to subsume relevance under strength, it is far from clear how this is to be done. Even without this subsumption, however, something might be said to justify running the two cases (16)–(17) and (18)–(19) together, along with their covering rules, in terms of the nature of language *acquisition* and *use*. The principle of relevance seems essential to both, while the principle of strength certainly has a role to play in accounting for language-utility, and maybe even has a role in language-acquisition. This is a speculative, though not unpromising, line of thought, and I shall not pursue it.

We are anyway in a position to see a little more clearly the difference in the nature of the principles explaining conversational implicatures and the principle involved in the Devonian case. Whatever the contextual variables involved in the notion of strength might be, they are unlikely to include the particular language used by the speaker, let alone some specific construction or idiom. As the speculative line of thought just gestured at explains, the principles underlying conversational implicatures are meant to be, as it were, language-transcendent; and they are language-transcendent rules, not language-transcendent empirical generalisations. The rules are operative except in cases, like many games, where they are evidently suspended; this claim is not refuted by the discovery that people disobey the rules most of the time.

Grice's work on conversational implicatures is meant as a refinement, and is indeed an important refinement, within traditional analytical methods. Our *a priori* understanding of the semantics of our native language is to be heightened: our initial *a priori* intuitions about meaning-consequences are to be refined by further, supposedly *a priori*, discriminative capacities that we possess. We begin with an *a priori* consequentialist intuition that there is something wrong with saying '$p \,\&\sim q$'; that intuition is then subjected to further, *a priori* considerations, primarily the tests of cancellability and detachability, along with consideration of the general character of the ground of the consequential relation. Within our perspective of the theory of meaning, any role for the apparatus of conversational implicatures must be radically different: for the possibility of *a priori* intuitions about consequential relations is rejected along with the possibility of *a priori* refinement of those intuitions, especially when those intuitions are meant to work in a piecemeal, sentence by sentence, way. But this apparatus still has an important role to play once we have tentatively constructed a theory of sense for the language.

The theory of sense delivers interpretations of the indicative contents of sentences uttered by native speakers. Those deliverances then combine with the theory of force to issue in redescriptions of the linguistic actions of native speakers, redescriptions of forms like: 'He asserted that *p*', 'He ordered that *q*', and so on. From these redescriptions we *standardly* move to the attribution of propositional attitudes to speakers: 'He believes that *p*', 'He desires that *q*', and so on. The word 'standardly' is not idle here; part of its force emerges by considering the role played at this point by conversational implicatures.

Suppose the combined outputs of the theories of sense and force issue in one case in the following redescription:

(16*) He asserted that his wife was in the bedroom or the bathroom.

Then, generally, we shall attribute to the speaker the belief that his wife is in the bedroom or bathroom; further, on the basis of the general *a priori* reflections suggesting that the rule of strength, like that of relevance, will be operative in a language, we shall perhaps withhold from attributing to him any belief about the particular room she is in at present. But suppose *other* observations of the circumstance of his utterance suggest that this withholding is implausible – say, because as he speaks on the telephone in the bedroom his wife is in full view in that room. Then we shall take the general conversational implication from his asserting that

(16) His wife is in the bedroom or the bathroom

to

(17) The speaker does not know which of the rooms the wife is in

not to obtain; by observation, along with the implausibility suggested by that observation of various propositional attitude ascriptions, we shall see the implication from (16) to (17) as cancelled. We shall therefore be led to attribute a modified belief on the basis of the speaker's utterance: viz. the belief that his wife is in the bedroom, rather than the weaker belief his utterance would standardly license. But it should be obvious that this manoeuvre is only open to us *after* we have an interpretation of the original utterance.

Or, again, suppose the combined outputs of the theories of sense and force issue in another case in the following redescription of the speaker's action:

(18*) Grice asserted that Jones has beautiful handwriting.

Suppose further that we have gained enough other insight into the context of utterance – say, from the redescription of *other* linguistic actions in the surrounding context – to realise that Grice's assertion should be about Jones's philosophical ability. Suppose further that our previous observation of Grice, including the redescription of other verbal actions, suggests the following hypothesis: Grice would not hesitate to express a favourable opinion upon a student's abilities (charity), nor would he hesitate to express ignorance on such a question (modesty). Then we shall be led to attribute to Grice, not, or not just, the belief that Jones has beautiful handwriting, but, rather, the belief that Jones is no good at philosophy – this, in part, because we have *a priori* grounds for believing that the rule of relevance is standardly acknowledged in the community, and we have no reason to believe, perhaps every reason not to believe, that Grice is merely attempting to change the subject. Whether or not we shall *also* attribute to Grice the belief that Jones has beautiful handwriting will depend upon a number of other factors: principally, whether Grice is *in a position* to have beliefs about Jones's handwriting (whether he's ever seen any of his essays), and whether the belief that Jones has beautiful handwriting is either true or explicably, for one in Grice's position, false (perhaps a friend always copies out Jones's rough essays for him). Depending upon such observations and reflections, we may be led to view Grice's assertion recorded in (18*) as *facetious* or *rhetorical* in its literal content. Similar considerations about Grice, now a teacher of calligraphy, might lead us to see that assertion as *sarcastic*. With such an utterance, the belief attributed to the speaker will be the opposite of that which would standardly be attributed on the basis of his utterance. But the role of redescription through the theories of sense and force of the speaker's, and other speakers', utterances in forming a view upon these further relevant factors suggests that we could only interpret an utterance as sarcastic on the assumption that other utterances standardly were not. A community that was consistently sarcastic in the expression of its beliefs would be indistinguishable – to us *and* them – from one that had some peculiar linguistic way of recording negation – say, by the omission of the word 'not' rather than its inclusion. The assumption that a speech-community is consistently sarcastic in the expression of its beliefs would be an idle addition – idle from the viewpoint of making intelligible their linguistic behaviour.

The role briefly sketched for the apparatus of conversational implicatures is firmly *a posteriori*: that apparatus comes into play only after the tentative, empirically grounded, adoption of theories of sense and force, and is crucially determined in its role by observations grounding the plausibility of propositional attitude ascriptions. We have such residual *a priori* considerations as there are suggesting that

D

the rules of strength and relevance will be acknowledged in the community; but the question of when these rules are obeyed and when flouted is resolvable only in a stubbornly empirical manner.

3 The Role of Intentions in the Theory of Language Use

The thought has often been expressed that the account of meaning developed so far is crucially incomplete. (See, e.g. Strawson, *Logico-Linguistic Papers,* pp. 170–89, and Peacocke in Evans and McDowell, *Truth and Meaning,* pp. 162–88.) I shall not discuss all the diverse ways in which this thought has been expressed, nor all the semantic morals that have been drawn from this supposed incompleteness. Rather, I shall cast the anxiety in an immediately relevant form, and attempt to show its groundlessness; the application of my discussion to other ways of expressing this anxiety should be comparatively straightforward.

Suppose we have constructed a theory of meaning for a language, a theory meeting our specified constraints. Then for any sentence in that language, we have an acceptable interpretation of it; that interpretation will specify, non-decompositionally, the truth-consequences of that sentence. We might still feel a matter of *explanation* to remain. What makes it the case that that sentence has those consequences? How does the inanimate sentence *come to have* that meaning, to carry those truth-consequences?

Posed like that, the matter invites the following thoughts: sentences have meaning because people *use* them in ordinary linguistic exchange; in so doing, people give sentences the meanings that they have. These thoughts are vague, and need to be sharpened before they will help. One way of sharpening them is to see the references to *use* and to *people giving sentences meaning* in terms of intentional activity. A sentence has meaning because people give it meaning by uttering it with certain intentions; the sentence carries the truth-consequences that it does because people utter it with certain intentions. These still vague thoughts are natural enough granted the evident connections in usage between 'to mean' and 'to intend'.

Fortunately, we need not consider the full range of possible intentional theories, for it has been compellingly shown by Grice that one kind of intentional theory is by far the most plausible (Grice, 'Meaning'; 'Utterer's Meaning and Intentions'). This kind begins with a crucial distinction between *sentence-meaning* and *utterer's meaning*: the distinction, roughly, between 'Sentence *s* means that *p*' and 'Person *x* by his utterance of sentence *s* means that *p*'. The theory then proceeds to define *utterer's meaning* in terms of *utterer's intentions*; it then finally aims to define *sentence-meaning* in terms of the notion of *utterer's meaning* previously defined. In standard developments of this theory, the notion of *utterer's meaning* exhibits a certain tension: for, on the one hand, it is presumed that this is a notion pre-theoretically accessible to competent speakers, captured by a pre-theoretically existent idiom in natural language; and on the other hand, its character is constrained by the theoretical role it has to play in connecting the definition of sentence-meaning with the notion of utterer's intentions. It is not at all clear that those two pressures upon the notion of utterer's meaning will prove to be compatible with the coherence of that notion.

Still, Grice's distinction, or distinctions, between sentence and utterer's meaning is, or are, crucial. Of comparable importance is his discernment of the kind of intentional structure that has to be invoked in defining utterer's meaning, at least in the context of our pre-theoretical grasp of that notion. It is not sufficient for me to mean by my utterance of sentence *s* that *p* that I intend to induce in my audience the belief that *p*, or the belief that I believe that *p*, or the belief that I have said that *p*. Grice's distinctive contribution is to have seen that it is also necessary that I have a further (higher level, as it were) intention to induce that belief through the audience's *recognition* of that first intention. That first intention must be open, must be fully avowable. But the chain of intention does not stop here: as Strawson, amongst others, has pointed out, subtler cases suggest that there must be a yet further intention to the effect that the desired response be secured through the audience's recognition of the higher level intention that the effect be secured through recognition of the first level intention (Strawson, *Logico-Linguistic Papers,* pp. 149–69). This chain of intentions, each requiring that the immediately preceding intention be recognised, can proceed without limit. The achievement of the desired effect should come about through the recognition on the audience's part of this chain of intentions.

Two points should be noted here. David Lewis, in his admirable work *Convention*, has elegantly demonstrated that it is distinctive of conventional activities that they reflect a background structure of participants' intentions of *precisely* the kind just outlined within the concept of utterers' meaning. Thus a first tentative connection is made between utterer's intentions and their conventional, sentence-meaning, realisation. Second, the appearance of the chain of intentions proceeding without limit may be misleading: it may not be necessary for that indefinite chain to exist so long as all those intentions that do occur are avowable, are open. Rather than requiring each intention to have an appropriate higher intention, we require that each intention *not* have a higher intention that it not be recognised. There must *not* be intentions that the speaker would wish to conceal. In this way the possibility is left open that a community of dullards, perhaps incapable of forming highly complex higher level intentions, will still be capable of *utterers' meanings* by their utterances.

The Gricean programme requires, then, an exact definition of utterer's meaning, along with a detailed explanation of quite how sentence-meaning is to be defined in terms of that notion. Grice's successive attempts at the definition of utterer's meaning have received much attention; without immersing ourselves in the detail of those attempts and attentions, I think it true to say that Grice has managed to amend his definition to meet nearly all objections. The reason I pass this complex area over is this: many of the objections which appear to be aimed at this definition of utterer's meaning have little relevance to it, being concerned, rather, with the relation between utterer's and sentence-meaning. This is as it should be, since the substantial interest in the definition of utterer's meaning lies not in the capture of some pre-theoretical notion we are presumed to possess, but in the construction of a definition, quite possibly adequate only for a term of art, which serves to bridge the gap between sentence-meaning and utterers' intentions. For example, Searle and Ziff have raised cases of utterances of nonsense, utterances which however have an intentional point (Searle, 'What is a Speech Act?' and Ziff, 'On Grice's Account'). These may have *some* relevance to the definition of utterer's meaning, though since they involve deceit, that definition is readily modified to handle them. More substantial worries are raised by comparable cases – coinings, as it were, of nonsense – where there is no deceit involved. In these cases, we find utterer's meaning as defined because of the absence of deceit. But what is important about these cases is not whether they intuitively fit the pre-philosophical formula 'Person x by his utterance of u meant that p', but is, rather, the fact that in such cases we do not necessarily yet have cases of sentence-meaning. Someone might non-deceitfully mean by his utterance of u that p without it yet being true that u means anything, let alone that p; for u might be literal gibberish.

Rather than trying to modify the definition of utterer's meaning to exclude such cases, it seems likely that Grice will simply deny that utterer's meaning is sufficient for sentence-meaning – which seems true on our pre-theoretical grasp of the notion – while still holding it to be necessary. This raises the proper anxiety about Grice's programme: what more is needed for sentence-meaning? One could try adding the requirement that *uptake* be secured, that the audience discern the utterer's intentions, and, perhaps, that it form the appropriate belief. Yet this does not appear sufficient, since it could obtain in the case of gibberish coining without the utterance yet being anything but gibberish. A further clause might be added about *how* uptake is secured; but the only obvious way of blocking the gibberish case in this way would be to require that uptake is secured *via* the audience's recognition of sentence-meaning, which would be blandly circular. An obvious second shot is this: there must be a *regularity* in the connection between the sentence and the utterer's meaning or between the sentence, utterer's meaning, and uptake secured. (We need not now choose between these options, for the same difficulty will emerge for both.)

But how could there be such a regularity? This is an obscure question, but it can be made a little more manageable by a slight change of tack. On Grice's theory, sentence-meaning is defined in terms of the intentions with which the sentence is uttered, along, perhaps, with the response standardly secured in an audience by that utterance. Now, as an account of the meanings of sentences in natural languages this will not do for a simple reason: the majority of such sentences, natural languages containing a denumerable infinity of sentences, will never be uttered. They will therefore not be uttered with any intentions, nor will their utterance induce any response in an audience. What, then, can Grice say about these un-uttered sentences? The obvious move, perhaps the only possible one, is to hold the meanings of such sentences to be definable in terms of hypothetical intentions and hypothetical responses: in terms of the intentions with which they would be uttered were they to be uttered and the responses they would then induce. But now Grice faces a dilemma: either there is some constraint upon these hypothetical intentions and responses or there is not. If there is none, the meanings of unuttered sentences will be left completely indeterminate: they *could* mean anything, so they *do* mean nothing. There must therefore be some constraint. Wittgenstein at one point invites us to say 'It's cold here', thereby meaning that it's warm here (Wittgenstein, *Philosophical Investigations,* sec. 510). It is unclear whether Wittgenstein thought this an impossible thing to do; David Lewis thinks it possible for himself only with a little help from his friends (*Convention,* p. 177). What help Lewis has in mind I know not; but at first sight little is needed, since sarcasm does not usually rely heavily upon others' assistance. Still, that may only be at *first* sight, since it is not clear that when I sarcastically say 'It's cold', I *mean* 'It's warm'; an alternative would be to say that I *mean* that it is cold, but mean it sarcastically. However, we need not now decide whether Wittgenstein's anxiety about the possibility of performing this specified action rests in the specific point just made or, perhaps, in the more general difficulty, discussed earlier, that a community that was consistently sarcastic in its utterances would be indistinguishable from one that had simply changed the meaning of the relevant sentence. What matters now is that the *source* of difficulty in obeying

89

Wittgenstein's instructions, or in responding to such an utterance by believing that it's cold here, or by believing that the speaker believes it cold here, or in recognising the speaker's communicative intention, is obvious: it is the meaning of the sentence he utters. This meaning constrains what we can mean by uttering the sentence, and it constrains likewise our response to such a sentence. Generally, the constraint upon the hypothetical intentions with which a sentence can be uttered, and upon the audience's responses to such an utterance, is precisely the meaning of the sentence. This constraint may not be invariable, as cases of sarcasm and counter-suggestible audiences *may* show; but it is standard, and it is the only constraint. If this is correct, the attempt to define the meanings of unuttered sentences in terms of hypothetical intentions and responses is hopeless: for it presupposes a prior notion of sentence-meaning.

Returning to our obscure question about regularities, we can say this: there can be, and there usually is, a regular connection between a sentence, utterers' intentions in uttering that sentence, and an audience's response to such an utterance. But that regularity is not mere chance, it is rule-determined: it is determined, namely, by the rules which determine the strict and literal meaning of the sentence uttered, those being merely part of the complete set of rules which determine the literal meaning of every sentence in the language, both the uttered and the unuttered. It is this notion of literal meaning, as readily applicable to unuttered sentences and to sentences on the first occasion of their use as to frequently uttered sentences, that must be pursued – pursued, precisely, by the determination of the general character of the rules that determine its specific instantiations. That pursuit would lead us to rehearse the considerations adduced in the first two chapters of this book.

Other difficulties, closely connected with the preceding, face the Gricean programme and merit brief mention. First, it is unclear that the utterances of any given sentence will standardly be accompanied by any one set of intentions on the parts of speakers. Reflection upon the diversity of circumstances of utterance – including the diversity of speakers' beliefs, speakers' beliefs about the audiences' beliefs, and speakers' desires – suggest the unlikelihood of speakers uttering that sentence standardly intending to induce the appropriate belief in the audience or even to induce the belief in the audience that the speaker has the appropriate belief. About the only plausible candidate for the intention regularly accompanying the utterance of sentence *p* is that of *saying* that *p*; but importation of this notion of *saying* at this point would again render the Gricean programme circular.

Suppose, however, that there *is* some standard intention accompanying utterances whose content is specifiable without employment of semantic notions. Then a second problem arises. The problem is not that such a specification will be trivial because it is likely, in the homophonic case, to rely upon the very sentence whose meaning is ultimately to be given; the distinction between designation and use ensures that such a specification of the intentions standardly accompanying utterance of the sentence will not be trivial. Rather, the problem is that the theory leaves completely unexplained *how* this pairing of designated sentence and accompanying intention is to be arrived at, and is to be arrived at for any of the infinity of sentences in the language. Given the intensionality that accompanies talk of intentions, the prospects of a plausible logical account of this generation of designated sentence and standard accompanying intention seem dim.

Third, *if* uptake is required as part of the Gricean ascent from utterers' meaning to sentence-meaning, we shall need an *explanation* of *how* this uptake is achieved by the audience. Utterers' intentions are not recognised by unfailing intuition, nor do Acts of God figure large. It is perhaps possible that very simple intentions be detected quasi-behaviouristically; but for intentions of any fair degree of complexity, this is simply implausible, the behavioural guide being too *inexact*. Any explanation of how such intentions are recognised will inevitably rely upon the audience's recognition of the literal meaning of the sentence; that meaning is the route to the speaker's intentions, the reverse journey usually being impossible. This difficulty carries over to us as external theorists of the language. If the theory of meaning is to be empirical in the way outlined at the beginning of this chapter and in the preceding chapter, then the difficulty for Grice is clear: detection of sentence-meaning will require on his programme the detection of utterers' intentions, and, perhaps, of audiences' responses. But again, for any except the simplest of intentions and simplest of responses, such detection will require both the verbal expression of those intentions and responses together with an *understanding* of those verbal expressions. This verbal expression of intention or response, if sufficiently precise, will standardly use, in part, the very sentence whose meaning we are trying to detect *via* the intentions held and responses induced. So to gain access to the appropriate intentions and responses we must first have knowledge of the meaning of the sentence concerned.

All of these anxieties issue in the same thought: there must be some prior notion of sentence-meaning fitted for a recursive characterisation of its infinite extension. This notion will be readily applicable to unuttered sentences; it will serve to explain such standard accompaniment as there is between the utterance of a sentence and utterers' intentions; it will generate, if anything can, the requisite pairing of designated sentence and content of intentions standardly accompanying the use of that sentence; it will explain how audiences secure

91

uptake of speakers' intentions; and it will explain how we, as theorists of the language, are able to recognise and identify native speakers' intentions and native audiences' responses. All these requirements on the prior notion of sentence meaning are met by the truth-conditions notion earlier developed.

In view of all these obvious difficulties, how have intentional theories of meaning gained such currency? This is not just an historical question; an answer to it may remove any lingering leanings towards such theories. The answer lies in part, I think, in a failure to distinguish the following (vague but distinct) claims:

(I1) A system of utterances would not be a language unless intentions were ascribed to the utterers; more specifically, an utterance is a piece of *linguistic* behaviour only if it is intentional.

(I2) The notion of sentence-meaning can be defined in terms of the notion of utterers' intentions.

(I3) The meaning of any particular sentence in a language can be determined by reference to the intentions with which it is uttered.

In (I1), I sense grains – perhaps sufficient for a heap – of deep truth about the notions of language, linguistic behaviour, and meaningfulness; but there is no way in which it implies either of its companion theses (I2) and (I3). Moreover, it is difficult to avoid the suspicion that any attempt to establish such implications would involve a crude shift from matters of meaningfulness to matters of meaning. The invalidity of such a move is testified to by the truth of (I1) and the falsity of the other two claims.

(I3) has been argued against completely explicitly; there remains the possibility of defending (I2) by construing Grice's theory as an attempt at an analytic definition of the term 'sentence-meaning'. We need not now challenge the notion of definition that this defence rests upon; all we need do is to ask what *interest* such a definition of a term would have which in no way, as shown by the falsity of (I3), helps to determine the application of that term in particular instances. What would be the interest of a definition of 'the meaning of a sentence' which is of no use in completing 'the meaning of this sentence is . . .'? If the analytic definition that (I2) gestures at is to be of any interest, it must have implications for the determination of meanings of particular sentences. What could these implications be but the *kind* of meaning-specification indicated by (I3), the kind of specification we have seen to be inadequate? So the claim (I2) is either wrong or uninteresting. This failure of intentional theories thus has two aspects: the failure to see the independence of (I1) from its companion theses (I2) and (I3); and the failure to see the essential connections between these two companions. Once these failures are acknowledged, the temptation of these theories becomes minimal.

The ground of these failings is rather deeper than that, however. The notion of sentence-meaning that is to play a useful role in any systematic account of linguistic behaviour is inherently unsuited to the kind of analytic definition, answering to our unreflective *a priori* intuitions about the structure of the notion as revealed by semantic decomposition, envisaged in (I2); rather, it is a notion constrained by its role within that overall account of linguistic behaviour, and that role requires that any 'definition' proffered must be applicable in the extension-yielding way envisaged by (I3). We can fully accept that the linguistic behaviour that is our starting point is *intentional*; if it were not, it would not be suitable for the *kind* of explanation by redescription our theory envisages. But we have seen that the way in which we are so to *understand* that behaviour requires the construction both of a theory of force and of an abstracted recursive theory of sense – a theory of sense with a form that intentional theories of meaning cannot have. The place within our overall theory of linguistic behaviour where intentions have a role to play is not, and cannot be, within the theory of sense, but is, rather, within the theory of force; specifically, within that component of the theory of force which enables us to identify the *mode* of utterance of a sentence. It is a 'harmless and salutary thing to say' that what distinguishes assertions from commands and questionings is the intention with which the utterance is issued; the presumption is that our theory of force can detect those intentions, can detect the requisite differences in the intended responses. But that is *quite* different from the presumption that we can detect, prior to the construction of a theory of meaning, the specific content of the intention so generically identified. It is also quite distinct from the presumption that all utterances within the same mode will share anything but the most schematically similar intentional accompaniment. It also does not rule out the possibility that in view of the overall deliverances of the combined theories of sense and force, together with the plausibility or implausibility of the propositional attitudes then ascribed, we shall be led to revise our original mode assignments to the utterance, and so shall be led to revise the schematic intentional structure attributed to the utterer.[2]

Grice's work, like Austin's earlier first exploration of this territory (Austin, *How To Do Things With Words*), will play a crucial role in our understanding of one element in the theory of force; but it is inherently ill-equipped to play any role within the theory of sense.

[2] That is to say: it is no part of the present 'concession' to intentional theorists that we can identify the mode of utterance prior to a theory of interpretation.

D*

Does this mean, then, to return to our starting point, that no explanation is to be given of how it comes about that a certain sentence has the meaning, the truth-consequences that it does? Of course not: that fact is explained by the observations of usage which our theory begins with and then enables us to redescribe, along with the observations constraining plausible propositional attitude ascription which serve to constrain that theoretical redescription. The success of the overall theory of linguistic usage serves both to justify and to explain the theory of sense which forms part of that overall theory. Given the role of that theory of sense, no further justification or explanation is needed.

Part Two

Some Structures of Meaning

Chapter IV

The Logical Form of Quantified Sentences

1 Standard Truth-Theories for the Universal and Existential Quantifiers

Appreciation of the importance of quantificational structure is one of the persisting effects of Frege's work. Discernment of the extent of the structure of quantifier and bound variables, recognition of the difficulties raised by multiply quantified sentences: since Frege inserted these into the philosophical consciousness, the proper treatment of quantified sentences has been a central issue in philosophical logic. If the methods of truth-theoretic semantics can shed new light upon this topic, the value of those methods will be shown.

Earlier, when presenting a rough and ready truth-definition for the predicate calculus language, I presented in effect a possible semantic analysis of two quantifiers, the universal and the existential. The relevant clauses of that definition are:

(I) A sentence is true if and only if it is satisfied by all sequences.

(II) A sequence S satisfies the existential quantification of a formula A with respect to the k-th variable v_k if and only if A is satisfied by some sequence S' such that S' differs from S in at most the k-th place (symbolising, $S' \underset{k}{\approx} S$).

(III) A sequence S satisfies the universal quantification of a formula A with respect to v_k if and only if A is satisfied by every S' such that $S' \underset{k}{\approx} S$.

Beyond this, all hangs upon the formula A, with additional clauses in the truth-definition specifying when that *kind* of formula is satisfied by a sequence. The workings of this truth-definition were illustrated in an informal manner, placing heavy reliance upon the all or nothing character of satisfaction, the fact that a closed sentence is satisfied by all sequences or none.

There are two questions that the truth-definitions for these quantifiers might prompt, one good, one bad. The bad one is this:

97

the definition of satisfaction for the existential quantifier includes the term 'some', that for the universal quantifier includes the term 'all'. Yet, surely, these are the expressions we want explicated? The definitions merely transfer the applications of these terms to sequences. The second question, the good one, is this: how do we determine the logical structure *within* the formula *A*, the logical structure which then fixes which *other* parts of the recursion for satisfaction are to be involved? Consider, for example, the sentences 'All men are mortal' and 'Some men are mortal'. Quite how is *A* to be represented in each of these cases? The orthodoxy, earlier adopted *en passant*, is that the representation of the former involves the material conditional, thus

$$(x) (Fx \to Gx),$$

where '*F*' is 'is a man' and '*G*' is 'is mortal'; while the second is orthodoxly taken to involve conjunction, to be represented as

$$(\exists x) (Fx \ \& \ Gx)$$

The rationale for these orthodoxies is clear. Suppose we assume that these quantified sentences do involve a sentential connective; suppose further, as looks to be the case, that the only plausible sentential connectives for such sentences are the material conditional and conjunction. Then the universally quantified sentence must involve the material conditional, since employment of conjunction would issue in insane ontological claims – in the case cited, the claim that *everything* is a mortal man; while the existentially quantified sentence must involve conjunction since employment of the material conditional would issue in claims which, if they make sense at all, would avoid the requisite ontological commitment – in the example given, the claim that there is something which, *if* it is a man, is mortal.

Putting the good and the bad questions alongside each other reveals *why* the bad one is bad. First, there is nothing *trivial* about the clauses given, for the expression focused upon is *used*, not mentioned, on the RHS of the satisfaction clauses. Such clauses therefore express contingent, learnable, forgettable facts about the predicate calculus language. Even if we were giving such clauses for the *English* expressions 'all' and 'some', the charge of triviality would likewise be avoided. Second, *whatever* the significance of 'all' and 'some', whatever meaning attaches to them, the problem of the logical structure of quantified sentences, the problem of the structure to be discerned *within A*, remains. Let us say, then, that this is the problem of the *logical form* of quantified sentences, while the problem of giving any *further* account of the universal and existential quantifiers beyond that given by pairing them, as is done in (II) and

(III), with the *usage* of 'all' and 'some', is the problem of the *analysis* of the quantificational expressions. Then there are two reasons for holding the bad question bad. First, it confuses questions of logical form with problems of analysis; and second, it blandly assumes, what might well be false, that some *further* analysis of the meanings of the quantificational expressions '(x)' and '$(\exists x)$' can be given other than their pairing with *uses* of 'all' and 'some'; that is, the question assumes, what might well be false, that these quantificational expressions, and their English counterparts, can be given correct decompositional analyses.

Let us focus, then, on the good question and the orthodox answers to that question. These orthodoxies were assumed correct in the earlier informal derivations of T-sentences for quantified formulae. I shall briefly rehearse that for the universal quantifier.

On the orthodoxy, the correct representation of 'All men are mortal' is

(1) $(x) (Fx \rightarrow Gx)$.

By clause (I) above, we have this:

(1) is true if and only if (S) (S satisfies $\overline{(x_3) (Fx_3 \rightarrow Gx_3)}$).

(I take the third variable to be the appropriate one; as we saw earlier, nothing hangs on this. Overlining represents a *naming* of the overlined expression.) Since satisfaction is an all or nothing matter, we know that the named expression is satisfied by all sequences if and only if it is satisfied by some arbitrary sequence; so consider sequence S_1

$\langle \sqrt{16}, \text{Quine, the moon, Nijinsky}, \ldots \rangle$

Then,

(1) is true if and only if S_1 satisfies $\overline{(x_3) (Fx_3 \rightarrow Gx_3)}$.

By clause (III) above, we then have this

(1) is true if and only if (S') ($S' \underset{3}{\approx} S_1 \rightarrow S'$ satisfies $\overline{Fx_3 \rightarrow Gx_3}$).

Since '$p \rightarrow q$' is equivalent to '$\sim p \lor q$', we have:

(1) is true if and only if (S') ($S' \underset{3}{\approx} S_1 \rightarrow S'$ satisfies $\overline{\sim Fx_3 \lor Gx_3}$).

Using the star-function introduced earlier, we have it that

S_1 satisfies $\overline{\sim Fx_3 \lor Gx_3}$

is equivalent to

$\sim F (S_1{}^*\overline{(x_3)}) \lor G(S_1{}^*\overline{(x_3)})$.

Now the fact that 'F' is 'is a man' and 'G' is 'is a mortal', together

99

with the range of admissible substitutions in S_1 to obtain S' (viz. *all* substitutions such that S' differs from S_1 in at most the third place), and so to obtain $S'*\overline{(x_3)}$, makes it obvious that (1) will be true if and only if there is no object which is both a man and is not mortal, which, intuitively, is the correct truth-condition for the sentence.

With existentially quantified sentences, assuming the orthodox conjunctive treatment of their logical form, we again saw earlier that no problem arises: the derivation upon that assumption produces the correct truth-conditions. But two points should be noted. First, generations of students of formal logic have found puzzling the shift in the sentential connective, from conjunction in the existential case to the material conditional in the universal case. Second, the only rationale that generations of logic teachers have been able to give to these students is the argument sketched just now; and that argument simply *assumes* that there is some sentential connective to be found within these quantified sentences, even though that connective is discovered to vary with the kind of quantification involved.

2 The Problem of Non-Standard Quantifiers[1]

'All' and 'some' are not the only quantifiers to occur in English. Two other prominent ones are 'most' and 'many', which I shall call the *majority* and the *manifold* quantifiers respectively. Consider, for example, the sentence 'Most men are mortal'. Part of the truth-definition covering such a sentence is apparently given easily:

(I) (as before): A sentence is true if and only if it is satisfied by all sequences.

(IV) A sequence S satisfies the majority quantification of a formula A with respect to variable v_k if and only if A is satisfied by most sequences S' such that $S' \underset{k}{\approx} S$.

What remains to be settled is the structure to be found *within A* for a majority quantified sentence. Assuming there to be a sentential connective present in A, and using an obvious enough notation, there seem only two candidates:

$$(Mx)\,(Fx \rightarrow Gx)$$

and

$$(Mx)\,(Fx\ \&\ Gx).$$

But the latter cannot be correct. One can hold that most men are mortal without holding that most things are both men and mortal:

---

[1] I owe my appreciation of the problem raised here to David Wiggins; it is, I think, first raised by Nicholas Rescher in 'Plurality – quantification', *Journal of Symbolic Logic*, 27, 3 (1962), pp. 373–4.

think of all the grains of sand! So the material conditional is the only remaining candidate for the sentential connective to be discerned within A.

Combining this with (IV) produces an account that prompts three anxieties. The first is the bad, old thought that the account is trivial because the term 'most' occurs in (IV). But this is beside the point: the term is *used* in (IV), and our concern, anyway, is with the matter of logical form, not with the possibility (or impossibility) of analysis. The second worry is technical and difficult. In (IV), the application of 'most' is shifted to sequences. But we have seen that there is a non-denumerable infinity of sequences, and it might well be doubted whether the term 'most' has any application to such a totality. What is required is that, in some way, 'most' be attached to objects, not sequences, while keeping a definition that relies upon the apparatus of sequences. The third difficulty is non-technical, and decisive: the proposal yields the wrong truth-conditions, and so often the wrong truth-values, for majority quantified sentences. The proposal indeed makes it true that in this world most men are mortal; but it will also make it true in this world that most men are immortal; it will even make it true that most men are both mortal and immortal.

This is readily seen by examining the informal derivation of a T-sentence upon this proposal. The claim is that 'Most men are mortal' can be represented like this:

(2) $(Mx) (Fx \to Gx)$.

By clause (I) above, we have it that

(2) is true if and only if (S) (S satisfies $\overline{(Mx_3) (Fx_3 \to Gx_3)}$).

As before, we need only consider some arbitrary sequence since the all or nothing character of satisfaction ensures that a closed sentence is satisfied by any one sequence if and only if it is satisfied by all sequences. Consider, then, sequence S_1, where S_1 is

$\langle \sqrt{16}, \text{Quine, the moon, Nijinsky}, \ldots \rangle$

Then,

(2) is true if and only if S_1 satisfies $\overline{(Mx_3) (Fx_3 \to Gx_3)}$.

By clause (IV), we obtain

(2) is true if and only if (MS') ($S' \underset{3}{\approx} S_1 \to S'$ satisfies $\overline{Fx_3 \to Gx_3}$).

Using the equivalence of '$p \to q$' and '$\sim p \vee q$', we thus have

(2) is true if and only if (MS') ($S' \underset{3}{\approx} S_1 \to S'$ satisfies $\overline{\sim Fx_3 \vee Gx_3}$).

The trouble now is obvious: most sequences S' will indeed satisfy

101

$\overline{\sim Fx_3 \vee Gx_3}$ because the appropriate (in this example, the third) member of most S' sequences will indeed satisfy $\overline{\sim Fx_3 \vee Gx_3}$, that is, x_3 is not a man or is mortal; but they do so for quite the wrong reason – viz. their third members are *not* men, and so satisfy the first disjunct. Most things are *not* men! But this means that *whatever* the other predicate in the sentence – 'is mortal', 'is immortal', 'is neither mortal nor immortal', 'is both mortal and immortal', 'is a flea-ridden aardvark' – the sentence remains true. It is thus revealed to be the case, not just that most men are mortal, but that most men are immortal, and so on! The point is simply put: 'Most men are mortal' is *not* equivalent to 'Most things either are not men or are mortal', for such an 'equivalence' would systematically yield the wrong truth-conditions, and in most cases, the wrong truth-values for majority quantified sentences.

We might note in passing that, in rather unlikely cases, this logical form proposal could yield the wrong result in another way. Consider a universe in which there are twenty objects, eleven of which are men. Five of these men are mortal, the others immortal. So it is not the case that most men are mortal. Still, if the other nine objects – say women – are all mortal, the logical form proposed will yield the result that most men are mortal: for in the universe described, most things either are not men or are mortal. But this recherché case is not needed; the logical form proposed is quite evidently wrong for *this* world.

The sentential connective in majority quantified sentences cannot be the material conditional; but there is no other plausible candidate for this role. Exactly the same point is readily seen to be true of sentences involving the manifold quantifier 'many'. 'Many men are fat' is not equivalent to 'many things are either not men or are fat', nor is it equivalent to 'many things are men and are fat'. The small minority of men in the universe precludes both proposals. Since, for neither of these non-standard quantifiers is there a plausible sentential connective available, the moral is obvious: sentences involving these quantifiers do *not* include a sentential connective. But this negative moral leaves wide open the question of what the logical form of such sentences is.

It is clear that this is not just a problem for the formal semanticist. Indeed, three paragraphs back I put the difficulty in terms quite independent of formal semantics. The general logical problem is this: what is the structure of sentences involving 'most' and 'many' when such sentences are represented in the predicate calculus? The formal semantical problem is: what is the full truth-definition for such sentences? This latter problem can now be seen in two stages: because of the problem with counting sequences, (IV) cannot be correct for the majority quantifier 'most'; because of the minority position of men, the first shot at representing 'most' and 'many' sentences as containing the material conditional cannot be correct. The general logical problem is thus just the second stage of the formal semantical problem; yet, within the context of truth-conditions theory, the test of a proposal for handling this second stage, the general logical problem, is that it combine with a proposal for handling the first stage to produce an acceptable truth-definition. Just solving the second stage, the general logical problem, in some *technical* way without this further element of the truth-definition would be a shabby success at best. So while *part* of the problem posed by these sentences can be appreciated outside the favoured theory of meaning, location of that part *within* that theory of meaning requires a deeper solution of that part.

3 The Beginnings of a Solution

We cannot represent sentences involving 'most' and 'many' using a sentential connective. How, then, are they to be represented? Harking back to a thought of Frege's, the most promising idea seems to be this: sentences containing these quantifiers do not include a sentential connective, and so do not include an open sentence; rather, they are *relational* sentences, to be construed on the analogy of 'Tom is next to Bill', canonically represented as 'Rab'. So we might represent 'Most Fs are Gs' as '$(Mx) (Fx, Gx)$'. But whereas 'is next to' is a 'first order' relational property of individuals, sentences involving 'most' contain a 'second order' relational property of concepts. That second order relational property could be expressed, clumsily, thus: that relation between two properties such that most of the individuals falling under the first fall under the second. Just as no one looks for a *sentential* connective within 'Tom is next to Bill', so no one should look for a sentential connective within 'Most Fs are Gs'; for, as we have seen, there can be no such connective.

Thus is the general logical problem solved! But if anything is clear, it is that this proposal is obscure and useless *until* it is combined with a solution to the other stage of the problem facing the formal semanticist; that is, it is obscure and useless until combined with a proposal that produces an adequate truth-definition for these constructions. So much the worse for attempts to treat of the general logical problem outside the framework of formal semantics: for all that attempt issues in are *typographic* solutions.

The distinctive problem located by the formal semantical approach was the inapplicability of the term 'most' to the non-denumerable infinity of sequences. The moral, again, was in outline clear: some-how, 'most' must apply initially to objects, not sequences. But how is this moral to be concretised?

The best attempt at this I know of is owed to David Wiggins. Let S_z^i for each i (where i is a number) and each z (where z is an object) and each S (where S is a sequence) be the sequence obtained by putting the object z in the i-th place of S. For example, take S_1 as the sequence S; take z as Venus, and i as three; then S_{1z}^i is

$$\langle \sqrt{16}, \text{Quine, Venus, Nijinsky}, \ldots \rangle$$

Now we replace the defective clause (IV) by

(IV') A sequence S satisfies the majority quantification of a formula A – say, '$(Mx)(Fx, Gx)$' – with respect to v_k if and only if most z (S_z^k satisfies $\overline{Fx_k}$, S_z^k satisfies $\overline{Gx_k}$).

This last clause should be read thus: most objects which when placed in the appropriate place of a sequence produce a sequence that satisfies 'F' when placed in the same place in a sequence produce a sequence that satisfies 'G'. Or, more simply, most F-satisfiers, most objects which satisfy 'F', are also G-satisfiers. It should *not* be read thus: most objects when put in the appropriate place of a sequence produce a sequence which, if it satisfies 'F', satisfies 'G'. For *that* uses the conditional 'if . . . then . . .', and represents the very problem we have to avoid.

This proposal apparently solves *both* elements of the formal semantical puzzle; thus its solution to the traditional logical problem – that of the logical representation of majority quantified sentences – is endorsed.

This kind of proposal is naturally extended to embrace the quantifier 'many'. Sentences involving this quantifier cannot involve the material conditional; nor, it seems, can they involve any other sentential connective. Rather, they are second order relational sentences. (IV') is easily modified for this quantifier by the substitution of 'many' for 'most' in the last clause, and in the informal readings of that sentence presented. Employment of the thus modified (IV') for 'many' may not be essential, for the other difficulty discerned for 'most' does not carry over with quite the same force: for it is not clear that the non-denumerable infinity of sequences precludes the possibility of applying the notion of *many, sufficiently many*, a *manifold*, to them. We do not need, *per impossibile*, to count up to half of the non-denumerable infinity to apply the notion of *many*. Still, it is not clear that an analysis of 'many', if such an analysis be possible, will yield much insight into the applicability of this term to such a domain; further, we might well wish in general to have concrete truth-theoretic proposals for constructions *prior* to considerations of matters of analysis. For both these reasons, it is reasonable to carry over the apparatus employed in the truth-definition of 'most' to that for 'many'.

It is a quite different order of question whether we should go on to apply this *kind* of analysis to the standard quantifiers 'all' and 'some'. We have seen that there is no difficulty facing the presentation of an adequate truth-definition for these quantifiers upon the assumption that sentences containing these quantifiers *do* include a sentential connective. But the idea that the four quantifiers – 'all', 'most', 'many', 'some' – function in quite different ways – the poles in one way, the intermediaries in another – is not an idea with intuitive or theoretical backing. If we wish for a uniform *kind* of account of these quantifiers – and there seems no good reason to prefer a non-uniform treatment – we shall extend the proposal sketched to all quantified sentences. All such sentences are relational, concern relations between concepts; and the simple replacement of 'most' by 'all' or by 'some' in the last clause of (IV') produces an acceptable truth-definition for the standard quantifiers so viewed. Frege and Russell hit upon special cases, cases where we could frame the appropriate sentential structure: but once we see that this puts us on the wrong track for other quantifiers, there is no reason to hold to their treatment of these special cases.

We should also note how readily this proposal is extended to the 'comparative' quantifiers 'more' and 'fewer'. Thus, the logical representation of, say, 'More frogs are happy than are sad' will be:

$$(More\ x)\ (Fx\ \&\ Hx,\ Fx\ \&\ Sx)$$

with the obvious interpretations of the predicates. The appropriate clause of the truth-theory, (IV'), is readily modified to handle this distinct quantifier. Orthodox treatments of quantificational formulae face formidable difficulties, comparable to those sketched for the manifold quantifier, in handling such sentences.[2]

This relational treatment of quantifiers is not, of course, without its difficulties. I have given two informal readings of the crucial last clause in the truth-definition, (IV), for quantifiers upon this treatment, and have indicated one reading that should not be imposed upon it. This might be thought to suggest that that clause is not altogether pellucid; and as long as this is not merely the stubborn demand for the reintroduction of a sentential connective, this is not an unreasonable thought. Further, the proposal does not handle quantifiers in sentences like '$(Mx)\ (x = x)$', for here there are no concepts to be related. Nor does the treatment given apply to sentences like 'Tom is the most happy person in the room', 'Tom is a

---

[2] Given that all occurrences of 'most' (except those mentioned in the next paragraph) can be rephrased in terms of 'more' – 'Most frogs are happy' becoming 'More things are happy frogs than are unhappy frogs' – but not vice versa, and given the intuitive plausibility of the relational treatment of 'more', indirect support is given to the favoured treatment of 'most'.

most happy individual', or 'Tom is more happy than sad'. It is not that there is any great difficulty in handling at least the first of these sentences; and it might well be that 'most' and 'more' have at least two quite different logical roles. It would, however, be reassuring to discern at least some common logical elements in these seemingly different occurrences of these expressions.

4 Logical Form and Inference

For any construction in the language under study, the aim of a theory of meaning is to construct a finite set of axioms and rules which assign to the constituents of that construction truth-bearing properties, and which also assign to the overall construction a logical structure with specified semantic import. We have followed Davidson in saying that the structure revealed within a sentence in the process of its incorporation within a truth-theory for the language is its *logical form*.

It is a matter of importance that the motivation behind the assignment of Davidson's logical form differs from that governing traditional assignments of logical form. Traditionally, logical form was assigned to facilitate, or to reveal as reasonable, *inference*: as little or as much structure was assigned as was necessary to license the inferences held to be reasonable. There were still differences over the assignment of structure to various sentences: partly for the relatively trivial reason that different logicians were concerned with different kinds, or levels of inference (hence the difference in logical representations of the same sentences as between the propositional and the predicate calculi); but also for the more important reason that there can be, and there has been, dispute over quite which inferences are reasonable or worth licensing. The difficulty within traditional logical form assignment was that in any area of intelligent dispute, any area where either side could with apparent reasonableness be maintained, it was utterly unclear how such disputes should be settled; hence the anxiety prompted by what David Kaplan has called 'the run-it-up-the-axiom-list-and-see-if-anyone-deduces-a-contradiction method'. Intuitions about validity of inference are not enough; the inner voice can mislead if it can lead at all; and intuitions about the *values* of inferences, about which are *worth* preserving, are even less decisive, especially when the *interest* prompting such assignment is unclear.

As said, our interest in assigning logical structure is initially quite different: we assign as much, or as little, structure as is necessary to facilitate formulation of an adequate truth-theory for the language of which the construction is a part. But it is also important to see that our interest governing logical form assignment is *not* unconnected

106

with the foundations of traditional assignments: for our logical form assignments are part of the construction of a truth-theory for the language, and validity of inference, the key notion of traditional assignment, is defined in terms of truth. Some of the complexities this connection produces can be seen in the following remarks by Davidson:

> To say a second sentence is a logical consequence of a first is to say, roughly, that the second is true if the first is no matter how the non-logical constants are interpreted. Since what we count as a logical constant can vary independently of the set of truths, it is clear that the two versions of logical form, though related, need not be identical. The relation, in brief, seems this. Any theory of truth that satisfies Tarski's criteria must take account of all truth-affecting iterative devices in the language. In the familiar languages for which we know how to define truth the basic iterative devices are reducible to the sentential connectives, the apparatus of quantification, and the description operator if it is primitive. Where one sentence is a logical consequence of another on the basis of quantifica-tional structure alone, a theory of truth will therefore entail that if the first sentence is true, the second is. There is no point, then, in not including the expressions that determine quantificational structure among the logical constants, for when we have characterised truth, on which any account of logical consequence depends, we have already committed ourselves to all that calling such expressions logical constants could commit us. Adding to this list of logical constants will increase the inventory of logical truths and consequence-relations beyond anything a truth definition demands, and will therefore yield richer versions of logical form (Davidson, 'On Saying That', p. 160).

Davidson's thought here appears in part to be this[3]: because of the role of truth in our assignment of logical form, the constituent constructions picked out by our assignment will be truth (or satis-faction) iterative devices; they will therefore carry truth-inferential consequences which will be taken over by the traditional logician – *if* he is interested in that *kind* of inference. But the traditional logician may *choose* to go beyond this. We select all, and only, those iterative devices necessary for the construction of an adequate truth-definition, and assign to them all, and only, those truth-bearing properties needed for such a definition. But there may be other iterative devices carrying interesting inferential consequences; and those

[3] The thought also includes a distinctive view of *logical constants*; I shall not discuss this here.

iterative features that we do single out may have *further* interesting inferential consequences. The traditional logician may choose to go beyond the formal semanticist either in terms of discerned inferential structure (additional inferentially motivated decomposition) *or* in terms of inferential properties of the structure discerned by the semanticist (additional axiomatisation). So there could be an adequate truth-theory which does *not* reveal as valid *all* those inferences we hold to be valid, and which does not reveal as valid all those inferences we hold to be valid and to be important enough to be worth preserving: the additional structure, or the additional inferential powers, may be unnecessary from our perspective.

An example of this is provided by the truth-definition given for the majority quantifier 'most'. Construction of derivations of T-sentences for sentences involving this quantifier, using that definition, shows the definition to satisfy the constraints we have placed upon truth-theories. But while doing this, the proposal does *not* license the pre-philosophically sound inference from 'most' sentences to 'some' sentences; for example, that from

'Most aardvarks are fat'

to

'Some aardvarks are fat'.

Such inferences are readily enough validated by additional axiomatisation, by the insertion of an appropriate rule of inference into the meta-language; they might even be validated by further, decompositional, analysis of 'most'. But none of this is required for the truth-definition to satisfy our stated constraints. Validation of inference can wait upon additional axiomatisation or upon the analysis of terms treated as primitive within the truth-theoretical logical form. Only the *short-sighted* demand for semantic decomposition or the *irrelevant* demand for additional axiomatisation could see this as a deficiency in a logical form proposal.

Chapter V

Reported Speech: The Problems of Intensionality

1 Reported Speech: The Problems

Reported speech figures large in the recent history of semantics, principally because it raises in a vivid form difficulties attendant upon a large, and important, area of language, that concerned with the mental life. It has also provided a major motivation for a radically different conception of semantics from that being expounded here. A truth-definition for this usage, or these usages, of language, adequate within our specified constraints, could both eliminate that motivation and pave the way for the incorporation into our semantic theory of the important, mental area of language.

Traditionally, reported speech has been held to take two forms, the direct and the indirect. Usage of quotation marks is taken generally to indicate that the former is being used, so that the accounts given of direct discourse have evolved in terms of the account given of quotation marks. This need not much concern us now, since our initial concern is with the other construction, indirect discourse – sentences like 'Galileo said that the earth moves', 'Phyllis said that Henry was in love with her'. Schematically, these are sentences of the form

'*A* said that *p*',

where '*A*' is replaced by an expression referring to a speaker, and '*p*' by a full, declarative sentence. I shall call '*p*' the *content-sentence*. Similarly, direct discourse is schematically of the form

'*A* said "*p*" '.

Our initial problem is easily stated: what is the logical form of each of these varieties of reported speech? At first sight, the answer for direct discourse is obvious: such sentences are simple relational sentences between speakers and sentences, the relation being that

109

of *said*. Such sentences are true if and only if the speaker stands in that relation to the very sentence quoted. This simple thought is not really so simple, both because of the need for an adequate treatment of quotation marks as *names* of the sentences quoted, and because *saying* is an *action*, so that our account must fit with an adequate treatment of action sentences generally. But what matters now is to see the obviously greater difficulty in handling indirect discourse. The analogy suggests that sentences of this form, too, are relational: but what, then, is the second term of the relation, the analogue of the sentence in direct discourse?

Putting aside the analogy with direct discourse, it seems that a significant part of the semantic structure of a sentence of indirect discourse must be its content-sentence. We can produce any of a potential infinity of sentences of this grammatical form as different sentences are substituted for p; we believe that we can understand each such sentence and assess it for truth or falsity; and we believe that each such sentence is semantically distinct. Unless these beliefs are false, it seems that the content-sentence must be a significant unit. But how?

We certainly cannot treat '*A* said that . . .' as a truth-functional sentence-forming operator on sentences, comparable, say, to 'It is not the case that . . .'; for a true sentence of the form '*A* said that p' can be made false by substitution for 'p' of another sentence with the same truth-value. My once having said a truth does not license the attribution to me as a saying of any other truth you care to think of. However, it is not just that the construction is not truth-functional: it creates, quite generally, an intensional context, one in which co-extensive substitutions do not preserve the extension of the whole. Consider 'Galileo said that the earth moves'; this is a true sentence of indirect discourse. But suppose we substitute for 'the earth' the co-extensive expression 'the planet that moves around the sun every $365\frac{1}{4}$ days'; then we obtain 'Galileo said that the planet that moves around the sun every $365\frac{1}{4}$ days moves'. But that is false, placing the price of suffering unduly low: Galileo did not achieve fame, or notoriety, with *that* kind of remark! A moment's more reflection suggests that this failure of extensionality infects, not just singular terms and whole sentences, but also quantifiers, variables, predicates and connectives. This is crucial: first, because we are attempting to work with a thoroughly extensional truth-theory; and second, because there are good, independent reasons for our doing so.

Given the intimate connection between Davidson's notion of logical form and the inferential notion of traditional logicians, it is unsurprising that customary inferences break down with indirect discourse. Normally, if someone utters a sentence containing the words 'the earth moves', we feel entitled to attribute to the speaker the commitment that *something* moves. This we clearly cannot do when his total utterance was 'Galileo said that the earth moves'. In this case, we would also have to be convinced that the *speaker*, not Galileo, believes that 'the earth' refers to something – say, through his belief that what Galileo said was true. The truth of 'Galileo said that the earth moves' does not suffice. We thus both lack any structural semantic understanding of sentences of indirect discourse, and have little confidence in inferences involving them.

2 Quine's Proposal

Given the truth of the claim that Genet said that crime is the highest form of sensuality,[1] all we initially feel entitled to conclude is that Genet said something, that somebody said that crime is the highest form of sensuality, and that someone said something. In the first and third of these inferences, we feel entitled to draw the same conclusion no matter which saying of Genet's is being reported; while in the second, there is no structure within the content-sentence involved and the same *pattern* of inference would work *whichever* saying of Genet's was being reported. The content-sentence, as regards inference, seems unstructured and inert. This reflection provides the starting point for an instructive proposal, first made by Quine (*Word and Object*, chapter VI).

Since, on many occasions, there seem to be no intuitively acceptable inferences involving structure within the content-sentence, Quine saw no point in assigning logical structure to that sentence. And if we do assign structure to that content-sentence, we may find ourselves forced to embrace inferences which, intuitively, we are unwilling to accept. In barest outline, Quine's proposal was this: combine 'said that' and the content-sentence to form a one-place predicate 'said-that-p', true or false of utterers, of persons.

This proposal has a number of consequences of varying degrees of unacceptability. One is that we cannot now immediately draw one of the conclusions that intuitively we wish to draw, namely that the person referred to said something. Still, this would be a small price to pay: as Quine has it, there may need to be *regimentation* of an idiom if it is to be incorporated within an adquate semantic theory, and this process of regimentation *need* not be conducted with an eye solely to conferring respectability upon our customary intuitions. However, the price in terms of inference of accepting Quine's proposal is much greater than is suggested by this objection: for while the content-sentence often functions inertly in inference, there are occasions when, like the inert gases, it behaves in a more active manner. For example, if alongside the claim that Galileo said that the

[1] The claim is in fact false.

earth moves we accept the additional premiss that everything that Galileo said is true, we wish to conclude that the earth moves, that something moves, and, perhaps, that the earth does something. To obtain these inferences, it is essential that structure be revealed within the content-sentence.

There is another aspect of indirect discourse, which I shall call the *detachability* of the content-sentence, which reinforces the view that the content-sentence is a significant unit and which suggests that it cannot be, as it were, buried within a Quinean predicate. At the very least, there is a usage that Quine's account does not directly apply to. As I stroll with a friend, I notice, chalked on the walls of All Souls College, the slogan 'Crime is the highest form of sensuality'. Pointing it out to my companion, I say 'Genet said that'. Such a sentence is a complete, declarative sentence. In another case, I notice the slogan, but, my friend being blind, I remark 'Genet said that crime is the highest form of sensuality'. The obvious similarity between these cases suggests that the content-sentence is *separable*, and so a significant unit. The example also shows us one usage of indirect discourse – 'Genet said that', as a complete declarative sentence – that Quine's account does not apply to (cf. Davidson, 'On Saying That', p. 158).

The anxieties about inference are not yet decisive, for our interest in assigning logical form is not that of the traditional logician. (Although, when Quine first presented his proposal, that did appear to be his main interest.) For our purposes, it does not matter if there are pre-philosophically valid inferences not licensed by a logical form proposal; although it would matter if the proposal *precluded* the possibility of validating such inferences. But maybe Quine's proposal can be supplemented to avoid any appearance of such preclusion. Nor, as it stands, need the point about separability be decisive: Quine could just present some *other* account of the detached attributions of sayings, and deny that the analogy just explored is semantically significant. What does matter in the present context is the question of whether Quine's proposal can be incorporated within a truth-theory of the kind required. Now, if Quine's predicates – 'said-that-p' – were unstructured, this would clearly not be the case: for there would be an infinity of such unstructured predicates. But, as Quine has recently emphasised, these predicates are not unstructured:

> I attributed a logical grammar to the intermediate contexts. I construed 'that' as an operator that attaches to a sentence to produce a name of a proposition. Then, switching to an alternative approach which shunned propositions, I construed 'believes that' rather as an *attitudinative*: a part of speech

that applies to a singular term and a sentence to produce a sentence. More complex operators came into play in the analysis of polyadic belief (in Davidson and Hintikka, *Words and Objections*, p. 344).

These comments about belief-constructions are meant to apply also to saying-constructions; Quine's predicates of the form 'said-that-*p*' are not unstructured, and so do not offend immediately against the requirement of finiteness. However, as Quine himself concedes (*ibid.*), it does not appear possible using his proposal to characterise a truth-predicate that applies to all sentences of indirect discourse. So, on that proposal, no coherent truth-theoretical account can be given of indirect discourse.

Quine concedes this at the same time as emphasising the *structure* to be discerned within his predicates. In part, this may just be to correct a misunderstanding of his earlier proposal, while conceding that that proposal ultimately will not do. But there may be a more interesting motivation behind Quine's emphasis upon the structure within his account. Suppose that sentences of indirect discourse are unintelligible, that no coherent semantical account can be given of them. Still, some *explanation* must surely be given of our, *ex hypothesi*, false belief that they are intelligible. By endowing these sentences with some *kind* of structure, we can account for this belief. It is true that we could attempt to account for this belief simply by reference to the *surface* similarity amongst the class of indirect discourse sentences. But this embodies a premature pessimism: the *kinds* of consideration invoked cannot play any part in a final semantic account of the idiom, if such an account be possible. Whereas an explanation relating to the *logical* structure is at least the right *kind* of explanation to play such a role, even if ultimately that role cannot be played. Even if Quine's proposal does not detect a logical structure facilitating the incorporation of indirect discourse within a truth-definition, it still reveals the kind of logical consideration that might have had some bearing upon such an account. So if we wish to combine the belief that indirect discourse is incoherent with *either* an unstructured analysis *or* with Quine's analysis, explanatory requirements favour the latter. Thus a possible further motive for Quine's emphasis upon the structured character of his admittedly inadequate proposal. But, of course, we should not embrace the first belief – that indirect discourse is incoherent – except as the last resort; especially since the construction is a common, apparently readily learnable one, which none of the language-users encounters much difficulty in handling, and over whose correct usage there is no great debate.

3 The Fregean Proposal

The difficulties raised by indirect discourse were presented, in part, in terms of the apparent failure of extensionality, especially with regard to singular terms and complete declarative sentences. One possible thought is that this appearance arose only because it was assumed that expressions have their *usual* reference when within the content-sentence. The strategy then would be to assume the opposite, that terms within the content-sentence do *not* have their customary reference, and then to posit some other entities to which the terms do refer in such contexts, for which referents extensionality does not break down. Then we would have an explanation of the appearance of non-extensionality together with a demonstration of how that appearance is illusory. This will have to be done for all expressions occurring in the content-sentence, but it will simplify matters if attention is restricted to singular terms and whole sentences.

What entities, then, are to be posited as referents of expressions within the content-sentence of indirect discourse sentences? A definite description usually refers to the object satisfying that description; a name usually refers to the object bearing that name; a declarative sentence, if we wish to speak of it having a referent at all, usually refers to its truth-value (this being a simple consequence of the standard criterion of *sameness* of reference, viz., substitutivity *salva extensione*: in, for example, '*p & q*', the truth-value of the whole sentence remains unchanged if, say, for '*p*' we substitute any other sentence with the same truth-value). But, putting aside the case of names, it is natural to say that definite descriptions and sentences also have a *sense*: two descriptions can present the same object, refer to the same object, in different ways, where the difference is not just typographical but semantic. Likewise two sentences can present the same truth-value but in different ways. This notion of the *sense* of an expression is introduced by Frege as the *mode* of presentation of the referent (Frege, *Philosophical Writings*, p. 57). The notion so introduced, whatever its initial intuitive appeal, soon becomes complicated by the diverse roles it is called upon to play, the diversity of which will be explored in more detail a little later in connection with the semantics of proper names; the initially intuitive, albeit vague, talk of *mode of presentation* of referent is supplemented by the desire that the notion of sense:

(a) should account for the meaningfulness of sentences containing expressions lacking any customary referent;

(b) should in some way provide a *route* to the referent, an explanation of how it is that the expression has the referent it does;

(c) should figure in any plausible account of the competent speaker's understanding through the requirement that such a speaker must *know* the sense rather than, or perhaps as well as, the referent of an expression;

(d) should account for the differences in both logical properties and informative content that can issue from truth-value preserving substitutions of co-referential expressions;

(e) should *explain* truth-value changing substitutions of expressions that are usually co-referring;

(f) should, for singular terms, account for the meaningful, and non-trivial, character of existence statements involving such expressions.

It is not at all clear that *any* notion could remain coherent under these diverse pressures; but for the moment all that need concern us is (e), the thought that difference of sense combined with sameness of customary referent can *explain* changes in truth-value that substitution of expressions having these properties can issue in.

Suppose, for example, that 'the oldest bachelor in England' has the same reference as 'the richest bachelor in England'. That fact does not ensure that if it is true that

(1) Tom said that the oldest bachelor in England is rich

it is also true that

(2) Tom said that the richest bachelor in England is rich.

But suppose that 'the oldest bachelor in England' has the same *sense* as 'the oldest unmarried man in England'; then it seems that (1) will have the same truth-value as

(3) Tom said that the oldest unmarried man in England is rich.

Thus such substitution of co-senseful singular terms preserves truth-value. Likewise, assuming the content-sentences in (1) and (3) to have the same sense, but that in (2) a different sense, it emerges that substitution of sentences with the same sense, or of sentences which express the same *proposition*, in the content-sentence of indirect discourse will preserve truth-value. If the referent is then defined by the criterion for sameness of referent of substitution preserving extension, we shall say that within the content-sentence of indirect discourse sentences, definite descriptions have as their referent their customary senses, while sentences have as their referent their customary senses, the propositions they usually express.

In the semantic theory expounded and defended earlier, entities like *senses* and *propositions* played no role. Indirect discourse, like other apparently non-extensional constructions, has provided a primary motivation for those who would wish to see truth-conditions semantics supplemented by (or, in some cases, replaced by) the invocation of such entities. Such invocation would drastically change the character both of the meta-language and of the proof-theory originally envisaged in defending truth-theoretic semantics; it is therefore a matter of importance to determine whether such invocation is coherent, let alone well-motivated.

Whatever the entities posited in supplementation of our austere semantics, they must be assigned to expressions *systematically*; otherwise, there will be no question of recursively characterising a truth-predicate meeting the conditions we have placed upon such a characterisation. This appears to be the major failing in Frege's own development of this kind of account: any referring expression can refer to any of an infinite number of entities in different contexts on the basis of their reference in simpler contexts. For example, there is no systematic way of moving from the reference of 'the earth' in 'Galileo said that the earth moves' to that in 'Tom believes that Galileo said that the earth moves'. No one could believe that the later stages of Frege's classic *On Sense and Reference* could form part of a *systematic* theory![2]

The appropriate manoeuvre seems obvious enough, although its full implementation soon becomes a matter of some complexity: posit just *one* kind of these entities, senses, concepts, propositions, and the like, to function as the referent of each *kind* of term within intensional contexts. (In some neo-Fregean theories, like Church's, the assigned entity or range of entities functions as the referent in *all* contexts, intensional or otherwise; but this is unimportant for present purposes.) As remarked, the full development of such an account is a complex matter, which fortunately need not delay us; let us concede to this neo-Fregean that it can be done, and that it is then possible recursively to characterise a truth-predicate meeting our stated constraints. Making those concessions, we shall be able to see the difficulties in principle facing this approach.

First, there is what appears a purely *ad hoc* difficulty. Suppose we follow Frege in his original inclination to say that within the content-sentence in indirect discourse terms have as their referents, not the entities they customarily refer to, but rather their customary *senses*. Then, in such contexts, substitutivity preserving extensionality must hold for terms that have the same customary sense. But, now, if any two expressions have the same sense, 'oculist' and 'eye-doctor' do. Suppose that JJ says 'An oculist is an eye-doctor'. We can truthfully report him thus: 'JJ said that an oculist is an eye-doctor'. But now the Fregean theory commits us to the truth of this report: 'JJ said that an oculist is an oculist'. But that is surely wrong. Likewise, suppose we hold that the whole sentence refers, not as on Frege's

[2] But see Dummett, *Frege, Philosophy of Language*, pp. 267–8, in which a way of avoiding this difficulty is presented.

theory it usually does to its truth-value, but to the proposition expressed. This would be the beginning of a theory that treats indirect discourse sentences as relational, upon the model of direct discourse, treating propositions as the second *relatum*. Let us also assume the Fregean principle that the proposition expressed by a sentence is a function of the senses of its constituents, such that that proposition will be unchanged by substitution for any expression occurring in the sentence of another expression with the same sense. It then follows on the Fregean proposal that if 'JJ said that an oculist is an eye-doctor' is true, so is 'JJ said that an oculist is an oculist'. But it is not, so that proposal is wrong.

This difficulty might appear purely *ad hoc*, showing only that we have so far failed to find the appropriate assignment within intensional contexts. But it is difficult to know what to make of this suggestion in the absence of a further concrete proposal; the failures of substitutivity with the ordinary reference and with the ordinary sense appear parallel, and invite the suspicion that it would be possible to engineer a similar failure of extensionality for any proposed assignment. Of course, this suspicion will only achieve much force if blessed with supporting argument; but it will certainly be reinforced by the discovery of an adequate alternative theory.

There is another difficulty with the Fregean theories. We need to be given adequate identity and individuation conditions for the occult entities posited by these theories. The entities posited are meant to be *particulars*: and understanding of the notion of a ϕ, of a kind of particular ϕs, requires understanding of the notion of *a ϕ*. Clarification of the notion of a particular, as opposed to an abstract, feature precisely requires that we give identity and individuation conditions for these particulars. But this is notoriously difficult for propositions and senses; at least, it is so *if* we hold, with the Fregean tradition, that sameness of sense and identity of proposition can be discerned *a priori*. It is true that our proposal at the end of the second chapter can be turned to give an *a posteriori* notion of sameness of sentence-meaning; but that will issue only as the *output* of an adequate theory, and so cannot be presumed as part of the input of such a theory. So there seem no grounds for optimism about the possibility either of *a priori* identity and individuation conditions or of useful *a posteriori* conditions; the resultant pessimism could only be removed by the successful provision of such conditions.

4 Davidson's Proposal

With that excursion into intensional exotica behind us, let us turn to a more mundane proposal for indirect discourse recently presented

E

by Davidson ('On Saying That'). This proposal will shed incidental light upon his contrast between matters of logical form and problems of analysis.

Davidson makes two quite distinct proposals. The *initial logical form* proposal is this:

> sentences in indirect discourse . . . consist of an expression referring to a speaker, the two-place predicate 'said', and a demonstrative referring to an utterance. Period. What follows gives the content of the subject's saying, but has no logical or semantic connection with the original attribution of a saying.

So the most perspicuous way of showing the logical form of 'Galileo said that the earth moves' is this:

> 'Galileo said that. The earth moves.'

This *initial logical form* proposal is meant merely to remove the appearance of non-extensionality, in a way shortly to be explained. Any full logical form proposal must also assign structure to each of the sentences the initial proposal distinguishes: that for the content-sentence is determined by our truth-theory for that *kind* of sentence, while that for the sentence attributing a saying to a speaker will be determined by our general manner of handling action sentences. Assuming the logical form of the attribution sentence to reveal, in some way, the relational predicate 'said' as a significant unit in the sentence, the question of analysis remains: can we interpret that relational predicate only by pairing *mention* of it with *use* of it, or can some more informative *decompositional* analysis be given? Davidson presents a *gloss* on 'Galileo said that' which incorporates a view upon the proper treatment of action sentences along with an informal, heuristic account of 'said' which is *not* meant as an analysis. That gloss is this:

> 'Some utterance of Galileo's and my next utterance make us samesayers.'

Dangerously combining this heuristic gloss with the initial logical form proposal, we shall obtain the following reading of 'Galileo said that the earth moves':

> 'Some utterance of Galileo's and my next utterance make us samesayers. The earth moves.'

Davidson's gloss on 'said' in terms of *samesaying* is not meant as an analysis proposal. But if it were, or if it were replaced by an austere non-decompositional analysis proposal, what would be the relation between the analysis proposal and the logical form proposal? The

118

answer seems to be this: if we have a correct account of the *logical form* of sentences of indirect discourse, we have shown how, given his grasp of the rest of the language, if a speaker can understand any one sentence of that variety, he can understand an indefinitely large number of sentences of that variety. An acceptable analysis proposal would combine with such a correct logical form proposal to establish the antecedent of this conditional: it shows how, assuming the logical form proposal to be correct, a competent speaker can understand at least one sentence of the grammatical *oratio obliqua* form. Successful completion of both projects – which interact, since final acceptance of a logical form proposal must wait upon its supplementation by an adequate analysis proposal – shows how speakers can understand any of an indefinitely large number of novel sentences of this form.

Another important aspect of this relationship between these proposals explains Davidson's claims for the priority of the logical form proposal ('On Saying That', p. 158). Starting from our observation of utterances of complete sentences, the logical form proposal is clearly temporally prior to any analysis proposal in that, until we have some logical form proposal before us, we can have no rational view upon the *subject-matter* of analysis. Until we have such a logical form proposal before us, we shall have no idea, for example, of the primitive groupings of words, of the groupings of words to be subjected to analysis. A logical form proposal tells us which of the expressions, or which groups of expressions, are the primitives to be analysed. For example, Davidson's initial logical form proposal, in combination with his logical form proposal for action sentences, tells us that one of the primitives in sentences of indirect discourse is the relational predicate 'said'; intuitions as to whether that would be so *prior* to those proposals are empty. Doubtless much of the philosophical interest *might* focus upon the analysis of terms treated as primitive in the initial specification of the logical form; but that interest must wait upon plausible claims as to what those primitives are.

Let us start, then, with the logical form proposal. The novel point is the logical independence of what follows 'that' from the attribution of a saying. Given this independence, there can be no general rules relating the effects of substitution in the content-sentence to the truth-value of the attribution of a saying; but since the 'that' refers to the utterance of the content-sentence, any change in that sentence changes the reference of the 'that', and so *may* change the truth-value of the attribution of a saying.[3] Division of *oratio obliqua* sentences

[3] But see McFetridge, 'Propositions', for reasons for believing that this is not quite the correct account (at least, not in all uses of 'saying that') of the referent of the demonstrative.

into two component sentences immediately solves the problem posed by the apparent failure of extensionality for such sentences. The problematic substitutions are made in one sentence, the content-sentence, while it is the other sentence, the attribution of a saying, the utterance of which may change in truth-value. But for the second sentence, if the reference of the demonstrative is to an utterance, the substituted term is not co-extensive with the term it replaces. So for either sentence alone, extensionality is preserved.

Now for the partial gloss upon 'said'. Davidson's gloss on 'He said that' is this: 'Some utterance of his and my next utterance make us samesayers'. This gloss cannot be a serious analysis proposal, although it could be improved even as a gloss, because of a simple point. Davidson acknowledges that 'He said that' can function as a complete declarative utterance; we can say 'Genet said that' while pointing to a wall on which is written 'Crime is the highest form of sensuality'. Yet in such cases Davidson's gloss could not apply since Genet and I cannot be samesayers, because *I* have not said the appropriate sentence. But there is a strong temptation, presumably shared by Davidson, to think that 'He said that' should be given the same analysis, and perhaps even the same heuristic gloss, in this case as in cases with an attached content-sentence. Something along the following lines looks to be the solution:

'Some utterance of his and that utterance of someone's make them samesayers.'

More perspicuously,

'$\exists x)\,(\exists y)$ (His utterance x and that utterance of y's make him and y samesayers)'.

The first quantifier ranges over utterances, the second over utterers. This account can apply both where the reference of 'that' is some utterance of mine (as the special case), and also where it is the utterance of another.

Given that this account arises naturally out of the aspect of indirect discourse that is Davidson's starting point – an anecdote about Oscar Wilde – it might seem surprising that he himself does not develop it. Perhaps the following argument deterred him; it may anyway deter others. If we drop the definite description 'my next utterance' replacing it by the demonstrative 'that utterance', we have to take account of available theories of demonstratives. Many find it plausible to hold that any reasonable theory of demonstratives must be partly intentional, must make reference to the utterer's intentions. If this is right, then our proposed analysis seems to commit us to the view that when we say 'He said that Tom is bald', we have the appropriate intentions regarding the demonstrative,

120

even though we do not intuitively recognise that 'that' is a demonstrative in such utterances. Hence, I suppose, the attraction of Davidson's use of a definite description to secure reference.

Others may have doubts about the intentional account of demonstratives; but it is anyway worth showing that even without calling that account into question, it is possible to meet this objection. We might begin to do this, negatively, by demanding some account of the key notions of a speaker's *intentions* and of what a speaker *realises or recognises*. But it is more positive to point out how very plausible it is that those intentions should have lapsed into dormancy, taking with them the realisation of the demonstrative character of 'that'. For given that the sentence the utterance of which the demonstrative refers to standardly follows it, there can be no doubt as to what the referent is, and consequently no need to consider the speaker's intentions, or for the speaker to focus attention upon his intentions, in order to determine the referent of the demonstrative. As the awareness of those intentions becomes dormant, so awareness of the demonstrative character of 'that' becomes dormant. Compare, for example, the role of 'that' in the sentence 'No one wants to eat a six-course dinner and play rugger after that'; again, the structure of such uses of the demonstrative is one in which the referent is clear, and there is a consequent blinding to the demonstrative character of 'that'. The exception in the case of indirect discourse is represented by precisely those cases where there is room for doubt as to the referent – namely, many cases involving the utterance of 'He said that' as a complete declarative utterance. Hence the plausibility of the generalised account.[4]

A commonly voiced objection to Davidson's gloss proposal should be mentioned at this point. Consider double *oratio obliqua* sentences, such as 'He said that you said that it was raining'. The Davidsonian logical form is this:

'He said that. (You said that. It was raining.)'

When we combine this with Davidson's gloss on 'said', we obtain the following:

'He said that. (Some utterance of yours and my next utterance make us samesayers. It was raining.)'

Yet this does not appear correct: he did not say *that* at all, he did not say that an utterance of mine made me and you samesayers, for he was not referring to any saying of mine. He may not even know of my

---

[4] Ultimately, this response concedes too much to the objection; for it concedes that we have some worthwhile intuitive understanding of the sub-sentential semantic structure of our language. The price of this undue concession is an excessive psychologism in the response given (see chapter IX).

existence, let alone of Davidson's notion of samesaying. So any report of his saying is bound to be false; and this surely cannot be correct.

The problem, however, is not with the gloss proposed but with the failure to apply this to both occurrences of 'said'. If we do so, we obtain this:

> Some utterance of his and my next utterance make him and me samesayers. (Some utterance of yours and my next utterance make us samesayers. It was raining.)

The problem now disappears. The point of the samesaying relation is that it does not require us to preserve the original speaker's form of expression. The problem would only remain if this charitable nature of samesaying were subject to this constraint: samesayers' utterances must make only the same references. There are clear counter-examples to such a rule. Take a case of single *oratio obliqua*: someone says of a steam-engine 'It's vermilion'; later, having forgotten the word, I report his saying by pointing to a vermilion pagoda, saying 'He said that the steam-engine was the colour of that'. My samesaying utterance makes a reference that his did not make, yet this does not affect my claim to have samesaid. My extraneous reference to the pagoda is a reference to a *sample*, playing an analogous role to that played by the content-sentence in customary *oratio obliqua* sentences.

This objection from embedded indirect discourse sentences is mistaken. It does bring home, however, the lack so far of any detailed discussion of samesaying. This notion is posited to incorporate, to capture, all the vagaries of indirect discourse that arise independently of the apparent failure of extensionality; it can thus be no more sharply constrained than is indirect discourse itself. The question of what these constraints are – the question of which substitutions in the content-sentence will preserve the truth-value of the attribution of a saying – need not delay us for the moment. What matters first is to see that Davidson's logical form proposal removes the apparent failure of extensionality while leaving the specification of these constraints open. This is in sharp contrast to the Fregean approach which, by continuing to view sentences of indirect discourse each as logically but one sentence, effectively identifies the problems of preserving extensionality and specifying substitutivity *salva veritate* conditions for the content-sentence. Davidson separates these questions as he separates his initial logical form proposal from problems of analysis; and it is his first word, the initial logical form proposal, that still needs further attention.

The apparent failure of extensionality is only half of the problem with indirect discourse; the other half is raised by problematic inferences involving the idiom. Davidson's proposal clearly licenses the following inference:

> Galileo said that. The earth moves.
> ∴ Galileo said something.

However, the proposal's ability to handle other inferences is less clear; for it is one thing for a proposal not to license an inference, it is another for it to *preclude* an inference. In an assertoric utterance of a sentence of indirect discourse, the content-sentence is *said*, not *asserted*: if I assert that Galileo said that the earth moves, *I* do not assert that the earth moves. In certain circumstances – given various other truths I accept – I can, however, be committed to the truth of the content-sentence. This is why the following inference is intuitively sound:

> Galileo said that. The earth moves.
> Everything Galileo said is true.
> ∴ The earth moves.
> ∴ Something moves.

Intuitively, there is nothing puzzling about this inference. If we quote, or mention, a sentence, we prepare ourselves for talk about language; but if to the quoted sentence we attach the predicate 'is true', we produce a sentence suitable for talk of the non-linguistic world (except, of course, in the special case where the sentence quoted is itself about language). This *disquotational* property of the truth-predicate is what makes it a device, to plagiarise and modify Quine, suitable for *semantic descent*: a device which enables us to move from talk about language to talk about the non-linguistic world. The content-sentence in indirect discourse is not quoted; but if we broaden our conception of the *levels* through which semantic ascent and semantic descent are possible, the inference above becomes thoroughly intuitive. The levels, working downwards, are these: designation (or mention); saying; asserting. If we now view the semantic descent that the truth-predicate makes possible as the move from *either* of the first two levels to the third, then the inference's validity is intuitively explained. What remains utterly unclear, however, is quite how on Davidson's proposal the inference is to be revealed as valid in virtue of its *form*.

The difficulties do not end here, however. Even without accepting that *what* Galileo said (let alone everything that Galileo said) was true, we might, in various circumstances, wish to accept the commitment that there is something which Galileo said moved – viz. the earth. Such a commitment apparently involves *quantifying into* the content-sentence from outside the content-sentence. It apparently involves, that is, a commitment not to

123

(4) Galileo said that. $(\exists x)$ (x moves)

but rather,

(5) $(\exists x)$ (Galileo said that. x moves).

The idea is that someone who asserts the latter is committed to the existence of *something* such that Galileo said that it moves, while someone who asserts the former is not. If a latter-day Galileo had said that Vulcan – the planet posited in the last century as causing the Mercury perihelion's properties – moves, *we* should not now accept the latter quantified-in assertion on the basis of the latter-day Galileo's assertion.

For Davidson, however, (5) cannot be the correct representation of the quantified-in sentence. The quantifier in (5) cannot be objectual: not because of the (vague) doctrine that such quantification is tied to *use*, not mention, for we have no good reason as yet to deny that saying *is* using; but, rather, because if the quantifier is objectual then the quantified-in sentence, if true, is true in virtue of there being an *object* such that Galileo said that it moves, it therefore mattering not *how* that object is (truly) described. We should therefore be committed to the truth of

Galileo said that . . . moves

where the referential slot is filled by *any* designation of the earth. But this commitment we do not want, because of the intensionality of the indirect discourse construction; we do not want, for example, to accept as true the claim that

Galileo said that the planet that moves around the sun every $365\frac{1}{4}$ days moves.

The quantifier cannot, therefore, be objectual, since if it were so, the quantified-in sentence, if true, would be true in virtue of an object *however described*. But nor can the quantifier be substitutional, since this leaves the sentence without the ontological commitment we, as asserters of the quantified-in sentence, wish to take upon ourselves. We do not wish our assertion to be true merely if there is an *expression* which when substituted for the second occurrence of 'x' in '$(\exists x)$ (Galileo said that x moves)' makes the whole sentence true – we want our utterance to be true if there is an *object* which Galileo said moves.

If (5) is not the correct representation of the quantified-in sentence, what is? Because of the intensionality of ordinary indirect discourse sentences, it seems clear that a quantified-in indirect discourse sentence cannot have the same overall logical form as such a sentence. A family of proposals which minimise this overall difference see the

124

quantified-in sentence as involving a *three*-place predicate 'said' rather than the two-place predicate occurring in ordinary, non-quantified indirect discourse; beyond that, the logical form is the same, with, in particular, Davidson's *initial logical form* proposal, that designed to save extensionality, being carried over. Thus one candidate for the quantified-in sentence would be:

(6) $(\exists x)$ (Galileo said of x that. x moves).

Here, the worry about the connection between objectual quantification and use is heightened: for of the two occurrences of the bound variable, one is in an *asserted* sentence, the other within a *said* sentence. Connectedly, it is unclear that we can still accept the quantifier in (5) as objectual, since it is unclear that we should wish to accept the truth of

Galileo said of the planet that moves around the sun every $365\frac{1}{4}$ days that the planet that moves around the sun every $365\frac{1}{4}$ days moves.

Indeed, we might even doubt the *grammaticality* of such a sentence. This points to a further peculiarity that (6) shares with (5): in both, the binding quantifier occurs in one, asserted sentence, while at least one of the bound variables occurs in a supposedly distinct *said* sentence. It is not clear how this could be; but if we try to avoid this by using

(6') $(\exists x)$ (Galileo said of x that.) x moves

nonsense results. For now the variable in the content-sentence is quite unconnected to the existential quantifier – we seem not to have quantified-in at all.

These considerations doubtless prompted a suggestion of Quine's about Davidson's three-place indirect discourse (in Davidson and Hintikka, *Words and Objections*, p. 335). Quine says that an *instance* of the quantified-in formula might be

(7) Galileo said of the earth that. It moves.

The quantified-in formula would then presumably be:

(8) $(\exists x)$ (Galileo said of x that.) It moves.

This use of a pronoun in place of a bound variable in the content-sentence sidesteps the previous worries; it does, however, require a semantic treatment of that pronoun whereby (8) does not collapse immediately into, and does not imply immediately, (6). Not knowing of such a treatment, the tentative conclusion must be that Davidson's indirect discourse proposal cannot be extended to cases of quantified-in indirect discourse. The problem, it is worth emphasising, is not

Davidson's silence upon when we can quantify in, upon when we can move from the two-place 'said' to the three-place 'said', for that is a quite distinct problem; rather, it is that it remains unclear *how* the quantified-in sentence, whatever the circumstances of its correct usage, is to be represented. We do not yet know its logical form.

5 The Varieties of Reported Speech

The problems facing the Davidsonian proposal in handling quantified-in sentences are instructive in making us realise the full varieties of reported speech. Direct discourse is constrained by the condition that the reporter of a saying uses the same form of expression as the original speaker: this will amount to phonetic or typographic identity, or an appropriate mapping from one to the other, depending upon the circumstances of the original utterance and the report. Indirect discourse requires that the reporter reproduce the meaning of the original utterance: the content-sentence employed by the reporter should be a correct translation of the original speaker's utterance, with homophonic translation as but one case. Many sentences of reported speech are a mixture of those two constructions. One use of quotation marks is to indicate the extent (sometimes total) of the direct discourse element; but only one usage, since the thought that a quoted expression is never translated is simply wrong.

Objectual quantification into the content-sentence in reported speech indicates the employment of a third, distinct variety. Let us call this *objectual* discourse. The possibility of objectual quantifying-in implies that objectual discourse is constrained by the distinct requirement of sameness of reference. The existence of such objectual discourse is at least partly embraced by Keith Donnellan in the following passage:

> if a speaker says, 'Her husband is kind to her', referring to the man he was just talking to, and if that man is Jones, we may report him as having said *of Jones* that he is kind to her. If Jones is also the president of the college, we may report the speaker as having said *of the president of the college* that he is kind to her. . . . [In choosing the referring expression] we need not, it is important to note, choose a description or name which the original speaker would agree fits what he was referring to ('Reference and Definite Descriptions', p. 112).

Donnellan is talking here about the locution 'said of . . . that . . .'; it is not yet clear that this is the objectual discourse construction. Also, his attachment to the proposed substitutivity principle – coreferential expressions are substitutable *salva veritate* in the subject position in the content-sentence – is restricted by his contrast, to

126

which we shall return, between referential and attributive uses of referring expressions. So it would be premature to call this principle the Donnellan principle; I shall be premature.

The claim that such a principle exists runs counter to orthodoxy. Suppose Tom asserts this sentence:

(9) JJ is a thief.

In doing so, he refers to the individual JJ using the expression 'JJ'. I wish to report Tom's utterance using reported speech. The Donnellan principle suggests that a sentence of the form

(10) Tom said that . . . is a thief

can be true if the slot is filled by any expression that refers to JJ. But suppose that, unknown to Tom, it is true that

(11) JJ = NN.

Then the Donnellan principle commits us to the truth of

(12) Tom said that NN is a thief.

Yet given his ignorance of (11), Tom might dissent from

(13) NN is a thief.

So the principle leads us to accept the following conjunction: Tom sincerely denies 'NN is a thief' and Tom said that NN is a thief. But this is absurd.

This argument has been employed by Quine in connection with belief contexts (*The Ways of Paradox*, p. 187); its force might be thought greater in the context of saying. But maybe, to plagiarise Quine once more, there is less to this than meets the eye. (12), as objectual discourse, does *not* imply that Tom asserted sentence (13), nor even a sentence with the same sense. Why, then, hold it to imply that Tom would either assent to or neither assent to nor dissent from that *sentence*? The use of objectual discourse enables us to escape from actual forms of expression used in the past and from literal translation thereof; why then hold it to be constrained by assent-dissent behaviour to particular sentences or to particular sets of sentences (those having the same meaning) in the past, present, or future? Of course, if Tom asserts this sentence

(14) NN is not a thief

the Donnellan principle commits us to the truth of

(15) Tom said that JJ is a thief and Tom said that JJ is not a thief.

But this, again, is quite unobjectionable when both uses of 'said that'

127

are construed as objectual discourse. (15) may be misleading or un-fair; but that is a common fate of truths.

It is quite clear, against the orthodoxy, that ordinary English allows attributions of sayings according to the Donnellan principle. We can even report a saying using a *said that* construction in which the content-sentence would not be asserted or assented to by anyone. You and I believe Russell to be the cleverest person ever. Tom says that Russell was mentally retarded. I can truly report Tom's saying thus: 'Tom said that the cleverest person ever was mentally retarded'. Examples of this kind can be multiplied – 'Tom said that the man with the toupée has a full head of hair', and so forth. Difficulty only intrudes when the objectual character of the report is ignored. This can easily be done, for it is by now clear that 'said that' constructions are used in at least three different ways. But in cases like those we are now considering, disambiguation is eased by an obvious enough principle: if treatment of the report as one of the other forms of reported speech credits the original speaker with an insane saying, treat it as objectual discourse.

If it is objected that all these cases involve, not the *saying that* construction, but the *saying of . . . that . . .* construction, the re-joinder is simple. If English usage is our guide, *saying that* is used in these cases. If English has a *saying of . . . that . . .* construction in which the first slot is referentially transparent, and if we wish to use available English locutions in giving a logically perspicuous repre-sentation of other English idioms, then there is a point to rewriting these cases in terms of that idiom; but it is a *rewriting*. This is yet more evident when the favoured locution is a term of art. The dull fact remains that English uses *saying that* in the way I have labelled 'objectual discourse'.

There is a more substantial objection to the Donnellan principle. Suppose the logical form of sentences of indirect discourse is this: '*A* said that . . .' attaches to the content-sentence '*p*' to form one compound sentence '*A* said that *p*'. (This is meant to be vague, for a family of theories, especially the Fregean, are under scrutiny.) The Donnellan principle holds this context to be referentially trans-parent. But there is a standard argument, deriving from Frege and Church, showing that if such a context is transparent, it is also truth-functional.[5] Yet the context created by '*A* said that . . .' cannot be truth-functional. As remarked earlier, my once having said a

---

[5] This much-discussed argument is clearly presented in Mackie, *The Cement of the Universe*, ch. 10, and receives a suggestive treatment in Barry Taylor's paper in Evans and McDowell, *Truth and Meaning*. In this book, I rely upon this argument without presenting it or defending it. Should that argument subsequently be revealed invalid, all it means in this context is that there are more logical form proposals still in the field than I suggest.

truth does not make true the attribution to me as a saying of any other truth whatever in any form of reported speech.

Apparent transparency and apparent non-truth-functionality are found in many other idioms. One solution in all such cases is to present an alternative account of the logical form of such idioms. A rough first shot at the logical form of a report of Tom's saying of (9) which sidesteps the Frege-Church thesis is this:

(16) $(\exists u)$ (*Said* (Tom,u) & *Of* ($\langle$JJ$\rangle$, u) & *Predic* ('is a thief', u)).

The variable ranges over utterances, a species of events. '*Said*' is a two-place relation between speakers and utterances. '*Of*' is a two-place relation between sequences of objects and utterances. '*Predic*' is a two-place relation between predicates and utterances.

The need for sequences of objects rather than single objects in the first place of the '*Of*' relation reflects two points. First, there is the possibility that the positions occupied by both 'Bill' and 'Mary' should be transparent in an objectual discourse reading of

(17) Tom said that Bill and Mary were at the party.

This is represented as

(18) $(\exists u)$ (*Said*(Tom,u) & *Of* ($\langle$Bill, Mary$\rangle$,u) & *Predic* ('were at the party',u)).

The need for ordering is evident from a case like

(19) Tom said that Bill hates Mary.

This becomes

(20) $(\exists u)$ (*Said*(Tom,u) & *Of* ($\langle$Bill, Mary$\rangle$,u) & *Predic* ('hates',u)).

This will still not quite do however. As it stands, this proposal does not appear to bring the subject and predicate expressions in the content-sentence close enough together. This seems to be shown by the failure of the proposal to distinguish, except in the irrelevant ordering of conjuncts, between

(21) Tom said that Jack was at the party and Bill was upset

and

(22) Tom said that Bill was at the party and Jack was upset.

Both could be represented as:

(23) $(\exists u)$ (*Said* (Tom,u) & *Of* ($\langle$Bill$\rangle$,u) & *Of* ($\langle$Jack$\rangle$,u) &
Predic ('at the party',u) & *Predic* ('was upset',u)).

There are a number of ways of handling this: the one, for little reason, I favour treats Tom as having made two distinct utterances. Thus (21) would be

(24) $(\exists u)\,(\exists u')$ *(Said* (Tom,u) & *Said* (Tom,u') & *Of* ($\langle$Jack$\rangle$,u) & *Of* ($\langle$Bill$\rangle$,u') & *Predic* ('at the party',u) & *Predic* ('was upset', u')).

Other possibilities would be to *order* the predicates, so seeing (21) as

(25) $(\exists u)$ *(Said* (Tom,u) & *Of* ($\langle$Jack, Bill$\rangle$,u) & *Predic* ($\langle$'was at the party', 'was upset'$\rangle$,u)).

or to complicate the '*Predic*' relation, say, to an *attribution* relation, so obtaining:

(26) $(\exists u)$ *(Said* (Tom,u) & *Of* ($\langle$Jack$\rangle$,u) & *Of* ($\langle$Bill$\rangle$,u) & *Attrib* ($\langle$Jack$\rangle$, 'at the party', u) & *Attrib* ($\langle$Bill$\rangle$, 'was upset', u)).

(24) seems to me intuitive and simplest.

The Donnellan principle is equivocal as to whether the reporter should aim for the *literal referent* of the referring expression used by the original speaker, the item that satisfies the name or description used, or for the *speaker's* referent, the item that the speaker intended the expression to refer to and his audience to pick out. There are familiar cases involving false beliefs on the speaker's part where these diverge. Tom arrives at a party, glances around the room, and says 'The philosopher at the party is drinking martini'. There is a philosopher at the party happily drinking martini, but he is in the garden, well out of view. The person Tom means to refer to, say, with a striking resemblance to the philosopher, is in the centre of the room Tom has walked into, drinking water out of a martini glass. He is, in fact, an advertising executive. The literal referent is the philosopher in the garden, the speaker's referent is the advertising executive in the same room as Tom.

Should the Donnellan principle be read in terms of speaker's or literal referent? The question is which of the following is correct as objectual discourse:

(27) Tom said that the philosopher is drinking martini.[6]
(28) Tom said that the advertising executive is drinking martini.

Although I have no clear argument on this point, I am strongly inclined to hold that the latter is correct as objectual discourse, and only as objectual discourse. The former is correct as indirect discourse but not as objectual discourse. There seems no reason why there could not be a 'literal referent objectual discourse' construction in English, but there does not appear to be one. Apart from intuition,

---

[6] There are important complications about tense-changes in the content-sentence in different forms of reported speech, but I pass these over.

the only kind of argument available on this descriptive question is this. Suppose one accepts the idea, implicit in Donnellan, that the most perspicuous rendering of objectual discourse in English (though not the only correct one) is the 'said of . . . that . . .' construction. Then it seems clear that the first of the following is incorrect, the second correct:

(29) Tom said of the philosopher that he is drinking martini.
(30) Tom said of the advertising executive that he is drinking martini.

The claim is, then, that when in reporting a saying we depart from the syntax and semantics of the original utterance, we concern ourselves with the intended, not the literal, referent. An attribution of a saying using objectual discourse is constrained by the truth-condition that the subject expression of the content sentence literally refers to the item the original speaker meant to refer to. (This is, perhaps, implicit in the cited passage from Donnellan in the first sentence of which reference is predicated of a person.) Thus any semantic explication of the '*Of*' relation must make reference to pragmatic factors, the intentions and beliefs of the original speaker. *Of* is a pragmatic notion, objectual discourse a pragmatic construction. One way of registering this would be to treat '*Of*' as a three-place relation between speakers, sequences of objects, and utterances.

Donnellan draws a distinction between referential and attributive uses of referring expressions. The contrast can be exemplified by comparing two assertions of 'The man who invented the zip was a genius'. In one type of utterance, the speaker has identifying knowledge (either by acquaintance or by description causally connected with the man) of the referent independent of that used in the sentence asserted; he may or may not believe his audience to have comparable knowledge. In the other circumstance of utterance, the speaker has no such independent knowledge, and assumes his audience to have no such knowledge: his assertion is tantamount to 'Whoever the man was who invented the zip – I have no idea who or what he was – that man was a genius'. The first usage is referential, the second attributive. In the referential usage, it would make perfectly good sense for the speaker to add – 'not that that was why he was a genius'; in the attributive usage, this addition would (generally) be puzzling at best.

This is only a crude explication, but it may suffice. We need to see two points. First, the preceding discussion suggests that the contrast between speaker's and literal referent is crucial for the understanding of objectual discourse; yet this contrast seems only to be substantial in the case of referential usages, any divergence in attributive uses being the result of mere verbal error. Second, such intuitive grasp as we have on the 'said of . . . that . . .' locution suggests that this is only properly employed in reporting utterances containing referential usages. These thoughts combine to suggest that objectual discourse is only correctly employed when a referential usage occurred in the original saying.

Within objectual discourse, as characterised, the subject position in the content-sentence is fully transparent: it matters not for this idiom whether the subject position is occupied by a proper name or by a description, and the position so occupied is open to objectual quantification without difficulty. If it be asked when, and logically how, we can quantify into indirect discourse, the answer is that we never can! The question should rather be: when can we move from indirect discourse to objectual discourse, the move that opens up the possibility of a logically admissible step of quantifying in? The preceding discussion *begins* to answer this question. It is not enough, and is in fact quite irrelevant, that we be convinced of the existence of an object answering to the referring expression used by the original speaker. What is needed is at least that we be convinced that the referring expression was used referentially, rather than attributively, and that there was *not* a failure of *speaker's* reference. If we then quantify in, we do so in virtue of the speaker's referent, for it is the speaker's referent that determines the truth-conditions of the attribution of a saying. Development of this would require detailed discussion of the referential-attributive distinction and the speaker's referent-literal referent distinction; but what has been said should suffice to avoid sidestepping such discussion by dismissing these distinctions as 'mere' pragmatics.

Chapter VI

Names and Objects

1 The Object Theory of Proper Names: Objections

Any general view about the relation between language and reality will both determine and be determined by views upon the notion of reference: in particular, views upon the ways by which singular terms in grammatical subject positions in utterances of indicative sentences come to refer to objects in the extra-linguistic world. A crucial case of these mechanisms is provided by proper names, for, pre-philosophically, proper names do not *describe* their bearers in the way that, for example, definite descriptions do, instead 'purely' *referring*, 'directly' referring to those bearers. Any semantic theory of proper names will immediately abandon neutrality about the coherence and character of this intuitive distinction between reference and description; such abandonment will issue in a distinctive partial view of the relation between language and the world. But it is not a matter simply of *choosing* one such view. Any view of the relation between language and reality developed through a semantic theory of the language, and a theory of the mechanisms of reference in particular, will issue in a distinctive account of *understanding*, a distinctive account of the knowledge that would suffice for an understanding of the language. Given that what constitutes a natural speaker's understanding is not his possession of some body of propositional knowledge but is rather his practical unreflective skill, this connection between 'knowing the meaning' and commonplace understanding will not produce a simple, direct test of a semantic theory, and so will not produce a simple, direct decision procedure between alternative views of the relation between language and reality. Still, whatever the relation between the body of propositions in the semantic theory of a language and the commonplace under-standing of speakers of that language, the following appears a necessary condition of the acceptability of a semantic theory: it must be such that explicit propositional knowledge of the theory *would* suffice for understanding of the language. And this condition might be sufficient to adjudicate between some semantic theories, and so some quite general views upon the relation between language and reality.

'The meaning of a proper name is its bearer': this slogan embodies what might be called *the object theory of proper names*.[1] The best manner to convey the meaning of a proper name – say, 'Jean Genet' – is to pick up the object which it names and hold it before you; there may be many reasons why this cannot be done in a particular case, many reasons why in some cases (e.g. 'Aristotle') this cannot in principle be done; but the paradigm remains. On this view, a sentence like

(1) Jean Genet is bald

is understood as the *coupling* in predicative combination of an object and a property or set of properties, in this case, that of baldness. (The austere may choose to read 'predicates' for 'properties' throughout this discussion.) Since our present concern is not with the profound, and profoundly difficult, matter of explaining the mode of combination here involved – we are concerned, as it were, with one of the *relata*, not with the relation – we might represent this view of (1) as the ordered pair of the object and the property, thus:

(2) ⟨Jean Genet, the property of baldness⟩.

But while this is of some heuristic value, it does not help with the primary concern of characterising a truth-predicate for the language. The format for semantic axioms for proper names within a truth theory emerges if we see the object theory of names as suggested by two antecedent conditions upon a semantic theory of names: that it be *interpretative* and *austere*. That is, we want the theory to reproduce the structure of *designation* and *use* found within any interpretative truth-conditions theory; and, further, we want the *axioms* for names to give *no* explanation of how, or why, that interpretation is given, of how, or why, *that* used expression is paired with *that* designated expression. If we add to this the motivation behind this object theory of denying the assimilation of proper names to predicate expressions, we shall expect the semantic axioms for proper names to be of the form of

(3) 'Jean Genet' stands for Jean Genet

where 'stands for' is a primitive, unanalysable relation between name and object: no further explanation can be given of it suitable for insertion into the semantic axioms for proper names. To avoid any

[1] Better would be: giving the bearer of a proper name is giving its meaning.

appearance of explanation within the axioms, it would be safer, for present purposes, to invoke the star-function introduced earlier (see pp. 31–2), and to replace (3) by

(4) $(S)(S^*(\text{'Jean Genet'}) = \text{Jean Genet})$.

The rationale for the interpretative format, rather than a translational one, emerged earlier; the reasons favouring austerity will be given in a moment; the difficulties attendant upon the assimilation of proper names to individual constants will also shortly become clear. What matters for the moment is to see that these three conditions invite the use of (4) as the format of semantic axioms for proper names, the internally unexplained pairing of name and object.

What is wrong with such a treatment of proper names? I shall discuss merely some of the most forceful and frequent of the objections to this treatment.

(i) The most obvious objection is perhaps that posed by empty names, names which lack bearers. A standard example is 'Vulcan', the name assigned by scientists to the planet that caused the Mercury perihelion; investigations revealed there to be no such planet, investigations culminating in the Einsteinian revolution. If we replaced both occurrences of 'Jean Genet' in either (3) or (4) by 'Vulcan', what would result would apparently be incoherent; for the crucial point about such interpretative axioms is that the name is *used* on the RHS, and so stands proxy, as it were, for its bearer; but when there is no such bearer, this is incoherent. Putting the point more obviously, if the meaning of a proper name is its bearer, then empty names have no meaning. But they do, so the object theory must be wrong.

(ii) The doctrine that the meaning of a proper name is its bearer does not tell us the meaning of any specified proper name until we are shown how to *determine* its bearer. What is required in supplementation of the general object theory is an account of some *route* to the reference, to the referent. To rest with (3) or (4) as a full account of the meaning of the proper name 'Jean Genet' is to disregard this additional requirement: it is to rest with a quite unexplained, and therefore quite unfathomable, connection between symbol and object. The route to the reference, according to both Frege and, on occasion, Dummett, will be some *descriptive* specification of the object: an object satisfying that description will be the object named. This descriptive content, the *sense* of the name, will be at least part of its meaning, will be understood, or known, by any speaker with mastery of the name concerned. The simplest thought, then, is that this same sense will account for the meaning of empty names. Whether, with non-empty names, the referent, the

135

object, is also 'part of the meaning' of the proper name is a further somewhat obscure question.

This point, about the need for a route to the reference, is assimilated by Dummett to the thought that the object theory gives an impoverished account of speakers' understanding. On the object theory, it is sufficient for Tom to understand the proper name 'Jean Genet' that

(5) Tom knows that 'Jean Genet' stands for Jean Genet.

The point is not to reveal (5) to be insufficient by assimilating it to the quite distinct knowledge attributions

(6) Tom knows that 'Jean Genet' stands for the same object as 'Jean Genet'.

(7) Tom knows that ' "Jean Genet" stands for Jean Genet' expresses a truth.

It is rather that precisely because (5) is 'stronger' than, is more substantial than, (6) or (7), there is a substantial question about *when* (5) can be said about Tom; but the object theorist, so far, has said nothing about when such attribution can be made. Dummett's connection between these two points is this: (5) can be said about Tom when, and only when, Tom possesses a *route* to the reference of 'Jean Genet', when, and only when, Tom has a grasp of the *sense* of 'Jean Genet'.

(iii) If the meaning of a proper name is its bearer, then any two names of the same object have the same meaning. This issued in a famous worry of Frege's. A fundamental principle of Frege's theory – as of any even remotely plausible theory of meaning – is that the meaning of a sentence is a function of the meaning of its constituent expressions; the meaning of a sentence is unchanged if, for any expression occurring in that sentence, we substitute another expression with the same meaning. Only on the assumption of this principle is our capacity to understand an indefinitely large number of novel sentences explicable. But now consider any true identity statement, where the identity-sign is flanked by proper names – for example, Frege's classic example

(8) The Morning Star is the Evening Star.

(If it is thought that these are untypical, unparadigmatic proper names, then note that the same point would emerge with the substitution of, say, 'Dr Jekyll' and 'Mr Hyde', or 'Michael Innes' and 'J. I. M. Stewart'.) What makes (8) true is the fact that the proper names concerned have the same bearer; but then, by the Fregean principle, (8) must have the same meaning as

(9) The Morning Star is the Morning Star

which results from (8) by the substitution of a coreferential (and therefore, *ex hypothesi*, synonymous) expression. But (8) and (9) cannot have the same meaning, for they differ in crucial respects. (8) is a contingent truth, it could have been otherwise, whereas (9) is a necessary truth; (8) is an *a posteriori* truth, its truth can only be known by empirical investigation, whereas (9) is an *a priori* truth; and (8) is an informative truth, while (9) is uninformative. How could two sentences have the same meaning whilst differing in these properties? Frege's answer is that it is the difference in *sense* between 'The Morning Star' and 'The Evening Star' which accounts for (8)'s being contingent, *a posteriori* and informative: this difference of sense explains why (8) and (9) have *different* meanings, so showing the sense of a proper name to be part of its meaning.

(iv) On the object theory, assertions of existence using proper names are, if true, trivial. Suppose I assert: 'JJ exists'. Suppose my assertion is true. Then, on the object theory of proper names, what I have done is, first, to pick out an object, using the purely referential, non-descriptive proper name, and, second, I have gone on to say that that object exists. But if it did not exist, I could not have picked it out; given that it does exist, I can so pick it out, but my *then* going on to say that it exists is trivial. This general point is intuitively clear, even if more needs to be said about the *kind* of triviality involved (cf. Pears in Strawson, *Philosophical Logic*, pp. 97–102). Nor does the objection hang upon the supposedly tendentious treatment of 'exists' as a predicate; exactly the same worry infects the sentence 'JJ exists' if we represent it as

$(\exists x)\,(x = \text{JJ}).$

Similarly, false denials of existence are problematic on this account. (My reasons for passing over false assertions of existence and true denials will emerge later.) Suppose I falsely assert 'JJ does not exist'. Then, on the object theory, what I do is, first, to pick out, non-descriptively, an object, and, then, I go on to say that it does not exist. But if it did not exist, I could not have picked it out; so my whole utterance is comparable to some kind of contradiction.

2 The Object Theory: Some Responses

With one exception, each of these objections can be met at a fairly moderate price, in some cases at no price at all; in each case, matters of importance arise.

(i) The objection from empty names cannot be met by the assignment of some arbitrary entity – say, the null set – to all such names except at the excessive cost of making all such names equivalent in meaning. Another possibility, avoiding that cost, would be to deny that there are empty names by assigning to each some distinct entity: for example, in the case of 'Vulcan', a possible Vulcan or the concept of Vulcan or the idea of Vulcan. But aside from the ontological excess this invites, along with the consequent obligation to elucidate these new kinds of entity, it is clear that such a proposal simply distorts the functioning of these expressions. Those who talked of Vulcan as the cause of the Mercury perihelion did not mean to talk of some possible entity playing that role, let alone the concept or idea of such an entity: none of these is suited to causing anything. There might, possibly, be a case for a treatment in terms of some such extra realm of discourse in the case of fictional names, like 'Mr Micawber'; but for many empty names such a proposal is clearly wrong.

The most promising strategy, I think, is indeed to deny that there are empty proper names, but to achieve this, not by addition to our ontology, but rather by the simple expedient of denying that empty 'names' are indeed names! While such expressions are *syntactically* proper names, *semantically* they are not; thus the object theory, an account of semantic proper names, has no application to them. How these empty names are then to be treated, if treated at all, is a further question: perhaps sometimes by ontological additions of the kind discussed, other times as functioning as names of themselves (i.e. as names of symbols), and yet other times as equivalent in meaning to some set of descriptions. But for the semantics of semantical proper names these questions are irrelevant. The price of this proposal is that whether or not an expression is semantically a proper name is no longer known *a priori*; it depends upon whether the name has a bearer or not, a matter for empirical discovery. Thus the second of our initial objections, (ii), becomes more pressing, since some *route* to the reference is apparently needed to determine whether that route leads to anything. But aside from that extra burden on the dissolution of (ii), it is not clear that there is anything wrong with this consequence, nor is it at all clear why it should be thought objectionable that our treatment of an expression which functions syntactically as a proper name will hang upon empirical investigations aimed at establishing whether or not it has a bearer. An instructive parallel here is with Russell's notion of a *logically proper name*. Russell required that an expression be logically guaranteed of a referent before it be a logically proper name. Unfortunately, he was led to the conclusion that only 'this' and 'that' used to refer to present sense-experiences satisfied this stringent condition! This may have been a mistake on his part, since it is at least arguable that numerals satisfy, and satisfy in a more interesting manner, the stated condition; more importantly, Russell's discussion may well reflect the consequences of a failure to separate questions of semantic description from problems raised by sceptical epistemologies. But the point that now matters is to see that our condition for being a semantic proper name, one to which the object theory of proper names applies, is merely that the name *has* a bearer, as a matter of contingent, empirical fact, not that there be any necessity about its having one. And while this might be deemed a little artificial, it is clear that this artificiality alone would be a modest price to pay for a reasonable theory of proper names.

(ii) The second of the worries about the object theory was first expressed in terms of the need for a *route* to the referent of the name. The theory tells us that the meaning of a proper name is its bearer, but it is silent upon how we are to determine *which* object is its bearer; a consequence of this silence is that we are left ignorant of how to determine whether the name is empty or not, whether it has a bearer or not. This putative deficiency is apparently heightened by the multiple applicability of proper names, by the fact that many objects can share the same name. (There are, for example, racehorses in England called Aristotle, Wittgenstein, and Davidson; none is strikingly successful, the first-named tending to wander under pressure, the second seeming always on the point of giving up, and the third usually leaving his efforts too late.) The worry about multiple applicability requires that we treat proper names as 'ambiguous' individual constants on the object theory, indexing the names in the meta-language; so instead of

'Aristotle' stands for Aristotle

we have, say,

'Aristotle' stands for Aristotle$_1$ or Aristotle$_2$ . . . or Aristotle$_n$.

But this formal device does nothing to tell us *which* objects are named by the indexed meta-language names, *which* objects are named by the series of disjuncts; nor does it do anything to tell us, on an occasion of use in the object-language of a name, *which* of the indexed meta-language names is the relevant one.

Dummett assimilates this worry to that of the adequacy, or inadequacy, of the account the object theory issues in of what would suffice for *understanding*. It is not that the attribution to a speaker of the knowledge that 'JJ' stands for JJ is trivial; if it were, the account would indeed issue in a trivial, insufficient account of speakers' understanding. The point is rather that in denying the triviality of this attribution of knowledge, in pointing to its difference from other, more trivial, attributions, we avoid the charge of triviality at a price: if the attribution is substantial, so is the question of *when* such an attribution can be made. The object theory, as presented, is utterly silent upon this. The thought now is that any filling of this lacuna will be in terms of a competent speaker's having a *route* to the reference of the name, possession of such a route being

139

a condition of mastery of the name. The further thought is that this route must be built into the meaning of the name: if possession of that route is a condition of mastery of the name, then it must be part of its meaning, since meaning is precisely what grounds mastery.

This line of thought incorporates two muddles. First, even if for each speaker's utterance of a sentence using a name there must be a route to its referent, it does not follow that there must be some *one* route which must apply to *every* such utterance containing that name. The point is not the multiple applicability of proper names; it is, rather, the fact that names are acquired and used by speakers in diverse circumstances, by speakers standing in diverse relations to the referent. Consider the name 'Mark Platts' and the object that is presently writing this sentence; and consider the differences between the relations held to that object by different, competent users of that name: the relation *I* stand in to that object, the relation my parents stand in to that object, the relation the man who baptised me stands in to that object, the relations close friends, distant acquaintances, stand in to that object, the relation, or relations, of people whose acquaintance with the name is exhausted by its occurrence in some footnote, the relation, or relations, that someone who has just *seen* me for the first time stands in to that object. These diversities of acquisition and use by competent speakers constitute a strong *prima facie* case against the idea that there is some *one* route from name to referent that applies to all competent speakers. The second muddle is this: even if, contrary to the above, there must be some *one* route, it does not yet follow that the competent speaker in any plausible sense *possesses* that route, has knowledge, implicit or otherwise, of that route. A moment's reflection suggests that this *further* move is simply implausible, simply makes language use too reflective. Without these muddles, the picture is this: we, as reflective interpreters of native speakers' behaviour, will need, in determining the referent to be assigned to some given usage of a proper name, a way of determining the referent to be assigned, we shall need a *route* to that referent; but this route need not be *known* by the competent native speaker concerned, nor need it be a route common to all, unambiguous usages of that name within the native speech-community. It need not even be common to all usages by the one speaker through time: for with time the route can change for a given speaker.

The consequences of overlooking these muddles emerges if the muddled thoughts are developed; we shall also discover a deeper, theoretical error in those thoughts. The muddle is one motivation for positing a Fregean *sense* for each proper name, a sense which is at least part of its meaning. (Whether it exhausts the meaning depends upon whether the referent is to be retained as part of the meaning.) Frege conceived of the sense of a proper name as being represented by some set of descriptions, these descriptions in turn combining with the proper name to represent the content of various beliefs held by speakers. Thus it is speakers' beliefs which finally determine the referent of a proper name as used by them. Any development in detail of this approach, any detailed account of how speakers' beliefs are to issue in the descriptive part of the meaning of a proper name, would need to face, and overcome, one central difficulty: the variations *within* the same speech community of individual speakers' beliefs. This is a difficulty given that the meaning of a proper name is, for Frege, to be uniform *within* the speech-community, is to be *public*; the meaning of a proper name is not to vary from speaker to speaker. In outline, the resolution of the difficulty is clear: denial of any immediate connection between speakers' literal understanding and individual psychological facts. That is, there is no requirement that what, on the theory, constitutes understanding the meaning should answer to all, or even any, of the psychological states found in an individual speaker; at least, not if these states are understood in pre-philosophical terms as conscious, as items that issue immediately in the speech-behaviour of the individual. This leaves much room for manoeuvre in constructing the sense of a proper name: we might favour widespread beliefs; we might weight certain kinds of beliefs (e.g. about species-member-ship); we might have some *vague* computational sum finally to determine the referent – 'whatever satisfies most of the following descriptions: . . . '.

But we need not go into this in detail; for Saul Kripke has suggested, in a series of brilliant examples, that any such theory must fail ('Naming and Necessity'). It will fail because it will often give the wrong referent, and therefore will produce an incorrect clause in our truth-theory, an incorrect pairing of object-language name and object picked out in the meta-language. The pattern behind the examples is clear: however the belief set is chosen, the set that, in some way, will determine the sense, it can be riddled with error – with error that we can *discover* by investigating the object, the referent. We can *discover* that Aristotle did not do this, that, and the other; in so doing, we are not changing our view as to what is the *referent* of the name – if we were so doing, we should not be *changing* our beliefs about Aristotle, merely forming a new set of beliefs about some other being. If the sense is to provide a route to the referent, and if the sense is to be determined in however vague a way by speakers' beliefs, then the route can lead us astray.

Kripke has, of course, suggested an alternative way in which the referent might be determined, a way which can leave the referent constant through belief-change. From our present perspective, this can be seen as an attempt to retain the object-theory in its most austere, non-descriptive form, whilst satisfying the demand for some uniform account as to how the referent is to be determined. In barest outline, Kripke's causal theory is this: the referent of a proper name is to be determined by tracing back the causal chain from uses of that name until some initial baptism using that name is encountered; the object so baptised is the referent. Now, there are many cases – Kripke, again, has given several good examples – where this theory seems correct. But, equally clearly, there are cases where it seems incorrect, at least as stated. Gareth Evans gave a good counter-example (cited in Kripke, 'Naming and Necessity', p. 768): 'Madagascar' entered English *via* the acquaintance of early sailors with native African speakers; the name, like much else, was taken from them. It has become, of course, a name for an island off the south-east coast of Africa. But the sailors made a mistake; they thought they were taking over the name from, and using it in the same way as, the native speakers. These speakers, however, used it as a name of part of the mainland, not of the island. If causal ancestry determines referent, then *our* use of 'Madagascar' is to refer to part of the mainland; we merely have the (absurd) belief that it is an island. But that itself is absurd. There *are* cases where causal origin determines referent and truth-values of beliefs; but there are cases where it does not, and this is one. This could be met by trading upon what counts as a *baptism*: by holding, that is, that the sailors *baptised* the island 'Madagascar'. But this is just a verbal manoeuvre which does nothing to answer the substantial question as to when, and why, causality is dominant, and when, and why, it is more submissive to descriptive considerations. Nor, of course, would it help in this context to say that what is required is the following *kind* of causal connection: one that preserves reference; for we do not know that until we know the referent at each point of the causal chain, and that is what we want our theory to tell us.

Kripke himself does not see his causal account as a *theory* giving necessary and sufficient conditions for a name to refer to an object; rather, it is a *picture*. If this is designed merely to insulate the account from counter-examples, one would want to know why description accounts cannot be insulated in a similar way. A jousting contest between an unfalsifiable picture and a falsifiable theory seems a little unfair. But Kripke might have a deeper point in mind as to why his *picture* is preferable to a description picture. The causal picture achieves a greater divorce between reference and speakers' propositional attitudes than does a description picture: this not only introduces acknowledgment of the possibility of error, and of correction of error, in speakers' propositional attitudes, it also makes the act of referring to an object by using a name comparatively unreflective. To introduce in the causal picture the requirement that the speaker knows or believes the causal ancestry of the name would be wildly implausible and would also reintroduce the problems of erroneous beliefs. It is we, as semantic theorists reflecting upon the speaker's language use, who form the appropriate beliefs about the causal ancestry; thus the way is left open for the speaker *just* to refer to an object in the same way he *just* says things. If this is correct, Kripke's causal picture of the route to the reference appears inherently ill-suited to play the role of the Fregean notion of the route to the reference, the *sense* of the expression: for it is *knowledge* of the sense that, for the Fregean, grounds the competent speaker's understanding.

Be that as it may, the causal account no more issues in a universally applicable theory of the route to the reference than do description theories. One diagnosis of why this is so refers us back to the diversity of circumstances in which speakers acquire and use names, the diversity that apparently forces austerity upon us. But there is a deeper error in the attempt to insert *either* description *or* causal *or* causal-plus-description accounts of the route into the semantic treatment of proper names: for this is simply a *mislocation* of these elements. Seeing this, we shall see that our overall theory of linguistic behaviour does not totally *shun* elements of causality and speakers' beliefs; we shall also see how the previous *silence* upon when understanding of a proper name can be attributed to a speaker – the silence upon the conditions for attributing the sufficient knowledge of the austere axioms – can be eliminated without moving to either Fregean or Kripkean accounts of the route to the reference.

On the object theory of proper names, the meaning of a name is its bearer: the meaning is given by axioms like

'JJ' stand for JJ.

The sense of a proper name, for Frege, is what a speaker knows when he understands its meaning. Why not, then, say that the *sense* of a proper name is *given* by our austere axioms, since knowledge of them would suffice for understanding of the names concerned? Presumably, the Fregean thought is that we should *not* say this because any account of when such knowledge can be attributed will require a *stronger* concept of sense, founded upon descriptions derived from speakers' beliefs. But that rejoinder is incorrect: appreciation of the theoretical notion of the meaning of a proper name, derived from appreciation of the role of the theory of meaning in an overall theory of linguistic behaviour, shows that an alternative account of the circumstances of attribution of this knowledge can be given.

The theory of sense is only part of the theory of linguistic behaviour. It interacts with the theory of force to issue in redescription of native speakers' linguistic actions: redescriptions of the form 'He asserted that *p*', 'He commanded that *q*', and so on. These redescriptions are then standardly used to license the ascription of propositional attitudes to speakers: 'He believed that *p*'; 'He wanted that *q*'; and so on. This propositional attitude assignment itself interacts with the theories of sense and force, for, as explained earlier, such assignment can be intelligible or unintelligible in diverse ways. Unintelligibility *may* prompt modification of the theories of sense and force. The notion of the meaning of a proper name, like that of any other kind of expression, is fixed by this briefly sketched role.

How, then, can a speaker manifest his knowledge that, say, 'JJ' stands for JJ? A simple thought is this: by utterances that an acceptable overall theory of linguistic behaviour interprets as the expressions of propositional attitudes *about* the object concerned. If one of his utterances is reasonably interpreted as the expression of the belief *about* JJ that he is such-and-such, or as the expression of the desire *about* JJ that he be, or do, such-and-such; and if that is so *in virtue of* the occurrence of 'JJ' in his utterances; then the knowledge that 'JJ' stands for JJ can plausibly be ascribed to him. This does not *ignore* the elements of causality and belief, for it is crucial to the acceptability of the overall theory that the propositional attitudes ascribed be *plausibly* ascribed. If, with this in mind, we accept two principles about propositional attitude ascription, the roles played by beliefs and causality *at this stage* – the stage of considering whether attitudes ascribed are plausible or not – becomes clear. The first principle is that ascription of any propositional attitudes *about* an object requires the ascription of *beliefs* about that object. The second principle is that ascription to a subject of beliefs *about* an object is plausible only if the speaker can be seen to have *causally interacted* with that object in some way. I am not sure that these principles, at least as stated, are true; unlike most philosophers, I am rather more doubtful about the first than the second. But if both were true – or if more careful formulations of them were true – it would follow that understanding of a proper name of the hypothesised cognitive kind could only be attributed to a speaker if he held beliefs about the object named and therefore stood in some appropriate causal relation to the object so named. This would give us a tidy diagnosis of the error of those who wish to locate these elements of belief and causality *within* the theory of sense: the error is that of trying to incorporate into that theory elements whose role *only* comes into being after the theory is combined with a theory of force, together with the additional step of moving from redescription of verbal actions to ascription of propositional attitudes to speakers. A proper appreciation of the role of the theory of meaning, and so of the notion of meaning, should eliminate any desire to see austerity in the theory of meaning as a symptom of impoverishment.

We understand, as object theorists, *which* object to pair with a proper name in the theory of sense by seeing *which* object the speaker can plausibly be taken to have beliefs *about*. We understand, as object theorists, *which* object to pair on a given occasion of use with a native speaker's usage of a multiply applicable proper name by seeing *which* object the speaker can plausibly be taken *now* to be expressing beliefs about. In the 'plausibly' is to be found the role for other beliefs and for causality. But those roles are restricted to the sentential, not the sentential component, level; and they are so restricted because their role is at the point of assessing for plausibility propositional attitude ascription, which ascription is possible only on the basis of the usage of a complete sentence.

(iii) The third objection aimed at our austerely non-descriptive account of proper names stemmed from its consequence that co-referential proper names will have the same meaning.[2] For this combines with the Fregean doctrine that the meaning of a sentence is a function of the meaning of its constituents to ensure that if

(8) The Morning Star is the Evening Star

is true, it has the same meaning as

(9) The Morning Star is the Morning Star.

But (8), it is claimed, differs from (9) in being contingent, *a posteriori*, and informative; they cannot, therefore, have the same meaning; so the object theory, which implies that they do, must be rejected.

I shall not discuss the claim that (8) is contingent; the only even remotely plausible argument for this view stems from the claim that (8) is an *a posteriori* truth; but since it has been convincingly argued in many places that there can be necessary *a posteriori* truths, that is no argument at all (see, e.g. Kripke, 'Naming and Necessity' and Putnam, *Mind, Language and Reality*, pp. 196–272). Added to which there are Kripke's independent arguments against the view that (8) is contingent, arguments I shall not here rehearse (*ibid.*).

What of the claim that (8) is *a posteriori* while (9) is *a priori*? Here, I think, it is the claim about (9) that is doubtful. We need, as before, to distinguish carefully between the following claims:

(10) It can be known *a priori* that the Morning Star is the Morning Star.

(11) It can be known *a priori* that 'the Morning Star' refers to the same object as 'the Morning Star'.

[2] A subtler variant yet of the worries discussed here is well met in McDowell, 'On the Sense and Reference of a Proper Name', pp. 175–8.

(12) It can be known *a priori* that 'The Morning Star is the Morning Star' is true.

Crudely speaking, the difference between the knowledge claim specified in (10) and that in (11) is that for that in (10) to be known, it has to be known which object is the Morning Star (though not necessarily under that designation); and it is perfectly clear that, except for Russellian logically proper names, that itself cannot be known *a priori*.[3] So (10) is false. Nor anyway is it clear that (11) is true: for the knowledge claim specified in (11) to be known, it must be known that 'the Morning Star' does indeed refer to some object, as well as that the two occurrences of 'the Morning Star' have the same reference; and while the latter fact also constitutes, as we have seen, part of a general difficulty for the object theory, the former fact seems to imply the falsity of (11). It is not even indisputable that (12) is true: many have held that sentences involving empty referring expressions are neither true nor false; if that is correct, then in the event of there being no Morning Star, the knowledge claim specified in (12) would be false; yet, as before, it is not to an *a priori* truth that 'the Morning Star' indeed refers, so that (12) becomes false.

Not that it is necessary for present purposes to dispute any of the three claims but (10); for it is no part of the object theory to comment upon the behaviour of proper names, coreferential or otherwise, within quotation contexts. Such contexts can be considered only in conjunction with an adequate theory of quotation; this will provide enough leeway to save the object theory from considerations arising from the changes produced by the substitution in either (11) or (12) for one of the occurrences of 'the Morning Star' of 'the Evening Star'. All we need to consider at the moment is the simpler difficulty posed by (10); and that difficulty is no difficulty at all. That the Morning Star is the Morning Star is an *a posteriori* truth; it thus differs not from the truth that the Morning Star is the Evening Star.

The final claim of difference between (8) and (9) is that the former is informative and the latter uninformative. In this case our strategy is slightly different; it is to argue that the truth of this claim does not establish that (8) and (9) differ in meaning; for more general considerations require us to deny that difference in informative content implies difference in meaning. We are also led to see Frege's worries about identity statements as but a special case of a more general philosophical problem.

Consider the expressions 'an oculist' and 'an eye-doctor': if any two expressions in English 'have the same meaning', it is surely these. Which is why

(13) An oculist is an eye-doctor

[3] At least, not unless we have a different notion of *a priori* knowledge.

is a correct, complete analysis of the notion of an oculist. But this fact of sameness of meaning combines with the Fregean doctrine that the meaning of a sentence is a function of the meaning of its constituents to imply that (13) has the same meaning as

(14) An oculist is an oculist.

The very fact that ensures that (13) is a correct analysis – namely, that 'an oculist' has the same meaning as 'an eye-doctor' – combines with the Fregean doctrine to ensure that (13) has the same meaning as (14). But (14) is trivial; indeed, it follows that *any* correct analysis, in virtue of its being *correct*, will have the same meaning as a triviality! So the only way for an analysis to avoid triviality is by being wrong! (Cf. Langford, 'The Notion of Analysis').

This Paradox of Analysis, as it has become known, is peculiarly difficult to avoid. It is no good, for example, detecting 'covert' quotation in (13) so as to claim that it is equivalent to

(15) 'An oculist' means the same as 'an eye-doctor'.

For while this, on any plausible view of quotation, does indeed block the problematic substitution, it simply misrepresents the character of (13). This is best revealed by considering the relations between the knowledge of each of (13) and (15): knowledge of (15) is not sufficient for knowledge of (13), for one could know (15) while not knowing what *either* of the quoted expressions meant; nor is knowledge of (15) necessary, since someone utterly ignorant of English can know that an oculist is an eye-doctor.

The solution, I think, is to accept the claim that (13) and (14) have the same meaning, and to question why it should be thought paradoxical. The thought is, presumably, that someone who says that an oculist is an eye-doctor has not *said the same* as someone who says that an oculist is an oculist; the one has said something informative and, perhaps, interesting, the other something trivial and boring. But, then, it is clear that there is nothing paradoxical about this once we distinguish the question of whether two utterances are of sentences with the same literal meaning from the question of whether the two utterers said the same thing. Questions of sameness of meaning are distinguishable as it were in both directions from questions of sameness of saying; for the latter notion is essentially one of *pragmatics*, one whose elucidation would make reference to context of utterance, speaker's and audience's knowledge and intentions, and *form* of expressions as well as to literal content of expression. And questions of sameness of informative content are particular cases of questions of sameness of saying. Frege, as is well known, distinguished the *mode of presentation* of an object from the object presented; the latter is the referent of an expression, the former its sense. Thus 'The Morning Star' and 'The Evening Star' present the same object but in different modes. Trading on this metaphor, the point of the preceding could be expressed like this: we need to distinguish the mode of presentation of a sense, a meaning, or a proposition from the sense, meaning or proposition expressed. Two sentences can 'present' the same meaning, but in different modes. Adding the conjecture that questions of samesaying or of informational content are functions, not just of the literal meanings of the sentences concerned but also of the mode of their presentation, we can avoid the worrying putative consequences of the paradox.

The point of this is that this independent, puzzling case – whose puzzle is generated by simple Fregean principles – requires us to draw a sharp distinction between claims of sameness of meaning and claims of sameness of informative content; but once this distinction has thus been drawn, Frege's worries about identity-statements upon the object theory of names disappear. (8) and (9) do indeed, in most imaginable contexts, differ in informational content; someone who uttered the one would not have said the same as someone who uttered the other; but it does not follow that the two sentences differ in meaning. It therefore does not follow that the object theory is mistaken in implying that they do have the same meaning.

Frege wanted to introduce the idea of a proper name's having a *sense* as well as a reference, the sense being at least part of its meaning, to explain how (8) and (9) could differ in meaning; for on such a theory, proper names being co-referential would not ensure that they had the same meaning, and so could be substituted preserving meaning. We have seen that this ground for positing senses of proper names was misguided because such positing is unnecessary; but it must also be emphasised that it is far from clear that the diverse motivations we have touched upon for the positing of senses of proper names could issue in a standard, non-patchwork notion of sense. Sense as route to reference; sense as mode of presentation of reference; sense as grounding for competent speakers' understanding; sense as informational content and, more generally, criterion of samesaying: each of these points to diverse *kinds* of considerations. The attempt to patch them into a façade of unity is not an attractive enterprise.

(iv) The crucial difficulty for the object theory of names remains. Given our treatment of the first difficulty (i), that from empty names, there is no question of true denials of existence of the form

(16) P.N. does not exist

constituting a problem; for our theory, *ex hypothesi*, does not apply in such cases. Nor, at least from what has been said so far, will our theory be applied to false assertions of existence, like

(17) Vulcan exists

for our stipulation about the expressions to which the theory applies was concerned, not with native speakers' beliefs as to whether the name was empty, but with whether it is in fact empty – by our own lights, of course. There will be a puzzle with cases like (17) as to what the *speaker* meant; but that will merely be a parallel puzzle to the problem for the object theory in accounting for true assertions of existence, like

(18) Jupiter exists.

In such an occurrence, the meaning of the subject term, on the object theory, is the object concerned: the proper name serves *purely*, so to speak, to pick out the object concerned. But then to go on to say that it exists is trivial: if it did not exist, we could not have picked it out. A similar problem arises, though with less force, for false denials of existence, like

(19) Jupiter does not exist.

For here, by the object theory, an object is *first* picked out, and then its existence is denied: but if it did not exist, it could *not* have been picked out! Such cases are not, I think, so worrying, since although the object theory reveals the literal meaning of the sentences to be puzzling, we can at least begin to make sense of what the *speaker* meant: for, presumably, the sincere asserter of (19) believes 'Jupiter' to be an empty name, and therefore not to be one to which the object theory applies. But this distinction between literal and speaker's meaning is of no comparable help with true assertions of existence like (18). For even if some account can be given of an un-problematic speaker's meaning in utterances of (18), it is very unclear that we should wish to accept that the *literal* meaning of (18) is so paradoxically trivial.

Various attempts might be made to represent the literal meaning of (18), or to represent the standard speaker's meaning accompany-ing its utterance, in a *meta-linguistic* approach. One example of this kind of approach would be to treat (18) as

(20) 'Jupiter' is to be analysed according to the object theory

or, more simply,

(21) 'Jupiter' is a semantical proper name.

Such a meta-linguistic approach intuitively misrepresents, however: (18) is not about language but about an object. Translation of (18)

F

into another language shows that it is not about the English name 'Jupiter' in the way that (20) and (21) apparently are. This point of translation reflects the intuitive fact that the occurrence of 'Jupiter' in (18) is at first sight comparable to that in

(22) Jupiter is a planet.

Indeed, we feel entitled to conclude from (18) and (22) that a planet exists. Maybe by noticing the 'semantic' character of the predicates in (20) and (21), we could try to *reconnect* the occurrences of 'Jupiter' in them with the non-linguistic world, by analogy with the disquotational character of the truth-predicate; but I do not know how this can be done.

A further problem arises because of the multiple applicability of proper names. Suppose someone utters (18) while talking about the planet. (18) is, then, true. So, too, are both (20) and (21): but they are true, not just because (18) is true, but because there are *many* Jupiters in the world: planets, mountains, ships, racehorses, and even children. We could, of course, use the indexed meta-language name in modified versions of (20) or (21): but then we represent the speaker, not just as talking about language rather than the world, but as talking about the *meta*-language, for natural object-languages do not have indexed names.[4] More plausible would be to treat this indexical version as a representation of what the speaker meant, while treating what he literally said as 'ambiguous', as translatable into the meta-language as

(23) 'Jupiter$_1$' or 'Jupiter$_2$' or 'Jupiter$_3$' . . . or 'Jupiter$_n$' is a semantical proper name.

But since the *list* we quote here will be determined by the class of non-empty names, his utterance will be completed by *us* in a way that still reveals it to be trivial by our lights, as well as implausibly meta-linguistic. Lacking a solution, then, to this puzzle about true assertions of existence, we might well look for alternatives to the object theory.

3 Names as Austere Predicates

Given the variety of ways in which objects acquire names, and in which names are learnt and used, austerity in the abstracted theory of public sense – a silence upon the relation between name and bearer – is a desideratum in any semantic account of proper names. But such austerity combined with treatment of names as individual constants – which, in interpretative semantics, issues in the object

---

[4] Except for a peculiar English dialect, originating in Eastern Europe, and now found only in the London School of Economics.

theory – encounters grave difficulties in handling assertions and denials of existence involving proper names. That there is a general puzzle about such assertions is not a novel thought; traditionally, it has provided a major motivation for treating proper names as predicates. If a proper name – say, 'JJ' – were correctly interpretable as equivalent in sense to a uniquely satisfiable set of predicates – abbreviated, say, to the predicate 'is F' – then the statement that JJ exists and the statement that JJ does not exist could be represented, respectively, as

(24) $(\exists x)\,(Fx)$

and

(25) $\sim(\exists x)\,(Fx)$.

There is no puzzle about either (24) or (25): for the reference is carried by the bound variable of quantification, which ranges – promiscuously – over all the items in the world. Such sentences thus no longer purport to refer *directly* to some *particular* object while going on to say that it exists or does not exist (Quine, *From a Logical Point of View,* p. 6). This same uniquely satisfiable set of predicates, the sense of the proper name, can account for the meaningfulness of empty names, can provide a route to the reference of the name, can ground the competent speakers' understanding of the name, and can account for the differences produced in the character of a sentence by substitution for a name of another, coreferential name. We have cast doubt upon the *need* for these further roles of such a conception of sense; but if that notion is needed to account for existence statements, it would be reasonable to try to employ it in these further areas.

The difficulty facing this approach, however, is clear: it is to reconcile such a conception of sense with the requirement of austerity. Standard predicate theories, of the diverse kinds developed by Frege, Russell and Strawson, are all subject to the Kripkean objection employed earlier: the uniquely satisfiable set of descriptions, however vaguely characterised, can be riddled with error, can be founded upon *false* beliefs of native speakers about the object concerned. We can discover this error, and in so doing we change neither the referent nor the sense of the proper name; if such a change were the result, our new beliefs would lack the required property of being logically incompatible with our earlier beliefs. The possibility of such a relation holding between beliefs is central to realism, and is part of our intuitive understanding of the role of proper names in our language.

Considerations like these might prompt the thought that the sense, the predicative content, of a proper name should be as *thin* as

151

possible, in an attempt to insulate the account from the worries of error in that content. Frege, for example, at one point considers the possibility that the sense of the name 'NN' is 'is called "NN"'. But there are two difficulties with this. First, 'is called "NN"' is not a uniquely satisfiable predicate; thus something *more* must be said about *how* uniqueness enters into a normal assertion of, say, 'NN is bald'. The point is that 'The thing that is called "NN"' is a *definite* description, in virtue of the definite article, but is also an *incomplete* description – it neither is satisfied by, nor is thought to be satisfied by, only one object. Any predicate theory, in accounting for usual occurrences of proper names in subject positions, must rely upon some account of definite descriptions; this Fregean theory must rely upon some account of incomplete definite descriptions. The most developed theory of definite descriptions is Russell's, whereby, for example, the sentence

(26) The present king of France is bald

is equivalent to

(27) There is something which is a present king of France, is unique in so being, and is bald.

This theory cannot be applied directly to sentences containing incomplete definite descriptions, for the way of handling uniqueness in Russell's theory would falsify such sentences. If I say to you, as we recline in front of the fire with our pet dog in the Sunshine Home for Retired Philosophers, 'The dog is going to vomit again', it would be absurd to represent me as asserting the existence of one, *and only one*, dog. Likewise, if I say 'NN is bald', it would be absurd, using the Fregean proposal, to represent me as asserting the existence of one, *and only one*, thing called 'NN'. So this Fregean proposal would need supplementation with an acceptable account of incomplete definite descriptions.

The second problem with the proposal is more decisive: its plausibility, especially in insulating itself from the Kripkean worries of error, rests upon imprecision. If 'is called "NN"' is read as 'is generally called by most people "NN"', or even 'is generally called by me "NN"', then the problem of error remains: for the claims now made could be discovered to be false *of the object* NN. To block this, we should need to treat 'is called "NN"' as equivalent to 'is called by me now "NN"'. But this seems far too weak: if I say 'Queen Victoria is a virgin', can I plausibly be taken to be breaking the silence merely to say that there is something that I am now (uniquely) calling 'Queen Victoria' and that is a virgin? How does *that* differ from the claim that the universe is not free of virgins? The problem is clear: if we wish for 'informative' analyses of proper

152

names as predicates, we can free ourselves from the worries of error only by producing far too weak an analysis. The solution is clear: abandon the requirement of 'informativeness' and settle for the austere. But how?

Quine has proposed that a proper name be treated as equivalent to an artificially constructed predicate defined to be satisfied by a bearer of that name (*From a Logical Point of View*, pp. 7–8). Thus we might have in our truth-theory a clause of the form:

(28) α satisfies 'Socratises' if and only if α Socratises.

This account would either need supplementation by an account of incomplete definite descriptions or would rely upon the indexing of the otherwise multiply-applicable artificial predicate. But while this proposal seems austere, it faces an obvious difficulty: we simply do not, as native English speakers, *understand* the predicate 'Socratises'. The appearance of austerity is thus misleading, since we shall need some account of that predicate as it figures in the (artificial) meta-language on the RHS of (28). But what account could be given except something along the lines of

(28*) α satisfies 'Socratises' if and only if α is identical to Socrates?

Thus the puzzle of understanding usual occurrences of 'Socrates' re-emerges at the level of interpreting, of understanding the meta-language. It is certainly not that we *generally* need pursue the interpretation of that language: it is our language, and we understand it. But when it is not our language – when it contains *artificial* expressions, concocted for whatever purpose – such an interpretation has to be sought for. In that search, Quine's proposal, as it stands, leads nowhere.

Both the Fregean and Quinean thoughts just considered bring us close to a theory recently proposed by Tyler Burge ('Reference and Proper Names'). Burge starts by noticing a class of sentences that occur in commonplace English in which are found predicates which obviously bear a close relation to proper names. Examples are:

(29) There are three Smiths in Princeton.
(30) Another Jones joined the club today.
(31) He's a Smith, but he's not the Smith I was talking about.

In any plausible representations of these sentences, predicates will be discerned that apparently 'include' a proper name: 'is a Smith', 'is a Jones'.

Burge's thought now is that such predicates underlie all occurrences of proper names. Proper names *are* predicates, albeit predicates with one eccentricity. And they are predicates, naturally occurring predicates, for which *austere* satisfaction axioms can be given, of the form of

(32) α satisfies 'is a Jones' if and only if α is a Jones.

Sentences like (29) – (31) are naturally understood by competent English speakers; they therefore understand predicates like 'is a Jones'; there is thus no problem, comparable to that facing Quine's 'artificial predicate' theory, in resting with the austere (32). An informal *gloss* can be given on (32) that might make explicit our usual, unreflective feel for these predicates – say

(33) α satisfies 'is a Jones' if and only if α has been given the name 'Jones' in an appropriate way.

The vagueness of the gloss – the vagueness of the 'given' and the 'appropriate' – is prompted by the variety of ways in which names are acquired by objects and used by speakers; this same vagueness, together with the yet to be explained occurrence of the *semantic* expression 'name' in (33), is what prompts the use of (32) rather than (33) in our theory of sense, however useful the latter might be as an intuitive gloss.

The eccentricity of Burge's predicates is this: their applicability to an object is dependent upon *linguistic* facts. Something can be a cat whether or not the word 'cat', or even some translation of it, has ever existed in a language; but something can be a Jones only if the term 'Jones' has been used in some way as a *name* of that thing.

'Is a Jones' is a multiply applicable predicate. In handling sentences like 'Jones is bald', Burge therefore must rely upon some account of incomplete definite descriptions. Russell's theory will not work for the reason already given. However, an intuitive solution is not hard to find, even though the formal details of its incorporation within a theory of sense are problematic.

Many, perhaps even most, definite descriptions occurring in English are incomplete. We already have

(34) The dog is going to vomit again.

Other examples are:

(35) The bus is late as usual.
(36) The man on the bus is smoking too much.
(37) The man in the corner is drunk.

The intuitive clue is that in all such occurrences, the definite article (in (36) and (37), the definite articles) is naturally replaceable by a demonstrative, even if style is scarcely improved by doing so:

(38) That dog is going to vomit again.
(39) That bus is late as usual.

154

(40) That man on that bus is smoking too much.
(41) That man in that corner is drunk.

This suggests that uniqueness for incomplete definite descriptions is secured, not in the manner of Russell, but by means of a tacit demonstrative element. The further thought would be that in a sentence like 'Jones is bald', the grammatical subject-term is the result of the combination of a demonstrative and a Burgean austere predicate – 'That Jones is bald' (Burge, 'Reference and Proper Names').

Any treatment, therefore, of 'normal' occurrences of proper names as grammatical subject terms must wait upon an adequate treatment of demonstrative constructions. We shall need to consider, for example, whether the following sentences have the same, or provably equivalent, truth-conditions:

(42) That dog is happy.
(43) That happy thing is a dog.
(44) That is a happy dog.

We shall also need to consider whether each of these has but one set of truth-conditions. I do not now have an acceptable treatment of such demonstrative constructions; but it is clear that any adequate truth-theory for English will include such a treatment, and that this treatment can then be applied to account for occurrences of proper names in grammatical subject-positions.

One further point that such a treatment must take account of connects with the question of how Burge's proposal might handle the stubborn puzzles about assertions and denials of existence involving proper names. At first sight, Burge's proposal merely accentuates the difficulties. A sentence like

(45) Vulcan does not exist

will presumably be

(46) That Vulcan does not exist.

The demonstrative seems to raise more forcefully than ever the worry about how we can first refer to an object, and then go on to say of it that it does not exist (or does exist). If it does not exist, it cannot be *demonstrated*; and if it can be demonstrated, of course it exists. If names were complete definite descriptions, the matter of uniqueness could be handled in the manner of Russell without reliance upon demonstratives; the puzzle would thus disappear. But we have found no acceptable treatment of names as complete definite descriptions.

The beginnings of a solution might be found by recognising that

155

demonstratives function in two, broadly distinguishable ways, which Burge, on another occasion, has labelled the *referential* and the *pronomial* ('Demonstrative Constructions'). In the referential usage of a demonstrative, there is, so to speak, an *immediate* reference to the world; an example would be my picking up a book and saying 'This is mine'. In pronomial occurrences, such reference as there is to the world is *mediated* by the surrounding linguistic context. An example is this: you say to me 'Yesterday, a man at the railway station tried to sell me a Daimler'; remembering a similar experience of mine, I ask 'Did this man have red hair?' My demonstrative makes reference to the person concerned (assuming your story to be true), but the reference is *mediated* by your utterance. This distinction is, of course, as vague as the notion of the surrounding linguistic context; but it is intuitive enough. Any detailed account of demonstrative constructions would have to acknowledge and explain it. In referential usages, is the reference dependent upon an *act* of reference by the speaker? In what ways can such referential usages go wrong, and with what consequences for the truth-value of the sentence? How close is the parallel between pronomial occurrences and the familiar apparatus of quantifier and bound variable? Does the role of the accompanying predicate, if any ('that man'), differ in the two constructions?

I do not have a theory that answers these questions, and therefore can only gesture at the help this distinction might give Burge in dissolving the worries about assertions and denials of existence involving proper names. It seems clear that if the demonstrative in

(46) That Vulcan does not exist

were referential in character, all the puzzles about such a statement, or about the corresponding affirmation of, say, Jupiter's existence, would remain. Instead, however, we might see the demonstrative in (46) as pronomial in character, in this case, crucially depending upon the linguistic context (admittedly, rather distant) created by all the writings and utterances of those who first posited the planet Vulcan. We might then notice a crucial feature of pronomial occurrences: namely, that they can, as it were, pick up the reference from the surrounding linguistic context even though the user of the pronomial demonstrative does not believe there to have been a *successful* reference in that surrounding context. An example would be a cross-examination in a court of law where the defendant explains that the wad of used notes found on him was given to him by a man he met at a racetrack; the prosecuting counsel, although believing, and perhaps repeatedly asserting, that the defendant stole the money from a bank, might ask: 'What was the colour of this man's hair? What was the colour of the hair of the man on the track?' Such demonstratives could frequently be employed in an attempt to *destroy* the alibi, to show that there was no such man. Seeing the demonstrative in (46) as functioning in this way – whatever it is – there is, intuitively, no puzzle about (46). We also gain a tidy explanation of why (46) would indeed be puzzling if the surrounding linguistic context of speculation about Vulcan did not itself exist.

All of this would only carry much conviction if we had an acceptable truth-theoretic account of such goings on. I do not have such an account; but the combination of that (future) account with Burge's austere predicate theory of proper names seems to me much the most promising line of development in resolving the puzzles about existence statements involving proper names. Amongst the questions that need answers are these: to what extent, in the court of law example, is the intelligibility of the prosecuting counsel's questions to be explained by the role of *supposition* or *pretence* – 'Let's suppose (pretend) that there is such a man'? To what extent does the reliance upon the role of pronomials, together, perhaps, with this role of supposition, issue in a *meta-linguistic* (say, 'scare' quotes) account of sentences like (46)? In handling assertions of existence, is the puzzlingly referential role of the demonstrative in some way *reduced* by its reliance upon a surrounding context in which non-referential (suppositional) demonstratives occur attached to the same (name) predicate?

4 Names as Ambiguous Predicates

There is an interesting aspect of predicates like 'is a Jones', an aspect which might be thought to constitute a further serious difficulty for this theory of proper names. This is the ambiguity of the predicates.

Consider the following kinds of case. First, suppose I adopt the *nom de plume* 'Wittgenstein'. Then I have two names, 'Wittgenstein' and 'Platts', both acquired in an appropriate way and both in common usage *as* names of me, with 'Platts is Wittgenstein' being a true identity statement involving names. Still, someone doubtful of my pretensions might say of me: 'He's not really a Wittgenstein, he's a Platts'. A similar deflationary remark might be made of me even if more official procedures are involved in the change of name, as in a change by deed-poll. Second, suppose that as I stand by the Ascot racetrack parade-ring, a racehorse enters whose sire is the famous Hyperion. The animal, let us say, is called 'Loppylugs'. However, struck by the evident physical similarity between Loppylugs and his sire, I might say of Loppylugs: 'Now, there's a Hyperion for you'. Third, suppose I have an illegitimate child by the wife of a friend, the child being raised as one of their family and bearing their name. Noticing his striking resemblance to me, you might say: 'He's a Platts all right'; even if he lacks much resemblance, you might covertly whisper to a gossip: 'He's a Platts, you know'. Finally, suppose you are struck by the resemblance in point of character and behaviour between myself and someone of fame (or notoriety) for you – say, Wittgenstein or Hitler – you might say of me that I'm a Hitler, or a Wittgenstein.

As defenders of Burge, we cannot be too quick with the claim that these are metaphorical, or eccentric, usages of these predicates; for just the same might be said of the usages that are Burge's starting point. Without that over-hasty response, what these cases suggest is that the connection between *being*, say, a Wittgenstein and 'Wittgenstein' being one's name is not as simple as casual thought suggests. One way of being a Wittgenstein is indeed to have the *name* 'Wittgenstein'; but another is to be, ancestrally, of the *family* Wittgenstein; and a third is to bear some striking *resemblance* to Wittgenstein. Unsurprisingly, the middle of these readings of 'being a ϕ', where ϕ is a proper name, is less readily available when ϕ includes *given*, or *maritally acquired*, names as well as family names; but the distinction between *given* and *family* name, like that between *maritally acquired* and family name, is rarely secure enough to preclude that middle reading. And, as the first kind of case detailed shows, that middle reading is often heavily weighted in situations of 'competing' names.

These are simple truths about the operation of Burge's predicates in English; these predicates are ambiguous. If, now, we wish our theory of sense to disambiguate ambiguous predicates, we face a problem: for a major point of Burge's theory is to meet the condition of austerity since there are good reasons for doubting whether an adequate, non-austere analysis of what it is to be *named* so-and-so can be given. The requirement of disambiguation apparently forces us to reimmerse ourselves in this thankless task.

There is a simple solution which is not merely *ad hoc*, serving, rather, to illuminate an important point about the theory of sense. This is to deny that the theory of sense should disambiguate. Given an utterance like 'Another Jones joined the club today', the theory of sense should serve to deliver the truth-conditions of (the indicative content of) that utterance; but these truth-conditions will themselves be ambiguous. In combination with the theory of force, they will therefore lead us, at least at the first stage, to attribute an ambiguous saying to the speaker – say, 'He asserted that another Jones joined the club today'. This is as it should be: if the speaker uttered a sentence containing an ambiguous word or phrase, then *what he literally said* was ambiguous. The question of *what he meant* can arise, in general, only after we have an account of what he literally said; and it is at the point of what he meant, of the ascription of the propositional attitudes that he was *expressing*, that disambiguation occurs.

Which disambiguated propositional attitude we ascribe to the speaker will depend upon which it is most *plausible* to attribute to him of the range whose ascription is (standardly) licensed by the redescription of his action achieved through the theories of sense and force. The plausibility, as usual, will be determined by the other beliefs attributed to him along with the observed facts of his previous experience. We can secure the requisite disambiguation of the *content* of the propositional attitude ascribed either by relating it to the observations which make the ascription plausible or by helping ourselves to a formulation that would be unacceptably non-austere within the theory of sense itself. So we might say, for example, that he believes that another Jones joined the club today *because* he saw the name in the New Members Book (or, *because* he knows his natural father); or we might say that he believes that another person called (or named) 'Jones' joined the club today. There is then no harm in producing a further, more informal, redescription of the linguistic action performed: 'Because he had seen the name in the New Members Book, he said that another Jones had joined the club today'; or, 'He said that another person called "Jones" had joined the club today'.

The theory of sense itself, however, remains austere to the point of neglecting ambiguity; and the initial redescription of his linguistic action, relying upon the theories of sense and force, likewise remains blind to ambiguity. Only upon an incorrect perception of the role of the theory of sense within the overall theory of linguistic behaviour could the fact of the ambiguity of Burge's predicates be seen as a problem.

One final worry might be this: Burge claims that the grammatical subject-term in a sentence like 'Jones is bald' is the surface result of the underlying combination of a demonstrative and the predicate 'is a Jones'. But that predicate is ambiguous; so, therefore, on Burge's account, must be the sentence 'Jones is bald'. The worry is that this is wrong, that 'Jones is bald' is not ambiguous, the subject-term being understood *only* as a *name* of the object referred to.

This, I think, is an indecisive worry. First, it is not clear that the other readings of the subject-term – family membership, similarity to famous (or infamous) bearers of that name – cannot be plausibly imagined in various circumstances. Second, we can explain the *appearance* of non-ambiguity by reference to the comparative *rareness* of the other, non-naming readings. It is just as if (as is more or less the case in my usual speech-communities) the term 'bank' was nearly always used only in talking of money banks,

159

rarely of river banks; then 'I'm going to the bank' might pass as unambiguous for much of the time – just as the other reading might *appear* the only reading within a community of money-neglecting fishermen. Doubtless, there are interesting questions as to *why* the name-reading of 'Jones is bald' is so frequent and so natural; but no explanation of that will reveal this reading as the only correct one.

Chapter VII

Adjectival Constructions

1 The Predicative-Attributive Distinction

What are the best semantic treatments of adjectival constructions? In this chapter, this question is explored in great detail. One reason for this is that many major issues in moral and aesthetic theory turn upon a proper understanding of such constructions, most obviously, those involving 'good' and 'beautiful'. I shall not much consider the particular difficulties posed by these philosophically interesting expressions; but it is difficult to deny that a better grasp of constructions involving more mundane adjectives is likely to help in understanding, and resolving, these difficulties. Second, one major issue in logical theory might well have fresh light cast upon it by a proper understanding of adjectival constructions: namely, the fundamental subject-predicate distinction. Proper names are paradigmatically fitted for the subject role in a sentence: some adjectives seem peculiarly well-fitted for the predicate role, while others seem distinctly ill-fitted. Understanding *why* this is should clarify the nature of predication. Finally, and connectedly, the appearance of facile calm surrounding the Davidsonian notion of logical form is largely removed by seeing the complexities that arise in handling these apparently straightforward constructions; the full, tendentious complexity of that notion may then be better seen. To this end, I consciously attempt for much of the discussion to eschew views upon the fine detail of the proper form for a theory of meaning. I assume the general constraints specified earlier; beyond that, I deliberately suspend theoretical judgment. This is not because I have any desire to return to the days when anecdote passed as semantic analysis, when it was thought useful, and therefore presumed possible, to record linguistic data without theoretical commitment. Rather, the point is that the danger may now have swung to the other pole: we may be too quick to ignore recalcitrant data, or to

161

assume that they must be squeezed into our favoured, detailed pre-conceptions. Sometimes, at least, this direction of fit needs to be reversed. That reversal begins in this chapter.

I start from a contrast between attributive and predicative adjectival constructions. Typical attributive constructions involve 'tall', 'large', 'attractive', and 'good' – which is not yet to say that all constructions involving these expressions are attributive. Typical predicative idioms involve exact metrical predicates and, perhaps, colour words. There are theories which deny this contrast, assimilating one of these groups to the other; still, I shall pretend that all share my initial intuition of contrast and agree with the rough extensional characterisation given.

Two claims about attributives seem close to orthodoxy amongst philosophers of language. The first is that the positive form of attributives cannot be represented as one-place predicates. This is sometimes canonised into a test, or even a defining criterion, to be employed in detecting attributive constructions. The second claim (less widely accepted) is that the positive attributive is definable in terms of the corresponding comparative, the comparative is primary. There is a vagueness about this thesis. Is the claim that the logical form of a sentence whose surface structure involves a positive attributive involves the corresponding comparative? We need to distinguish the denial of the possibility of definition of positive in terms of comparative *tout court* and the denial of the *need* for such definition for purposes of logical form assignment. This clearly hangs upon the requisite understanding of *logical form*. Since, for reasons that I shall indicate, the first, stronger denial can be made out, this other claim, and its theoretical hanging, will not delay us.

The reason behind the first orthodoxy is clear enough. Suppose we treat the attributive 'large' in

(1) Theo is a large flea

as a one-place predicate. Then the logical representation of (1) will be

(1*) *Fa & Ga*

where '*F*' is the predicate '*is large*' and '*a*' is '*Theo*'. From (1*) it follows that

(2*) *Fa*

which is

(2) Theo is large.

But (2) is false: large fleas are not large. Yet Theo might be attributively a large flea, so (1*) cannot be the correct representation of (1) (cf. Wallace, 'Positive, Comparative, Superlative', and Wheeler, 'Attributives and their Modifiers').

As remarked, this argument is often embodied in a test. A sentence of the form

(3) This is a (adjective) (noun)

is a predicative as opposed to attributive construction if and only if it implies

(4) This is (adjective).

We thereby assume the exhaustiveness of the attributive-predicative distinction.

This test is far from happy. For example, by it the following sentence involves an attributive construction:

(5) This is a red head of hair.

Our hesitation over accepting this as an attributive construction is explicable and intuitively justifiable. There could be another term, characterising the appropriate colour of hair and with no other use in the language except to characterise that colour, which would be substitutable in (5) apparently preserving sense, and which would be predicative by the proposed test. Metaphorical origin, if that is what it was, need not yield attributivity.

Another batch of cases revealed as attributive by this test might induce further disquiet. Their characteristic is that for each of them a sentence of the form of (3) does not imply

(6) This is a (noun).

A list of such cases is given by Montague: 'false friend', 'reputed millionaire', 'ostensible ally', 'possible president', 'alleged intruder' (Montague, *Formal Philosophy*, p. 211). The reason for such cases failing the proposed test for predicativity is that the appropriate sentence of the form of (4) scarcely makes sense. A connected class of cases, labelled by Kamp *privative*, is constituted by those in which (3) implies the negation of (6) while (4) does make sense and is sometimes true; examples are provided by many uses of 'fake' and 'false' (J. A. W. Kamp in Keenan, *Formal Semantics*, pp. 123–55).

Finally, there are cases revealed as attributive by this test, which do not imply the equivalent of (6), but for which the equivalent of (4) does make sense. An example is 'is a white elephant'; an interesting, though very disputable one, is 'is a hard bargain'. The metaphorical character of such idioms makes the falsity of (4) as irrelevant as its meaningfulness and their failure to imply (6). I therefore disregard such cases from now on.

Such difficulties are far from decisive. We could just buy the consequence that all these cases are attributive; since it is not yet clear what hangs upon this expression, this is still an option. We might then subdivide the class of attributives to acknowledge the evident differences just noted. Or we could abandon the assumption that the attributive-predicative distinction is exhaustive. The simple test then suffices to demarcate predicatives, and gives a necessary condition for attributivity; what more is required for a sufficient condition for attributivity remains to be seen.

2 Implicit and Explicit Attributives: Semantical Attachment

Aside from these diverse problem cases, there is a further, apparently simple-minded, difficulty facing the proposed test. Crudely put, it is this: sentences of the form of

(3) This is a (adjective) (noun)

even when construed attributively, do imply sentences of the form of

(4) This is (adjective)

namely, when (4) is elliptical for (3)!

The obvious rejoinder is: a sentence of the form of (3) is predicative if and only if it implies (4), where (4) is not elliptical for (3). Crucially, this is not enough: for predicativity, (4) must not be elliptical at all. If it is, we face the problem not of distinguishing attributives and predicatives, but of distinguishing two kinds of attributive construction. It is a matter of surprising consequence that there are these two kinds. Consider

(7) Rudy is an attractive ballet-dancer.

This can be read in two sorts of ways, the second sort having many instances. One way reveals (7) as equivalent to

(8) Rudy dances ballet attractively.

On this reading, to know the truth of (7) we need to scrutinise Rudy while he performs. The other way, schematically, reveals (7) as equivalent to

(9) Rudy dances ballet and is attractive in some other way.

An instance of this second reading would be

(10) Rudy dances ballet and is an attractive person to look at whatever he is doing.

Read as (10), (7) does indeed imply

164

(11) Rudy is attractive

where (11) is not elliptical for (7). But, as I shall argue, (11) is still elliptical and (7) still involves an attributive construction.

A little jargon may help. If the adjective in a sentence of the form of (3) is semantically attached to the noun explicitly occurring in (3), I shall call it an *explicit* attributive construction; if it is attached to some other noun, I shall call it an *implicit* attributive construction. This would only be a clear explanation if I defined the notion of *semantic attachment*; the main point of my discussion will be that this notion is essential to attributive constructions, and must be explicated by any account of these constructions; but for the moment I am concerned to draw an intuitive distinction, not to ground it.

It might be thought that in adding the condition for predicativity that the implication (4) not be elliptical at all, the class of predicative constructions is being eliminated. A sentence of the form of (4), even when read as a consequence of a sentence of the form of (3) read 'predicatively', could still be treated as elliptical for

(12) This is a (adjective) thing.

But this is wilful silliness. The noun in (12) is, at best, a dummy. What counts as a dummy is another question, but this need not now delay us.

Once we recognise the distinction between two kinds of attributive construction, we are led to realise the paucity – though not the non-existence – of predicative constructions. Consider (7). Suppose this is read as implying (11), where (11) is not elliptical for (7). Still, (11) is always non-dummily elliptical, say, for

(13) Rudy is an attractive person to look at

or

(14) Rudy is an attractive person to have dinner with.

The filling-in of (11) will vary from context to context; but it is a matter of some importance that such a filling is required, that it will never rest with dummies. (These may be two points or one; I return to this later.) (7), by the proposed test, will be predicative if and only if it implies (11) where (11) is not elliptical at all; since (11) is never non-elliptical, it follows that (7) is never a predicative construction. This is a claim about the adjective *attractive*: it is a purely attributive adjective. Similar considerations suggest that most adjectives do not admit of predicative constructions. I return to *why* this is later, but for the moment we can conclude that what matters with most adjectival constructions is distinguishing implicit and explicit attributives.

What determines the noun to which the attributive is semantically

165

attached? That is, what determines whether it is an explicit or an implicit construction, and, if it is the latter, what determines which implicit construction it is?

The most obvious comprehensive answer is: the intentions of the speaker. I am unclear, as I shall explain shortly, that acceptance of this answer requires general acceptance of Gricean theory. I shall anyway pass by this answer with the following remark. Even were the answer correct, a problem remains. Our route to the intentions of others is usually mediated by our understanding of their utterances, together with broader contextual considerations; to study these contextual clues is neither to accept nor to deny the general intentional claim, nor is it to accept or to reject any general primacy claim about the relation between meaning ascription and propositional attitude ascription.

Which contextual factors, then, determine our assignment of a particular noun as that to which the attributive is semantically attached? There are many such clues, of which I mention only a few.

(a) Repetition of a noun already used, or tacitly involved, in identifying the item, or items, referred to. Thus if 'The elephant over there is a large elephant' and 'African elephants are large elephants' are not read as explicit attributives, the repetition seems pointless. Similarly, attachment of a noun which speaker and audience both know applies to the item concerned will invite an explicit attributive reading. This common knowledge may be founded upon a mutual acquaintance with the item concerned – 'Fidel is a large elephant' said by one elephant man at the zoo to another – or upon some standard connection between the name used and the kind of item referred to – 'Jumbo is a large elephant' said by almost anyone to almost anyone.

(b) General beliefs about the speaker, including beliefs about his beliefs and about his desires. Coming from many speakers, for example, the sentence 'Tom is an attractive rugby-forward' could only be read as an explicit attributive.

(c) At least in the case of purely attributive adjectives, there may be a principle of the following form: unless there is evidence to the contrary (e.g. of the kind indicated by (a), (b), and (d)) read any such construction as explicit. For there are other ways of conveying an implicit reading, no better way of conveying the explicit reading.

(d) Perhaps the most frequent, though not the most basic, is the surrounding linguistic context. If the preceding conversation is about attractive ballet-dancers in the explicit reading, an utterance of (7) will be taken as an explicit attributive, while an utterance of (11) will be taken as elliptical for (7) as an explicit attributive. The understanding of the preceding conversation will be based upon considerations like (a) to (c). Likewise, someone who argues in a logic class 'The elephant over there is a large elephant; so the elephant over there is large' or 'Jumbo is a large elephant; so Jumbo is large' will invite the reading of the conclusion as an ellipsis for the corresponding premiss, the understanding of which again derives from considerations like (a) to (c). Of course, the triviality of the argument, on such a reading, may invite in other contexts some other reading; but normal considerations of informativeness are often suspended in logical argument, and the belief that some principle of informativeness is operating is yet another contextual determinant.

The connections between these considerations and various Gricean principles of conversational exchange (pp. 81–3) should not need labouring, nor should the need to systematise such contextual considerations. What may be less obvious are the parallels with certain aspects of demonstrative usage. Burge, as we have seen (pp. 155–7), distinguishes two kinds of demonstrative construction, the referential and the pronomial. In referential usages, the reference of the demonstrative is determined by an extra-linguistic reference by the speaker; for example, a spontaneous assertion at a party 'That man in the corner is drinking too much'. In pronomial uses, any extra-linguistic reference is mediated by the presence of a surrounding linguistic context; you might tell me of a man who tried to sell you a Daimler today, and I ask 'Did this man have blond hair?', remembering a similar, recent experience of mine. There is, ultimately, an extra-linguistic referent; but my reference to it is mediated by your remark. This distinction, as Burge realises, is as clear as the notion of the surrounding linguistic context; the same is true of the class of considerations adduced under (d). This may not, however, exhaust the parallels between attributives and demonstratives, as we shall see.

3 Why Attributives are not One-Place Predicates

Let us return to the argument against treating attributives as one-place predicates; and let us approach it by asking why attributives must have a semantically attached noun. The answer is simple: that is what attributives are like. But a little more can be said. Consider the sentences

(2) Theo is large

and

(11) Rudy is attractive.

Until we know, or form beliefs about, the appropriate filling, we have no complete understanding of these sentences. We know (up

167

to a point) the meanings of the words they contain, and (perhaps) their syntactic structure; but we have no idea *which* conditions would make the sentences true or false. This (vague) thought is what I mean by saying that (2) and (11) are elliptical. It also explains why 'thing' is a *dummy* filling, since such filling effects no change in the deficiency.

An instructive analogy is with a sentence like 'He is bald'. Again, we understand in some sense the meanings of the constituents, along with their syntactic combination; but we have no idea of the determinate truth-conditions of the sentence. One general account of these conditions would make reference to the utterer's intentions; but we need a route to these intentions. That route is provided either by the surrounding linguistic context – the pronominal usage – or by the extra-linguistic context and an act of reference thereto by the speaker – the referential usage. Without such a filling-in of the reference, such sentences have no determinate truth-conditions.

'He' is an indexical, demonstrative expression; attributives, at least pre-theoretically, are not. But the point of the analogy can be seen by considering the following inferences: 'John is bald; so he is bald' and 'John is a bachelor; so he is unhappy'. In such cases, the clue as to the reference of the demonstrative lies in the preceding sentence. In the context of such arguments 'he is bald' and 'he is unhappy' have determinate contents, determinate truth-conditions. Without such a context, and without any extra-linguistic reference by the speaker, the sentences do not have determinate truth-conditions. Still, it is difficult to believe that 'he' functions as anything but a referring expression; it is simply that the reference is determined contextually in one of the two broadly indicated ways.

With this in mind, the argument against treating attributives as one-place predicates becomes less compelling. The offending conclusion – 'Theo is large' – offends only if it either has no filling-noun or has some filling-noun other than that specified in the premiss of the argument – viz. 'flea'. The former way of making the conclusion offensive has the effect of making it offensive quite independently because it leaves it with no determinate sense; it is not that the conclusion is false, rather, it is not complete enough to be either true or false. To make it complete, some noun must be read into it; and the obvious noun to read into it (by (d)) is 'flea'. Which leaves the conclusion true. Reading some other noun in may indeed make the conclusion offensive because false; but this is achieved only by ignoring the evident contextual determinant, the premiss, of the filling-noun. With such a reading, the thought might be, the conclusion no longer follows from the premisses alone, the argument is invalid; so the falsity of the conclusion matters not. While the former way of making the conclusion offensive transgresses the syntactic rule that another predicate must occur in the same sentence; so that move would not be valid either.

Resistance to this idea dies hard. For example, it might be thought that the proposal commits us to the validity of the following argument:

(A) Theo is a large flea
so (B) Theo is large.
(C) Theo is an animal
so (D) Theo is a large animal.

But this just reiterates the confusion. First, perhaps (D) could just about be read as an implicit attributive, the filling-noun being 'flea'. In that case the argument is valid, the conclusion unobjectionable. But if (D) is read as an explicit attributive and (B) is read as having its content determined by (A), the argument is simply invalid, and the falsity of the conclusion need not concern us. The argument is then comparable to

(A′) John is happily married
so (B′) He is happily married.
(C′) Derek is a miserable bachelor
so (D′) He is a miserable bachelor
so (E′) He is happily married and he is a miserable bachelor
so (F′) He is happily married and a miserable bachelor.

One way of reading (E′) and the steps thereto makes (E′) follow but be quite unobjectionable; the other way licenses the move to (F′), which is indeed false; yet on that reading (E′) simply does not follow from the preceding, the argument is invalid. Indexicals can pick up their reference from the surrounding linguistic context in pronomial occurrences; the claim being considered is that the determinate sense of attributive constructions can be fixed in just the same way.

If the difference between determining reference and giving determinate sense worries, the following argument is worth considering:

(A″) John is a graduate of Columbia University
so (B″) John is a bachelor.
(C″) John is happily married
so (D″) John is not a bachelor
so (E″) John is a bachelor and is not a bachelor
so (F″) John is and is not a bachelor.

Once again, either (E″) is read in a way that makes it unobjectionable and the argument up to that point valid, or it is read in a way that makes it objectionable (say, as implying (F″) on the assumption that (F″) is objectionable) but according to which the argument

169

is invalid. One way in which the sense of an ambiguous predicate is detected is through the surrounding linguistic context.

Indexicals and ambiguous predicates require delicacy in considering, and formalising, inferences involving them; but this does not show that indexicals are not referring subject-expressions, nor that ambiguous predicates are not predicates. Inferences involving such expressions frequently exemplify the importance in understanding natural language inferences of recognising a disparate set of phenomena that might (misleadingly) be lumped together under the title *linguistic cross-reference*. Recognition of this set carries with it recognition of the crude simplicity of the standard argument against treating the positive form of an attributive as a one-place predicate. Doubtless, uncertainty of reference and uncertainty as to disambiguation differ as markedly from failure of determinacy of sense as they do from each other. But this does not *yet* show the argument for the first orthodoxy to be sound.

That argument is a crude one, and I have met it crudely. Such argument and counter-argument is not much to the point except in so far as they lead us to the deeper matters involved in attributive constructions. The questions that matter are: what is the relation of semantic attachment? And quite how is this mode of combination to be represented in the chosen canonical notation for the theory of meaning in a manner consistent with general constraints of adequacy upon such a theory?

The idea that attributives are one-place predicates is, thus far, silent upon these deep questions. What is wrong with that idea is not that it saddles us with unacceptable inferences, but that once this silence is eliminated, that idea is demonstrably incorrect. So far, the claim of the one-place predicate theorist *might* be that there is *no* relation of semantic attachment, with the deep questions thus never arising. Now, one claim I have made repeatedly seems incompatible with this: namely, that a sentence containing an attributive requires *another* predicate to occur in the same sentence if it is to have determinate sense, determinate truth-conditions. For saying that attributives are one-place predicates but peculiar ones – their peculiarity being that they require the company of *another* predicate – seems utterly mysterious. *Why* do they require this other predicate? Any answer to *that* appears to lead to the abandonment of the one-place predicate theory – for example, in the direction of treating them as *predicate modifiers*, expressions that operate upon a predicate to form a new predicate, comparable, say, to predicate negation. The one-place predicate theorist must, then, either provide some other account of this peculiarity, or *deny* that attributives in fact have this peculiarity.

The only remotely plausible way I can see of substantiating this denial is as follows. I compared inferences involving attributives with others involving indexical expressions, like 'he', and ambiguous predicates, like 'is a bachelor'. There is a crucial difference between these comparison inferences and comparison expressions. The one-place predicate theorist must decide *which* he wishes to hold to be the closer parallel. The difference is this: roughly, indexical demonstratives are essentially *pragmatic* devices, devices a semantic account of which must make reference to pragmatic features, whereas ambiguous predicates are not. Our theory of sense, we have argued, need not disambiguate ambiguous predicates; but even if that is rejected, it is sufficient for semantic purposes to *index* ambiguous predicates so as to disambiguate them. Pragmatic considerations may enter into the question of how we *recognise*, so to speak, the index involved; but for the theory of sense itself, indexing suffices. It does not suffice for indexical demonstratives for there is no limit to the number of demonstratives, with distinct references, that distinct sentences of the language can contain. If our theory is to be finite, is to be one we can write down, the pragmatic treatment of demonstratives is essential.

The point, now, is this: the committed one-place predicate theorist might hold that attributives are *ambiguous* one-place predicates. There is nothing *incomplete* about the sentence 'Theo is large', it is merely ambiguous. What misled us into thinking it *incomplete*, in some sense *other* than ambiguity – what made us think attributives had the peculiarity of *requiring* another predicate to occur in the same sentence – is that any accompanying predicate *can* serve (not *must* serve, because of implicit attributive constructions) to disambiguate the ambiguous predicate. The peculiarity is a *pragmatic* guide, not an essential semantic feature. *Semantically*, there is no attachment to be explained.

However, assimilation of attributives to ambiguous one-place predicates will require an account of their disambiguation. It is not that such disambiguation *need* be done within the theory of sense; rather, it must at least be possible, however artificially, that such disambiguation be done. The parallel with other, clearly ambiguous predicates suggests that this be done by indexing. So, for example, for 'large' we shall have a *list* of indexed predicates, perhaps paired with the noun that would serve, pragmatically, to disambiguate them:

large$_1$ . . .   (flea)   . . . (large *for* a flea)
large$_2$ . . .   (elephant) . . . (large *for* an elephant)
large$_3$ . . .   (giraffe)   . . . (large *for* a giraffe)
. . .
. . .

The problem is clear: this list could never be completed. There is no *limit* to the number of nouns to which 'large' can be attached: the expression 'a large large elephant' makes perfectly good sense, and exemplifies the capacity of natural languages to generate an infinite number of terms to which 'large' can be attached. The predicate theorist, to avoid the offending inferences and to avoid the need to account for semantic attachment, must treat 'large' as a quite distinct predicate in each of its potential infinity of occurrences with different nouns. It is thus in principle impossible to disambiguate this ambiguous predicate in a manner compatible with the general requirement of finiteness.

Thus the analogy with ambiguous predicates and their pragmatic disambiguations is of no help to the one-place predicate theorist. Some further explanation – a *semantic* explanation – must be given of the peculiarity that attributives require another predicate to occur in a sentence if that sentence is to have determinate truth-conditions; that explanation will be the abandonment of the theory that positive attributives are one-place predicates. Likewise, if the theorist wishes to trade upon either the parallel with indexical expressions or the parallel with ambiguous predicates, it must be the former; but any way of taking that parellel seriously – say, by detecting a demonstrative element in positive attributives, perhaps, in a way I shall explain later, by treating them as *two*-place predicates – will also amount to the abandonment of the one-place theory. With that abandonment, the need to account for, not to deny, semantic attachment comes to the fore.

One last point should be mentioned. I said that a predicative construction of the form 'This is (adjective)' is not elliptical at all, and certainly not elliptical for 'This is a (adjective) thing' since 'thing' is a dummy. I held that 'Rudy is attractive' and 'Theo is large' always require a non-dummy filling, without which they have no determinate sense, no determinate truth-conditions; I thus held that if the apparent conclusion of an argument is a non-elliptical sentence of either form that conclusion is independently objectionable and could only follow from the premisses if inference is allowed to disregard the syntactic and semantic character of attributives. If we ignore the requisite filling, we inevitably ignore the way in which that filling is determined.

These claims about 'large' and 'attractive' might be denied; that is, it might be claimed that these expressions are not *purely* attributive adjectives. This could even be generalised to the claim that *all* attributives have a predicative usage. For example, 'Theo is large' just means 'Theo is a large thing'. The apparent counter-examples to this generalisation are irrelevant. At first sight, 'Rudy is attractive' is indeed hopelessly indeterminate in sense; I said that it must be elliptical for the attributive, say, 'Rudy is an attractive person to look at' or 'Rudy is an attractive person to have dinner with'. But, it could be claimed, it could just as well be elliptical for 'Rudy is an attractive thing to look at' or 'Rudy is an attractive thing to have dinner with'; and 'to look at' and 'to have dinner with' are not predicate constructions, and so are not the predicates to which 'attractive' is attributively attached. Even if we leave in 'thing' (or 'person'), we find something odd about 'Rudy is a thing (or a person) to have dinner with'. Rather, phrases like 'to have dinner with', which Lakoff calls *hedges*, serve to specify the relevant dimension of assessment; they are, roughly, attributive modifiers which function to narrow down the appropriate range of the (vague) adjective. So all adjectives have non-elliptical, predicative usages, although some require hedges to obtain sharper sense. Hedges may even be needed with 'large' *vis-à-vis* height, weight, and bulk. But my ellipsis claim, my claim of pure attributivity, was not just concerned to avoid the *vagueness* that hedges can reduce.

I need not deny this unless it is claimed that a sentence like 'Theo is large' must always be read in this pseudo-predicative way. But I anyway have doubts as to whether there is such a usage. The claim is that 'Theo is large' can be equivalent to 'Theo is a large thing', where *thing* ranges over all the items in the universe. But such a usage, even if intelligible, would rarely have any *point*, would rarely fit with the aim, role or function of 'large'; more importantly, the intelligibility of such a usage is unclear. In such a usage, we have pathetically little grasp upon either its verification or its assertability conditions; and this is not just a contingent, human failing, since the dummy noun 'thing' fails to provide any principle of grouping, of individuation, and so can be of no use in counting. How many *things* are there in this room? There is no answer; yet it is difficult to believe that we could begin to make sense of whether, say, a chair in this room is a *large* thing in this room until we have *some* idea how *many* things, of different sizes, there are in this room. There seems, in some way, to be an essentially comparative element in *all* applications of attributive adjectives; 'thing' gives us no *grounding* for that comparison, and so gives the adjectival construction no determinate sense. Quite *what* this comparative element is, and quite how it differs from the comparative element, if any, found within predicative constructions, is a further question, to which we shall return; but the invocation of 'thing' eliminates that comparative element only at the price of unintelligibility. Likewise, it is difficult to believe that we have any understanding of what it is to be an *attractive* thing. We have a grasp, yet to be explained, of what it is to be an attractive ballet-dancer, or film, or dinner-companion, or vase; but we have no idea at all – not just a

173

vague, hedge-reducible idea – of what it is to be attractive *tout court*.

4 Positive, Comparative, Superlative

What is the relation of semantic attachment? And how is that mode of combination to be represented in our chosen canonical notation? One direct answer to these questions is apparently given by definition of the positive in terms of the comparative. The comparative is treated as a primitive two-term relation.

(15) Jumbo is larger than Dumbo

is represented as

(15*) $L(j,d)$.

The superlative is readily defined in terms of the comparative. For example,

(16) Jumbo is the largest elephant

is

(16*) $E(j)$ & (x) $(E(x)$ & $x \neq j \rightarrow L(j,x)$).

With these readings, as Wallace points out, the inference from (16) and

(17) Dumbo is an elephant other than Jumbo

to (15) is revealed to be valid. The intuitive connections between 'larger than' and 'largest' are tidily, finitely represented. The aim, then, is to extend this by also defining the positive in terms of the comparative. Given a finite number of comparatives, the desideratum of finiteness is met; the intuitive connections between 'is large' and 'is larger than' are exhibited; and various intuitively valid inferences may be revealed as formally valid.

This programme can be carried out in one of two crudely distinguishable ways (or some combination thereof). The *statistical* method proposes translations of 'Jumbo is a large elephant' of the kind 'Jumbo is larger than most elephants', 'Jumbo is larger than many elephants', 'Jumbo is larger than the average elephant'. (All these apparently require the addition of 'and Jumbo is an elephant' to handle the ambiguity of 'Jumbo is not a large elephant', but I omit this addition for the moment for simplicity's sake.) The non-statistical method proposes translations like 'Jumbo is larger than the typical elephant', 'Jumbo is larger than the normal elephant', 'Jumbo is larger than the standard elephant', where the object of comparison is *not* determined in any straightforward statistical manner from the present distribution of elephant sizes.

Some of the failings of the statistical approach, although not, I think, its most basic deficiency, are familiar. Consider the following possible accounts of 'Jumbo is a large elephant':

(18) Jumbo is larger than most elephants.
(19) Jumbo is larger than the average elephant.
(20) Jumbo is larger than many elephants.

If (19) were the correct account, it would be a sharp, decisive matter, at least in principle, whether Jumbo is a large elephant; but the application of the positive form of attributives is a *vague* matter, and no correct account could sharpen away the vagueness. (Cf. Crispin Wright in Evans and McDowell, *Truth and Meaning,* pp. 223–47.) This vagueness of the positive form might provide a general motive for treatment of the comparative as basic: for if the comparative is, as seems to be the case, in general *less* vague than the corresponding positive form, we might well be influenced by the thought that it is easier to *introduce* vagueness than to eliminate it. Still, whatever the worth of that motivating thought, it is clear that (19) does involve an unacceptable sharpening of the positive form. Further, unless there are a surprisingly large number of elephants of the average size, and assuming 'small' to be defined in the same way, there will not be, on this account, the requisite gap between 'large' and 'small'; usually, many elephants will be neither large nor small. (19) brings large and small elephants far too close together.

Wallace raises the first of these objections against Langford's analysis of the positive, as exemplified by (18). He remarks of this account that it 'makes the extensions of "larger than" and "elephant" determine uniquely the extension of "large elephant" '. This only follows if 'most' is treated as 'any proportion larger than n', where n is a determinate number. The obvious value for n is 0.5. This seems literally correct, even though pragmatically, perhaps through conversational implicatures, usage of 'most' is often taken to suggest a larger, and vaguer, proportion. If this literal construction of 'most' is used, we also fail to obtain the desired gap between large and small elephants: both of the failings of (19) are found in (18). A modified Langfordian analysis, aimed at meeting these first two constraints, might run along either of these lines:

(21) Jumbo is appreciably larger than most elephants

or

(22) Jumbo is larger than shmost elephants.

Here, what counts as 'appreciable' can be a vague matter, as is what proportion counts as 'shmost'; and the gap between large and small elephants is introduced assuming a similar account to be given of 'small'.

However, Wallace's second objection to Langford's original proposal will be yet more decisive against both these modified Langfordian analyses. Wallace says: 'If I manufacture a distinctive line of lawn mowers that includes a special diminutive version for midgets and children, it may very well be true that most Wallace lawn mowers are large Wallace lawn mowers.' If this is correct, (18), (21), and (22) all bite the dust.

Wallace's point here can perhaps be clarified with the help of a diagram. Imagine that the following chart is a representation of the distribution of elephants according to size:

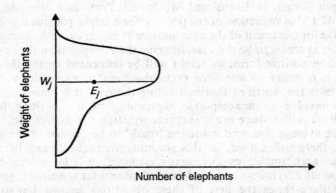

Let us call this kind of top-heavy distribution a Wallace distribution. Consider a particular elephant, E_j, of weight W_j. Because of the peculiarity of the distribution, it is not larger than most elephants; therefore it is neither appreciably larger than most nor larger than shmost. Yet, Wallace maintains, it can still be a large elephant; indeed, most elephants and even shmost elephants can be large elephants. If this claim is correct, all three of (18), (21) and (22) are wrong.

But is the claim correct? Can most, or even shmost, elephants be large elephants? Is E_j a large elephant? When we attempt to assess these claims, we encounter a difficulty; essentially, it is that of distinguishing explicit from implicit attributives. To see this, consider first the claim 'Most elephants are large'. With no views at all on the distribution of elephant sizes, most will readily assent to this. This is easily explained. Elephants are larger than most animals; elephants are large animals. When faced with the claim that most elephants are large, we tacitly consider the reference class of, say, animals, aided by the indeterminacy of the elliptical form. Which is why assent is yet more readily obtained for, say, 'Most dinosaurs were large'. Nor is the problem completely avoided by abandoning part of the ellipsis. For, to repeat, even 'Most elephants are large elephants' can be ambiguous between explicit and implicit attributive readings. It is more natural to read it as an explicit attributive, since otherwise there seems little point to the repetition of 'elephant'; but this pragmatic point cannot have an overriding logical force. Certainly, if the elephant is referred to by a proper name – say, 'Jumbo' or 'E_j' – the implicit attributive reading is readily available, even if it is not always the most natural. So it might be possible for a committed Langfordian or quasi-Langfordian to explain our assent to the possibility of most elephants being large elephants or to E_j being a large elephant as arising from a reading of the (intended) explicit construction as an implicit one, with a tacit shift in the reference class, and as therefore being quite irrelevant. Other comparable shifts in the reference class are easily imagined. Talking of improvements in child health over the last fifty years, I might say: 'Most children now are healthy children'. One natural way of taking the reference class here would be as all children in the last fifty years. More recherché reference classes are possible. Imagine a child whose previous experience of elephants is restricted to pictures of elephants isolated from background items. Taken on a tour of a Safari Park, he remarks: 'Most elephants are large'. The reference class here could be *animals*, or *animals found in this Safari Park,* or *pictures of elephants*; it might even be, crudely, *expected elephants, imagined elephants, typical elephants,* or even *possible elephants.* Another possibility would be to take the child as acquainted with different *types* of elephant, say Indian and African. What he is then asserting is that most elephants are of the larger type.

The point of this, remember, is to indicate a possible line of defence for the Langfordian, that of holding Wallace's counter-example to obtain its force only by equivocation upon the reference class. I do not have a decisive rejoinder to this defence, but I doubt if it can work *in general*. Pre-philosophically, there is something relevant to our assessment of the claim that most elephants are large in our knowledge of the distribution of the items concerned; the knowledge that a Wallace distribution obtains just does make that claim plausible. The relevance of this distributional factor is unacknowledged by the Langfordian analyses. Take, for example, my case of child health. Shifting the reference class to *children existing in the last fifty years* does not necessarily save those analyses. A population explosion could have produced a Wallace distribution, and, *knowing that,* I still assent to the claim that most children now are healthy children. I do not have a reply to the claim that either I am shifting the reference class again or my claim is false; but this is outweighed by the belief that only prior attachment to Langford's analysis could prompt this retort. I therefore tentatively agree with

177

Wallace's rejection of (18) as an analysis of (14), and am thereby led to reject also (21) and (22).

Of our initial candidates this leaves only (20), the 'many' analysis. This is given a measure of plausibility by the following distribution:

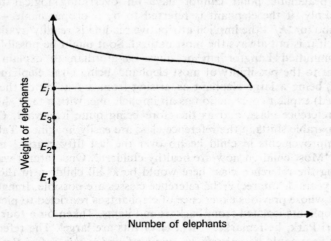

Here there are but three dwarf elephants, E_1, E_2, and E_3. Now, is Jumbo, E_j, a large elephant? He is not larger than most; but we have seen that this does not disqualify him from being a large elephant. But aside from equivocation upon the reference class, it seems that Jumbo is not a large elephant; he certainly would not be, it might be claimed, if only one of the dwarfs existed. But why isn't he? (20) as the analysis gives a neat answer: Jumbo is not larger than many elephants. Jumbo is a large elephant if and only if he is larger than many elephants.

This proposal readily handles the problems posed by the Wallace distribution. It also handles Wallace's other anxiety about the Langford analysis, the need to acknowledge vagueness in the application of the positive form. For *many* never has the sharpness that *most* literally has. What counts as sufficiently many, as a manifold, is a vague matter, determined partly by our interests in the case and partly by the size of the reference class. In most contexts, to have fifteen non-triers in a race field of thirty would be to have many non-triers in that race; but for there to be fifteen albino elephants would not usually be for there to be many albino elephants – unless, say, I have a scientific theory that precludes albino elephants.

But although this analysis handles both the Wallace distribution and the anxieties about vagueness, it obviously encounters other difficulties. In most distributions, there will be no gap between the application of 'large' and 'small', if we also accept a *many* analysis of 'small'; indeed, there will fail to be a gap in a striking way, for there may be many elephants that are both large and small on this approach. The analysis will also go wrong in a distribution that is the opposite of the Wallacian. Consider the following distribution which I shall call Plattsian:

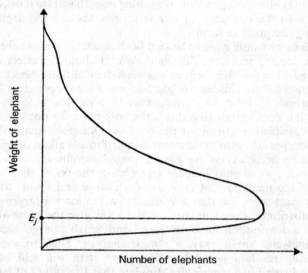

Is E_j, Jumbo, a large elephant? I take it that in any plausible account of a manifold, Jumbo will be larger than many elephants. Yet I also take it that Jumbo is not a large elephant. This bottom-heavy distribution counts against the *many* analysis just as the top-heavy distribution counted against the *most* analysis.

I can see only one remaining way of trying to save this *kind* of analysis of the positive in terms of the comparative. This is to abandon the attempt to give such an analysis without regard for the distribution of the relevant items; we specifically relativise our analysis to the kind of distribution concerned. What the positive form means depends upon that distribution.

We already have an outline account for two crudely characterised cases, the Wallacian and Plattsian distributions. In the former, the *many* analysis is correct, in the latter the *appreciably larger than most* analysis or the *shmost* analysis. So in a Wallacian distribution, this argument is valid:

Jumbo is larger than many elephants;
So Jumbo is a large elephant.

179

Whereas this argument is invalid:

> Jumbo is a large elephant;
> So Jumbo is larger than most elephants.

But in a Plattsian distribution, the second argument is valid while the first is invalid. As the meaning of the positive form varies with the kind of distribution at issue, so the validity of inferences involving that form is also so dependent. If nothing else, this at least draws our attention to the obscurity of our intuitions about valid arguments involving the positive form.

Much more would need to be said both about the precise character of these crudely indicated distributions and about the effect on the meaning of the positive form as any such distribution edges towards the normal before this idea could be turned into a concrete logical form proposal; I am very unclear as to how this is to be done, although it does appear that this is the only route for one committed to the statistical treatment of the positive. One point that will have to be incorporated into the account is this: if in a Wallace distribution of some numerous class, we gave a 'many' account for both 'large' and 'small', we should immediately obtain the result that at least some of the items in that class are both large and small; to avoid this we must recognise that a Wallace distribution for largeness is a Platts distribution for smallness. We do not give the same analysis in such a distribution for both 'large' and 'small': 'large' receives a *many*-analysis, 'small', say, a *shmost*-analysis. Then to avoid the apparently residual possibility that some item will still be both large and small, we specifically stipulate that the values of 'shmost' and 'many' must be such as to rule this out; indeed, these values must generally be such as to leave the desired gap between the large and the small, so that at least some items are neither large nor small. But however this point is formally captured, it is clear that by this point the analysis is not intuitively motivated, merely self-motivated.

It is thus clear that, fine detail aside, the statistical approach could only begin to work at the price of high artificiality. That this price is too high – especially in the absence of a detailed development of this account – is suggested by the quite evident fact that any account given along these lines will fail to connect in any way at all with how we learn the use of the positive form and with how we ground its application as competent speakers. If logical form proposals are to have any relation to learning or to understanding, this statistical approach fails; and without such relation, it is utterly unclear what the enterprise of logical form assignment is. When, finally, we notice that any statistical approach yields wildly counter-intuitive results when applied to sentences like 'Tom is more intelligent than he is kind', we shall reasonably feel entitled to abandon any such approach.

The other way of pursuing the programme of defining the positive in terms of the comparative was labelled the *non-statistical* approach. This proposed translations of 'Jumbo is a large elephant' of the following kinds:

(23) Jumbo is larger than the typical elephant.
(24) Jumbo is larger than the normal elephant.
(25) Jumbo is larger than the standard elephant.

Variants would use the relation 'is at least as large as' in place of 'is larger than'; these relations being readily interdefinable, there is no problem here. Nor is there much difficulty in seeing the kind of consideration that motivates this non-statistical approach. It is surely quite possible that *all* ballet-dancers be attractive ballet-dancers: this is because we do not assess – or, at least, need not assess – ballet-dancers by reference to their contemporaries, their ancestors, or such like. Dancing is an intentional activity with aims and purposes; central to the whole activity is a concrete set of standards. Such intentional activities can be assessed in terms of their success or failure in meeting these standards, without reference to the attainments of others. All can succeed – or all can fail. We can admit this without denying, of course, that our conception of the relevant standards may frequently be affected by the actual levels of success achieved: Nijinsky taught us something about attractive ballet-dancers, as did his namesake about attractive racehorses. Perhaps the reference to intentions, to aims and purposes, is too narrow; the sharpness of a knife can be assessed, not by reference to the intentions of the knife, but by reference to its function. The use and function of a knife determines the appropriate standard of assessment; all knives could be sharp, or none might be. Whether such references to *function* must all be grounded in considerations about human intentions – the function *given* to an item by its users – is a familiar question in the philosophy of science; but at first sight it seems that there need not be such a final grounding. Consider an *effective pancreas*: couldn't *all* pancreases be effective and efficient?

All of this is intuitively correct; but the problem with this non-statistical approach is that of finding some precise embodiment of these intuitions. We need to be told precisely *which* translation applies in a given *kind* of case, and quite *how* the 'object of comparison' is to be determined. This has never been done, such accounts have been left at a hopelessly vague level; thus it is impossible to know, for example, whether any of the failings of the statistical approach carry over to this non-statistical approach. Without much

G

more detail, this non-statistical approach, while perhaps of a certain low-level heuristic value, can be of no final substance.

One other, obvious enough, worry about these non-statistical translations is that they appear themselves to involve positive attributive constructions, constructions containing 'normal', 'standard', or 'typical': we have no understanding of what it is to be a normal, typical or standard *thing*, only of what it is to be a normal elephant, a typical Picasso painting, a standard knife. This raises an important question about the motivation behind theories that attempt to interpret the positive in terms of the comparative. The central question for any account of the positive form is: how does it handle the notion of semantic attachment? The original aim, I surmise, of theories treating the comparative as primary was this: because the comparative form does not involve semantic attachment, attributivity, such interpretation, if successful, would show there to be no real problem here; the aim, if you like, was explication by elimination. This obviously cannot work if the objects of comparison in the proposed interpretations themselves are specified using positive attributive constructions. Still, the aim might be, not to translate out all positive attributive constructions, but to reveal some basic, finite stock of such constructions out of which all other positive attributive constructions can be built. This would require a *further* account of the semantic attachment occurring in the basic stock, but would at least edge us towards a finite semantic theory of positive attributives.

This brings us, however, to a crucial point: the usually unrecognised failing of *all* theories that attempt to translate the positive in terms of the comparative. The central question is the explication of semantic attachment; the motivation, only partly achieved by non-statistical theories, is explication by elimination relying upon the absence in the comparative relation of any element of attributivity, of semantic attachment. Any such answer to the question about semantic attachment will fail simply because the comparative form is itself attributive. Sentences like 'Jumbo is larger than Dumbo' and 'Rudy is more attractive than Mischa' are themselves elliptical, are themselves hopelessly indeterminate in sense. This is readily seen by comparing them with the sentences 'Jumbo is a larger elephant than Dumbo' and 'Rudy is a more attractive ballet-dancer than Mischa'. These sentences cannot be represented merely as the conjunctions of the 'simple' comparative sentences with appropriate predications of the individuals referred to; we cannot represent

(26) Jumbo is a larger elephant than Dumbo

as

(26*) $L(j,d)$ & $E(j)$ & $E(d)$;

nor can we represent

(27) Rudy is a more attractive ballet-dancer than Mischa

as

(27*) *A (r, m) & BD (r) & BD (m)*.

For in these cases our *understanding* of the comparative relations – *is larger than* and *is more attractive than* – is critically determined, in a way left unacknowledged and unexplained by these representations, by the accompanying predicates – *is an elephant, is a ballet-dancer*. This is shown most strikingly by considering sentences like

(28) The Coliseum is a larger building than the Royal Opera House, but is not a larger theatre

and

(29) Rudy is a more attractive ballet-dancer than Mischa, but is not a more attractive dinner-companion.

For, using comparative translations like those in (26) and (27), these sentences are revealed as *contradictory*; but they are not, so the representations are wrong. Such sentences illustrate the stubborn fact of the attributivity of the comparative form: the fact that, for example, our *understanding* of the first *more attractive* in (29) is determined by the accompanying *ballet-dancer*, while our understanding of the second is determined by the accompanying *dinner-companion*. This difference in understanding is what makes the sentence possibly true, non-contradictory; and this difference in understanding is precisely grounded in the semantic attachment that still occurs in the comparative form, and that is left unacknowledged by standard theories treating the comparative as primary. Thus in the simple step of representing

(15) Jumbo is larger than Dumbo

as

(15*) *L (j,d)*

a crucial error has been made. This error is revealed most obviously by considering sentences like (28) and (29); but it is revealed also by comparing the standard representations of the comparative with the attempt to maintain that sentences like 'Theo is large' and 'Rudy is attractive' can be predicative constructions, with the dummy-filling 'thing'. Both the standard representations and that predicative claim share the failing of assuming that we have an *understanding* of the adjectival construction, have a grasp of its determinate (albeit vague)

183

meaning *in isolation from* any accompanying predication. But we have no such understanding.

5 Wheeler's Proposal

Semantic attachment occurring in both positive and comparative locutions, intertranslation will not alone suffice to elucidate this crucial semantic element. Such translations could, however, spell out the intuitive and inferential connections that considerations of finiteness require us to spell out; but the translations anyway fail. There is, however, a slightly different approach recently employed by Wheeler. This is to see the positive and comparative constructions as both being interpretable in terms of some distinct common element.

Wheeler's view is that both positive and comparative forms involve a primitive two-term relation between an individual and a class. The treatment of the positive can be illustrated by reference to

(1) Theo is a large flea

which is seen as

(1**) Large (Theo, $\hat{x}$ (x is a flea)) &
   Theo ε $\hat{x}$ (x is a flea).

The membership clause is held by Wheeler to be an addition, is not part of the meaning of the first conjunct, because of the ambiguity in the negation of (1). This means, as Wheeler acknowledges, that the two-term relation 'Large' has no natural reading in English: we cannot read the first conjunct in (1**) as 'Theo is large for a flea' since this already implies that Theo is a flea.

Wheeler's treatment of the comparative is exemplified by

(15) Jumbo is larger than Dumbo

which becomes

(15**) Large (Jumbo, $\hat{x}$ (x = Dumbo)).

There is no membership clause in this kind of comparative.

Wheeler develops his theory with great subtlety. He shows how intuitive and inferential considerations are met in terms satisfying requirements of finiteness; he also develops a novel and important account of attributive modification using expressions like 'very' and 'much'. But his account faces a number of difficulties, the first, and foremost, of which is that it does not explain semantic attachment.

We have seen reason to doubt whether *any* representation of (15) as a non-elliptical sentence could work. This is part of the general neglect of the attributivity of the comparative. Consider

(26) Jumbo is a larger elephant than Dumbo.

This presumably becomes

(26**) Large (Jumbo, $\hat{x}$ (x = Dumbo)) &
Jumbo ε $\hat{x}$ (x is an elephant) & Dumbo ε $\hat{x}$ (x is an elephant).

This is incorrect: the difference between (15) and (26) is not merely a matter of additional predications; it is, rather, the introduction of an attributively attached predicate giving the comparative adjective a determinate sense. This is yet more clearly so in the case of

(27) Rudy is a more attractive ballet-dancer than Mischa.

What hammers this home is that, like Wallace, Wheeler will be forced to view as contradictory the sentences

(28) The Coliseum is a larger building than the Royal Opera House, but is not a larger theatre

and

(29) Rudy is a more attractive ballet-dancer than Mischa, but is not a more attractive dinner-companion.

This unacceptable result is a direct consequence of the failure to see the role of semantic attachment in the comparative.

Nor is it clear that Wheeler adequately captures the attributivity of the positive form. Extensionality accompanies his usage of sets in the second place of the two-place relation. If Theo is a large creature with a heart, and if all and only creatures with hearts are creatures with kidneys, then, as Wheeler acknowledges, his analysis commits him to holding that Theo is a large creature with kidneys. The reason this causes concern reflects part of the motivation behind the non-statistical theories using the comparative to define the positive. When applying the positive, we are often concerned with, for example, the sizes of animals under normal conditions, even if these conditions virtually never obtain. But conditions might be abnormal as regards size development of creatures with kidneys, but normal, or abnormal in as it were the reverse direction, as regards size development of creatures with hearts. In such a case, the conclusion licensed by Wheeler's account can be false even though the premises are true. The semantic attachment in the positive form cannot be to a *set*. While Wheeler allows some non-extensional constructions by embedding the attributive within an intensional context, this approach does not seem plausible in this kind of case.

A further, distinct difficulty for Wheeler is the unavailability of any natural English reading for his two-place relation; this precludes the possibility of a thoroughly *austere* account in English of some

English construction underlying both positive and comparative. There is no great difficulty here, since Wheeler can simply *stipulate* that the offending implication – that the item in the first place is indeed a member of the set in the second place – does not obtain. But this worry connects with a much deeper difficulty. Wheeler's motivation for adopting his favoured, admittedly unnatural, reading of that relation is two-fold: first, his treatment of the comparative, as exemplified by (15) and (15**), clearly requires this stipulation, since when asserting that Jumbo is larger than Dumbo we do not wish to be committed to their identity; second, there is the clear ambiguity of the denial of a sentence like (1) – 'it is not the case that Theo is a large flea' – together with the three-fold ambiguity of the denial of a sentence like (26) – 'it is not the case that Jumbo is a larger elephant than Dumbo'. Since Wheeler's treatment of comparatives like (15) is mistaken, the first motivation has no force. The second is also tendentious. Why must a logical form proposal – where logical form is understood in the Davidsonian manner – reveal such ambiguities in denials of sentences? Adopting such a condition on logical form proposals seems tantamount to the demand for semantic decomposition, a demand we have seen reason to reject. But even if such a demand is reasonable – say, because some sense can be made of the claim that the ambiguities concerned are *logical* rather than semantic – it seems clear that Wheeler's way of meeting it is incorrect. The reason is simple, and connects with the point about the unavailability of any natural reading of Wheeler's two-place relations: namely, his reading (his way of recognising the ambiguity of the denials) requires that we can make sense of the claim that Jumbo is large for an elephant even though he is not himself one. Is my usual lecture-room large for a hospital ward? Am I attractive for a ballet-dancer? For a rugby-forward? Is Richard Nixon skilful for a philosopher? For a touch-typist? Such questions make no sense, and not just because of the 'offending' implication of the 'ϕ for a ψ' English construction that Wheeler wishes to deny. There are indeed *two* ways in which Jumbo can fail to be a large elephant; but one of them – his failing to be a *large* elephant – can be made sense of *only* if he has not failed the other – *only* if he is indeed an elephant. This fact seems to me strongly to support the view that attributives are predicate modifiers, expressions that operate upon a predicate to form a new predicate; but I do not have a truth-theory for predicate modifiers and so must look elsewhere.

6 Some Other Possibilities

Wheeler's account could be modified in the light of these difficulties in a number of ways. The point about the unintelligibility of his two-place relation could be met, at the price of an initial neglect of the matter of the ambiguity of denials, by adopting the usual *English* reading of the 'ϕ for a ψ' construction. The other point about positive forms – the unacceptability of the extensionality that accompanies Wheeler's reliance upon sets – could be met by modifying the second term of the (modified) two-place relation in a number of ways: we could place the predicate concerned in the second place; or we could place an expression that picks out the property picked out by that predicate, assuming that we have a reasonable semantic account of such 'property abstracts'; or, trading upon the earlier discussion comparing attributives to demonstratives, we could place a demonstrative in that second place, a demonstrative referring to an open sentence or to an utterance thereof. Thus,

(1) Theo is a large flea

might be seen as, with the non-Wheeler reading of the relation 'Large' either

(1***) Large (Theo, 'x is a flea')

or

(1****) Large (Theo, λx (x is a flea))

or

(1*****) Large (Theo, that): x is a flea.

There are a number of ways we might try to decide between these options. For (1****), as I have said, we shall clearly need an adequate truth-theoretical account of the property-abstraction device; for (1***), and for (1*****) on the reading where the demonstrative refers to the open sentence, not to its utterance, we shall need to defend the account against the standard worry that such representations distort (1) by construing it as being *about* the English language, a distortion revealed by the test of translation into another language. For these inconclusive reasons, I incline to the remaining reading of (1*****) whereby the demonstrative refers to the *utterance* of the open sentence. One *general* point at issue between (1*****) and the other two explains my vagueness in talking of sentences like 'Theo is large' being *elliptical*: the point is whether such a sentence is more correctly assimilated to a truly elliptical sentence, having no truth-conditions until the ellipsis is eliminated (which is how the first two options must view such sentences, lacking a term in the second place of the relation), or whether it is more correctly assimilable to a sentence like 'He said that', which is a complete declarative sentence, but one which requires there to be some *other* utterance, to which the demonstrative refers, before that indexical sentence can be assigned a truth-value. This is not a question with a clear intuitive answer, nor is it easy to see a significant theoretical issue in it. What is clear is that inclining to the second assimilation, to the quasi-Davidsonian reading of (1*****), we are led to see semantic attachment as a type of demonstrative construction; thus the final theory of semantic attachment, of attributivity, must wait upon a theory of that type of construction.

The extension of any of these lines of thought to the comparative attributive constructions is peculiarly difficult; I am unclear at present how the difficulties here can be overcome. Consider

(26) Jumbo is a larger elephant than Dumbo.

An initial schematic representation might be this:

(26**) More {Large (Jumbo, that), Large (Dumbo,
            that)} : x is an elephant.

This is, of course, purely schematic until we have interpreted, syntactically and semantically, the expression 'More'. Since the context it would create is both referentially transparent and non-truth-functional, it cannot, in the light of the familiar Frege argument (see p. 128 and the references there cited) be a sentential connective. Another possibility would be to borrow from Davidson's treatment of indirect discourse (see chapter V), reading (26**) in the following way

Jumbo is large for that. That is more the case than this.
Dumbo is large for that. x is an elephant.

The first and fourth demonstratives function as before; the second refers to the utterance of the first sentence, the third to the utterance of the third sentence. The reliance upon the demonstratives in the positive attributive sentences enables this proposal to avoid the discernment of contradictions in both

(28) The Coliseum is a larger building than the Royal Opera House but is not a larger theatre

and

(29) Rudy is a more attractive ballet-dancer than Mischa, but is not a more attractive dinner-companion.

Unfortunately, this will not do. The Frege argument shows that 'More' cannot be a sentence-forming operator upon pairs of sentences, just as it shows that 'He said that' in indirect discourse cannot be a sentence-forming operator upon a sentence. But there is another parallel between these idioms: just as the possibility of quantifying-in precludes Davidson's treatment of objectual discourse, so the same possibility with comparative constructions precludes this pseudo-Davidsonian treatment of the comparative. That there is such a possibility is clear: from 'Jumbo is a larger elephant than Dumbo', we can intuitively conclude that *something* is a larger elephant than Dumbo. The problem, on the present proposal, is clear: if, as the proposal suggests, 'Jumbo is a larger elephant than Dumbo' contains as a constituent the sentence 'Jumbo is a large elephant', then this constituent cannot be *asserted* but merely *said*: for Jumbo can be a larger elephant than Dumbo even though *both* are dwarfs. Restricting the quantifier to the first *said* sentence leaves it without the requisite ontological force; while appending it to the asserted sentence – there is something such that that is more the case than this – leaves the first said sentence an open sentence with no connection with the binding quantifier in the asserted sentence.

This same difficulty infects an otherwise elegant proposal, similar to Wheeler's. On this proposal, 'More' drops out of the picture, and

(26) Jumbo is a larger elephant than Dumbo

becomes

(26***) Large (Jumbo, that)): x is an elephant
      & (x is Jumbo or x is Dumbo).

(In Wheeler's terms, Jumbo is large for the set of elephants whose members are Jumbo and Dumbo.) The trouble is that the quantified-in version of this cannot be

(30*) ($\exists y$) (Large (y, that)): x is an elephant
     & (x is Jumbo or x is Dumbo)

since the name 'Jumbo' cannot occur in that sentence; but if we try to replace the *said* occurrence of Jumbo in the second sentence by a variable bound by the existential quantifier in the other sentence, the same problems arise as on the pseudo-Davidsonian proposal. Note that we cannot have a version yet closer to Wheeler's, viz:

(30**) ($\exists y$) (Large (y, that)): x is an elephant and x is Dumbo

since, although this neatly solves the problem about quantifying-in, it is incompatible with the stronger, natural reading of 'ϕ for a ψ' we have adopted. The object, Jumbo, does not satisfy the open sentence of the RHS of (31*).

189

Chapter VIII

Actions and Causes: Events

1 Understanding Action Sentences: Davidson's Proposal

At its most general, the substantial philosophical interest in the theory of meaning is this: any theory of meaning must embody a distinctive view of the relation between language and reality, and so of reality itself. Neutrality is not a possibility here. One way of assessing the plausibility of the view held of the relation between language and reality in a theory of meaning is to consider whether that view issues in an acceptable account of the competent speakers' understanding of their language.

That is a matter to which we shall turn in the final part of this book. But there is a more modest, though connected, matter to be considered first. Given a favoured general form of a theory of meaning, and supposing it to issue in a plausible general view of understanding, there remains the question of its proper application to particular locutions occurring in a language under study. This has been our concern in the preceding chapters in Part Two. But one matter arising out of such applications deserves a little more attention: this is the question of whether an application of the theory to a particular locution itself issues in a plausible account of native speakers' understanding *of that particular locution*. This seems a much more modest question than that about the general form of understanding embodied in a theory of meaning; but we have seen reason to doubt whether this modesty is matched by simplicity. Natural language use is *unreflective*: speakers just *say* things, and audiences just manifest their understanding by responding appropriately, in verbal or non-verbal ways. There is nothing yet to suggest an intuitive, pre-theoretical understanding by which applications of the general theory can be tested. Still, against this, there is a persistent tendency to believe that competent speakers – though not necessarily *all* competent speakers – do indeed have some privileged insight into the semantic structure of their own language.

The present chapter is concerned, in part, with the assessment of both the truth and the utility of this persistent tendency. The discussion is focused upon Davidson's proposals for the incorporation of action sentences within a truth-theoretical semantics (Davidson, 'The Logical Form of Action Sentences'); for this proposal has been deemed precisely to falsify native English speakers' understanding of the semantic structure of such sentences (Strawson, *Freedom and Resentment,* pp. 198–207; also in Evans and McDowell, *Truth and Meaning,* pp. 189–98). Our concern is not to consider the final acceptability of Davidson's proposal, but merely to consider whether this charge of falsification of native understanding has yet been substantiated. Doing so should clarify the general, modest question about the relation between applications of a semantic theory and speakers' understanding.

Consider a sentence like

(1) John kicked Bill.

Grammatically, and intuitively, this appears to be a simple relational sentence, of the form

(1*) *Rab*

where *R* is the relation of kicking, '*a*' is 'John', and '*b*' is 'Bill'.

Consider, however, a sentence involving adverbial modification, like

(2) John kicked Bill at 3 p.m.

Keeping to the idea that this, like (1), is a singular relational sentence, we shall treat it as involving a *three*-place relation, that of kicking at such-and-such a time, we might thus represent it as

(2*) *R'abc*

where *R'* is this new three-place relation and '*c*' is '3 p.m.'. Then considering

(3) John kicked Bill at 3 p.m. in the greenhouse

we shall treat it as involving a four-place relation, the whole sentence being represented as

(3*) *R''abcd*

where *R''* is this four-place relation, kicking at . . . in . . . , and '*d*' is 'the greenhouse'.

It is not difficult to see the problems with this approach. First, since *R*, *R'*, and *R''* are distinct, primitive relations, the validity of the inferences from (3) to (2) to (1) is not revealed. Still, we have seen that it is no condition of acceptability of a logical form proposal that it reveal all pre-philosophically valid inferences *as* valid; the condition is, rather, that such proposals should not (at least generally) *preclude* such validation. It might seem an easy enough task to insert a rule into the meta-language licensing the moves from (3) to (2) to (1) for the set of relations there occurring (with, perhaps, an exclusion clause upon certain *kinds* of adverbial modifiers).

This leads, however, to a second difficulty. It is not clear that there is any specifiable limit upon the number of *kinds* of adverbial modifiers which can sensibly be attached to distinct action sentences involving the 'same' kind of action. If there is no such limit, then treatment of each distinctly modified sentence as involving a distinct primitive relation will offend against the condition of finiteness: we shall be crediting speakers with a competence in the application of an indefinitely large number of primitive relations, a competence that we cannot (finitely) describe, let alone explain. Likewise, the list of additional meta-linguistic rules designed to meet the first anxiety will be indefinitely large, a list we could never complete. This is still indecisive, however, since there is no general reason as yet to believe the premiss of these arguments: viz. that there is no specifiable limit upon the *kinds* of adverbial modifiers within the language.

It is tempting, though not unproblematic, to rely upon a third worry to dismiss this kind of treatment of adverbial modification. Surely, as *reflective* speakers of English, as English-speaking semantic theorists of English, we *understand* (1), (2) and (3) as involving a common, semantically significant element, 'kicked'. As reflective theorists, we account for our understanding of these sentences through our (reflective) discernment of the words they contain, part of this process seizing upon the common contribution of the word 'kicked'. It is not, if you like, a *typographical accident* that that word occurs in each sentence, as it is, for our purposes, a typographical accident that the symbol 'can' occurs in 'You can do it if you try', 'Tom bought a can of beans', and 'The canary is singing'. This common element is not acknowledged in the treatment of adverbs being considered: the typographic fact that '*R*' occurs in '*R*', '*R''*', and '*R'''*' is not enough, for each of these is treated as an unstructured, primitive relation. The further thought is then that it is this semantically significant common element that explains, or figures essentially in any explanation of, our grasp upon the inferences from (3) to (2) to (1), and which reveals as spurious the threat of an infinite number of unstructured primitive relations.

At this stage of play, this cannot be a decisive objection. Either the understanding, the recognition, of the role of this common element is founded (at least partly) upon our competence as English speakers or it is not. The idea that it is so founded seems in tension with the unreflective character of natural language use; until more is said about the elimination of that apparent tension, that idea seems empty; while if our recognitional capacity is not so founded – if our natural linguistic competence does not give us *any* privileged insight into the significant semantic structure of English sentences – the objection is simply a bland assertion of the rejection of the treatment of adverbial modification proposed.

Suppose, however, that we underestimate the problems associated with talk of recognition of significant semantic structure within our own language; then we shall seek for some way of revealing the supposedly recognised common element in sentences like

(1) John kicked Bill.
(2) John kicked Bill at 3 p.m.
(3) John kicked Bill at 3 p.m. in the greenhouse.

Donald Davidson has put forward such a proposal, one which, revealing the common element, validates the requisite inferences in a manner meeting the requirement of finiteness. His idea, roughly, is to treat sentences like (1), (2), and (3) as existentially quantified, with the quantifier ranging over events; thus an extra place, for the bound variable, is introduced into each of the relations apparently involved in (1), (2), and (3). So (1) becomes

(1**) $(\exists u)$ $(Rabu)$

or, informally, '$(\exists u)$ (kicked (John, Bill, u))': 'there was an event which was a kicking of Bill by John'.

Adverbial modification is treated as the conjunction with (1) of an appropriate relation between events and the item (or items) specified by the modification; prepositions are seized upon as the standard surface embodiments of such relations. For example, (2) becomes

(2**) $(\exists u)$ $(Rabu \ \& \ ATcu)$;

informally, '$(\exists u)$ (kicked (John Bill, u) $\& \ AT$ (3 p.m., u))'
while (3) becomes seen as

(3**) $(\exists u)$ $(Rabu \ \& \ ATcu \ \& \ INdu)$

or,

'$(\exists u)$ (kicked (John, Bill, u) $\& \ AT$ (3 p.m., u) $\& \ IN$ (the greenhouse, u))'.

More informally still, (3) becomes: 'There was an event which was a kicking of Bill by John; that event occurred at 3 p.m.; and that event took place in the greenhouse.'

In this proposal, the common element in (1), (2) and (3) – the three-place relation R – is revealed, though it is worth noting that it is difficult to find natural English expression for this relation.[1] The inferences from (3) to (2) to (1) are immediately revealed as valid in virtue of &-elimination. Requirements of finiteness, in point both of primitive vocabulary and of inferential axioms, are tidily met.

In fact, as Davidson points out, common structure is revealed within verbs which, aside from consideration of *obvious* adverbial modification, might be handled without such common structure being revealed. Consider, for example,

(4) Amundsen flew to the pole

and

(5) Amundsen flew away from the pole.

Initially, we might be tempted to treat these as involving unstructured distinct verbs, 'to fly to' and 'to fly from'. Doing so, we shall represent them as

(4*) *Sab*

where 'S' is 'flew to', 'a' is 'Amundsen', and 'b' is 'the pole', and

(5*) *S'ab*

where 'S''' is 'flew from'. But bearing in mind Davidson's treatments of (1), (2) and (3), we might notice, first, the possibility of sentences containing the 'simple' verb 'to fly' – 'Theaetetus flies' – and, second, the validity of the inference from (4) or (5) to

(6) Amundsen flew.

We shall thus be led to reveal more significant structure within the sentences (4) and (5), focusing upon the (unobvious) role of prepositions in those sentences. Thus we might have

(4**) $(\exists u)$ (*Rau* & *TO* (the pole, u))

and

(5**) $(\exists u)$ (*Rau* & *FROM* (the pole, u)).

There is then no problem in handling sentences like 'Amundsen flew to the pole in 1906 and from it in 1907'. But, of course, the question still remains open of whether we are *required*, by considerations of finiteness or of understanding, to 'reveal' this 'significant semantic structure'.

Two points should be noted about Davidson's proposal. First,

---

[1] This will be a serious problem if austerity is required in the semantic axioms for such relational expressions.

objectual quantification over events requires that events be particulars. It is therefore incumbent upon anyone using such quantification that he take this *particularity* claim seriously and provide identity and individuation conditions for these particulars. For reasons we need not pursue – they quickly emerge if the project is attempted – reference to spatio-temporal location and path, the ground of material object identity, proves useless. Some other tack is required. The proposal favoured by Davidson is this: two designating expressions refer to the same event if, and only if, the event referred to by the one designator has the same causal ancestry and the same causal consequences as that referred to by the other designator (Davidson, 'The Individuation of Events').

'Same', in 'same causal ancestry and same causal consequences', cannot mean merely *qualitative similarity*: worlds in which there are parallel, qualitatively indistinguishable universes or in which there is a uniformly cyclical, qualitatively repetitive universe show the Davidsonian condition to be inadequate on this reading. So 'same' must mean *identical*. This requires, in turn, that we be given identity conditions for causes and effects. Davidson faces an apparent problem here, since, as we shall see later, he holds that causes and effects are also events. Circularity apparently threatens: to know whether an event referred to by one designator is identical to that referred to by another, we have to establish whether there is identity of causal ancestry and causal consequences, which is itself a matter of establishing whether there is identity of *sets* of events. But this appearance of problematic circularity might be illusory. Consider material objects: the ground of the identity of one such particular object is spatio-temporal continuity (though not just *any* such continuity) (cf. Wiggins, *Identity and Spatio-temporal Continuity*) To apply this, to determine whether two designators refer to the same material object, we obviously need to determine the spatio-temporal route of each designation. To do this, we need to *fix* the spatio-temporal framework. How do we do this? By identifying and reidentifying *other* material objects! Such circularity as there is here is unavoidable given that *material object* is a *basic* category of classification of particulars; a 'non-circular' account could only be given if the identity conditions for material objects could be given in terms of some other, independent category of particulars – which would just be to say that *material object* would not then be a basic, but a derived, category of particulars. Likewise, the defence against the circularity charge brought against Davidson's proposal for the identity-conditions for events is simply that it ignores the possibility that *event*, too, is a basic category of particular. For such a category, as the material object case shows, the discerned degree of circularity is unavoidable, what matters is that in both cases the circularity falls well short of a formal circularity in that the identity-conditions proposed do not presuppose the *particular* identity statement under consideration.

There are, of course, arguments that purport to show that *event* is a derived, not a basic, category, and which hence purport to show that the degree of circularity present in Davidson's account is still unacceptable. But since such arguments are dubious members of a doubtful species ('transcendental arguments'), this need not delay us. Likewise, we need not worry about the consequence of Davidson's proposal that *all* events lacking in both causal ancestry and causal consequences will be deemed one and the same event; such a consideration is somewhat recherché, and, anyway, the role played by causality in empirical knowledge ensures that such events could never be known.

The second point to notice about Davidson's proposal is that it is unclear how it is to be applied to adverbial modifiers like 'slowly' and 'deliberately'. The problem with 'slowly' is that it is *attributive*; under one description, an action, or set of actions, can be done slowly, under another quickly: 'She crossed the Channel in eight hours'; 'God, that was slow'; 'She was swimming'; 'God, that was quick!'.[2] The problem with 'deliberately' is that it is both intensional and intentional, ultimately making reference to the agent's mental states. Both of these cases illustrate serious general problems, although the remarks made earlier about attributive adjectives shed some light upon the first kind of case, and it may also be that Davidson's treatment of indirect discourse sheds some, more indirect, light upon the second. Doubtless, it would also help to have some *general* characterisations of such cases other than 'those to which the theory does not apply', along with, or embodying, some explanation of why the theory does not so apply. But there anyway seems to be everything to be said for *first* pursuing the apparently straightforward cases of adverbial modification.

2 Understanding Action Sentences: Some Problems[3]

A general worry about Davidson's proposal might be put like this. The account is motivated by the fact that the initial proposal considered – that treating action sentences involving distinct adverbial modifiers as involving distinct, independent relations – fails to acknowledge our intuitive recognition of, for example, 'kicked' as a

[2] Cf. Reichenbach, *Elements of Symbolic Logic*, pp. 301–8, where the problems here discussed are first raised.
[3] This section is partly meant as part of a reply to Strawson, *Freedom and Resentment*, pp. 198–207; another part of the reply is found in the considerations adduced in the second half of Chapter IX.

common, semantically significant element in (1), (2) and (3). Thus starting from intuitive understanding, the Davidson proposal cannot, *without further consideration*, proceed to flout it; and flout it the proposal apparently does. It does so by treating action sentences, with or without adverbial modification, as *general* sentences, as existentially quantified sentences, whereas initial intuitive understanding suggests that each such sentence is a singular, non-quantified sentence.

Of course, if the only alternative account were the initial, primitive relations treatment, this anxiety could not be decisive; for that initial account is held to offend against intuition too. But it is not clear that that account is the only way of holding to the view that action sentences are singular sentences. An alternative, similar to the possibility for attributive adjectives, would be to view adverbs as predicate modifiers, as expressions which, like predicate negation, operate upon a predicate to form another predicate. We begin with

(1) John kicked Bill

represented, as before, as

(1*) *Rab.*

But instead of treating

(2) John kicked Bill at 3 p.m.

as involving a distinct, independent relation, we see 'at 3 p.m.' as modifying the predicate 'kicked' to form a compound, structured, still two-place relation 'kicked at 3 p.m.'. Similarly with 'in the greenhouse' in

(3) John kicked Bill at 3 p.m. in the greenhouse.

Precisely because the predicates involved in (2) and (3) are now *structured*, are built up, by predicate modification, out of that involved in (1), the initial intuitive recognition of the element common to (1), (2) and (3) is acknowledged; but each of the sentences remains a singular sentence.

It is an open question whether it will prove possible to incorporate such predicate modifications within an acceptable truth-theory. It is unclear – just as it is unclear whether the initial, primitive relation treatment can meet the requirement of finiteness – whether a theory of predicate modification will be *required* to treat modifiers like 'at 3 p.m.' and 'in the greenhouse' as themselves structured, as being instances of schematic modifiers 'at . . .' and 'in . . .'. It is clear that while a truth-theory for predicate modifiers need not validate inferences like that from (2) to (1), it must not block the possibility of such validation by means of a finite number of validating axioms.

197

For our present theoretical purposes, fortunately, we need not wait upon the answer to the question of quite how, if at all, predicate modification is to be incorporated into an acceptable truth-theory. What matters is that the roughest idea of what such a theory would be like is sufficient to highlight the distinctive feature of Davidson's theory, that it treats action sentences as generalised, existentially quantified sentences. That rough idea is therefore sufficient to highlight the anxiety that Davidson's proposal falsifies our intuitive understanding of such sentences.

I have repeatedly expressed doubts about the worth of the claim that there is such an intuitive understanding; such understanding is accessible to us only as theorists, not as native speakers, for as native speakers we do not *work out* the meanings of sentences, and so do not discern the structure *needed* to work out, explicitly and reflectively, the meanings of sentences. But it is anyway worth seeing that a less extreme position, one which acknowledges (dubiously) and gives some weight to (dubiously) native speakers' semantic intuitions can still be compatible with the rejection of this worry about Davidson's proposals.

Davidson treats all action sentences as generalised, quantified sentences. Thus, on that treatment,

(1) John kicked Bill

could be true in virtue of any number of actions on John's part. Put like that, however, the point seems perfectly intuitive. The *range* of actions that could make such a sentence true can be, as it were, *reduced* through adverbial modification. Thus

(7) John kicked Bill in the greenhouse

can still be true in virtue of any number of actions on John's part, albeit a reduced range. While perhaps

(8) John kicked Bill in the greenhouse at exactly 3 p.m. on the 12 of March 1976

can be true only in virtue of *one* action of John's.[4] Exact time modification can ensure that, even though the sentence is a generalised, existentially quantified sentence, it can be true only in virtue of one action. But the sentence is still generalised. If very fully specified, the existentially quantified sentence will be made true by just *one* action; nevertheless, the sentence does not refer to some *particular* action since *any* action meeting the appropriate specification will do to make the sentence true.

Even, then, with such a full specification of the action, the Davidsonian treatment conflicts with the posited intuition that such sentences are singular, unquantified sentences: the intuition, that is,

[4] Assuming him to be one-legged.

198

that such sentences purport to refer to some one, particular action, not to any (perhaps unique) action satisfying the description given.

Put like that, however, both the existence and the worth of the intuition seem doubtful. Once the possibility that (1) could be true in virtue of any number of actions is pointed out, native speakers of English apparently see the point immediately. The only thing that might obscure this perception is a failure to distinguish what the *sentence* literally means, its literal truth-conditions, from what a particular *speaker* meant upon a particular occasion of utterance of that sentence. A sentence like (1) refers to *any* action meeting the appropriate description; a speaker uttering it might mean himself to refer to some particular action (meeting the appropriate description). The idea that a *sentence* like (1) purports to refer to some *particular* action has no intuitive appeal except for those whose (cloudy) intuitions fail to distinguish the semantic properties of a sentence from the communicative content that speakers standardly intend to transmit by an utterance of it. Our concern, all along, has been with sentences and their truth-conditions, not with what is *meant*, or what is *understood* as being meant, by a particular speaker on a specified occasion of utterance; for, in general, the literal meaning of a sentence, its literal truth-conditions, are an indispensable element in any explicitly formulated *route* to a speaker's communicative intentions. Of course, we need then to go on to show how a sentence with the specified truth-conditions can fulfil its role as part of that route; but there seems no reason to believe that Davidson's proposal could not be shown to satisfy this requirement.

If the objection is strengthened to the claim that speakers do not understand such sentences as involving the existential quantifier, and may not even be capable of doing so, the rejoinder is that this is quite beside the point. The claim that speakers understand these sentences as involving, say, predicate modification is no more plausible. Ordinary speakers have no such understanding, or misunderstanding, for such understanding is highly theoretical. If the issue moves beyond that of the general or singular character of sentences like (1), (2) and (3), it moves into the realm of theoretically founded ('educated') intuitions, and becomes quite irrelevant. While if the issue remains within the minimally theoretical area of singular *versus* general, the objection turns back upon itself.

Nor, for parallel reasons, will it help to focus upon speakers' intuitive understanding of the *grammar* of their language, even assuming there to be an area of understanding here distinct from the semantic. For such understanding, as a form of potentially expressible intuitions about the grammatical structure of the language, is either lacking, its positing being an (unsuccessful) act of wish-fulfilment, or is highly theoretical in character, being just as readily

199

accessible to the non-native linguistic theorist. As before, reference to 'what every speaker knows' proves vacuous (cf. Nagel, 'The Boundaries of Inner Space', and Stich, 'What Every Speaker Knows').

Even the modest concessions just made to those wishing to emphasise native understanding are dangerously excessive. Of course, native speakers *understand* their language. But they do so in a quite unreflective way, the manifestation of their understanding being the successful *use* of language both in making utterances and in responding appropriately to utterances. If we wish to detect in this practice a pool of potential evidence for assessing semantic proposals, we must be careful to shun both pseudo-psychological claims about how speakers constructively recognise the meanings of sentences from recognition of their components and their semantic structure, and also the temptation to prompt speakers into making explicit various 'implicit' propositional knowledge claims about their language. Either procedure is founded upon a false view of the phenomenology of language use, an undue psychologism, together with an incoherent conception of psychological processes.

If there is any content to talk of native understanding, other than that manifested by the success of ordinary linguistic exhange, it will receive *its* manifestation in further, observable facts of linguistic practice. Two *possible* areas of such observation are the circumstances of language acquisition and the procedures employed in determining the truth-values of sentences of various kinds. So, for example, observation of the methods of learning attributive constructions along with observations of the ways employed in determining the truth-values of such constructions count heavily against the attempt statistically to define the positive in terms of the comparative using the device of relativising the significance of the positive form to the kind of distribution of the relevant property found in the items concerned. Neither possible area of supplementation is unproblematic: the *relevance* of methods of language acquisition is not as obvious as it might casually seem, and reference to such methods produces a dangerous tendency towards (incoherent) psychologism; while reference to procedures for determining truth-values of sentences both introduces ominously idealistic elements of verificationism, and also encounters grave difficulties in the form of the familiar Quinean point that the procedures adopted are determined in part by the speakers' *beliefs*. Still, such procedures are *observable*, and are accessible in the same way to both native speakers and theoretical semanticists alike; the evidence they provide is therefore at least of the right, non-intuitive kind.

If we had an acceptable truth-theoretic account of predicate modification, I doubt whether the insight we might thus gain into

200

speakers' non-explicit understanding would settle the issue between that theory and Davidson's. But just because both such accounts can be incorporated within an adequate truth-theory, it does not follow that they can be incorporated with the same degree of ease. Such incorporation ultimately requires that there be a mapping of the underlying semantic structure on to 'surface elements' found in the ordinary English sentences; that mapping must finally *yield* the English surface sentence for each proposed semantic structure of that sentence. Now, it is obvious that the greater the disparity between underlying semantic structure and surface sentence, the greater will be the complexity of this mapping.[5] On Davidson's approach, for example, we shall need procedures that map, or transform, or systematically eliminate, each of the elements in the existentially quantified sentence on to elements of English so as to yield the appropriate surface English sentence. The same would have to be done for the predicate-modifier theory, if we had it. But it is clear that, precisely because the predicate-modifier account is closer to the surface English structure – it does not, for example, posit the additional underlying apparatus of quantifiers and bound variables – the combination of mapping, transformation and elimination rules will be far simpler for that theory. If, then, both theories are found to be adequate in handling truth-theoretic, inferential, and non-explicit understanding requirements, we can decide between them upon grounds of simplicity and technical ease. Like any other exercise in empirical theory-construction, our final decision may reasonably come to rest upon those, admittedly vague, considerations.

3 The Logical Form of Singular Causal Sentences

Logical form proposals carry more general philosophical consequences about ontology – as exemplified by the positing of events in Davidson's treatment of action sentences. It follows, then, that such proposals can be affected by arguments designed to show the derivative, non-basic character of various ontological elements. But, equally, if the only plausible semantic treatment of some locution requires a particular ontology, and if that locution is one we are reluctant to discard as incoherent, then we shall view with scepticism any arguments designed to establish the unacceptability of that ontology. The interaction is reciprocal.

A more difficult matter to become clear on is the relation between the activities of formal semanticists in considering specific locutions

---

[5] This matter arises, of course, for nearly all the logical form proposals previously discussed; I have merely chosen to postpone consideration of it until now.

and the epistemological issues, if any, associated with these locutions. One route to a partial view on this is provided by Davidson's proposals for the semantics of causal discourse, proposals with obvious similarities to those he presents for action sentences (Davidson, 'Causal Relations'). Again, we shall not be concerned with the final assessment of Davidson's proposals, using them, rather, as a stepping-stone to a view upon the more general issue of the epistemological connections of claims as to logical form.

Consider, first, a singular causal statement like

(9) The short-circuit caused the fire.

Unsurprisingly, traditional discussions of such a sentence have not been geared towards a logical form proposal, in our sense of that expression. Rather, the concern has been with the (vaguer) question of how the concept of causality occurring in it is to be understood. One long-standing approach to this has been founded upon the notion of necessary and sufficient conditions. We start from the (mistaken) thought that (9) says that the short-circuit was both a necessary and a sufficient condition of the fire's occurring: if the short-circuit had not occurred, the fire would not have occurred; and if the short-circuit did occur, the fire also occurred. We then realise, first, that the short-circuit cannot be a literally sufficient condition, that the short-circuit could occur without the fire occurring: for many other conditions are also needed, like the presence of oxygen, of inflammable material, and the absence of automatic fire-extinguishers. Second, we see that the short-circuit is not literally a necessary condition of the fire's occurring, that the fire could occur even though the short-circuit did not: for the fire could have been caused in many other ways. We are thus quickly led to the most plausible form of this kind of account: (9) says that the occurrence of the short-circuit was an INUS-condition of the fire occurring, an insufficient but necessary part of a condition that was itself an unnecessary but sufficient condition of the fire occurring.

This idea has been developed with great sophistication (see, e.g. Mackie in Sosa, *Causation and Conditionals,* pp. 15–38). But this idea was not developed within our favoured framework; it is therefore an open question whether it is of any use in handling our primary concern, that of the logical form of singular causal statements.

If discussions of this idea are to be construed (or misconstrued) as bearing upon the question of logical form assignment, the clue to that bearing will be found in the opaque notion of a *condition* there invoked. As my gloss upon talk of necessary and sufficient conditions suggests, that notion can apparently only be understood through the notion of a *conditional*. The thought must be understood (or misunderstood) as being that (9), contrary to surface appearances, is a *conditional* sentence of some kind, it must involve sentential components, since these are what conditionals connect. So, for example, (9) may better be written as, say,

(10) *The fact that* there was a short-circuit *caused it to be the case that* there was a fire.

The italicised components must be taken to be the conditional sentential connective required by any analysis invoking the notion of a *condition* in the account of causality; and if that analysis is to be construed (or misconstrued) as a logical form proposal, then that italicised sentential connective must be part of the logical form of singular causal sentences.

We need to be told at least two things before this proposal can be of any substantial interest. Quite what kind of conditional is involved in (10)? And quite what kinds of entity does this approach reveal causes and effects to be in virtue of their (*ex hypothesi*, most pellucid) specification by *sentences*? Unfortunately, as Davidson points out, it is utterly unclear that there is any kind of conditional that the italicised component in (10) can be plausibly construed as being, especially in view of the fact that (10) commits its asserter to the truth of both the 'antecedent' and the 'consequent'. Further, the Frege argument suggests that there cannot be any kind of sentential connective in (10), conditional or otherwise, for (10) is extensional for singular terms, but is not truth-functional. Connectedly, it is unclear that there is *any* kind of entity that the sentential components occurring in (10) can plausibly be construed as *naming*, for the idea that complete, asserted sentences name anything is of doubtful coherence.

If convinced by (detailed elaboration of) these points, we shall be led to reject the idea that singular causal statements can be represented, for purposes of logical form assignment, as conditionals of any kind. We shall thus see the rewriting of (9) as (10), which suggests the presence of such a conditional element, as misleading; (10) is further from the logical form of singular causal statements than (9). We see here a general difficulty facing claims, like those discussed in the context of action sentences, that a logical form proposal takes us far, perhaps too far, from the surface structure of the English sentences they represent. Let us suppose (9) and (10) to be equivalent in meaning; then whether a logical form proposal takes us far from the surface structure will depend upon *which* of the (*ex hypothesi* equivalent) (9) and (10) we are considering. Only if there is *no* way within ordinary English of expressing the sentence under examination in a way closely connected with the logical form proposal could this worry have any force: although even then, it does not yet follow that the proposal is mistaken, merely that it will be somewhat complicated in its final form.

(9) appears to be a simple relational sentence, asserting a relation between the items picked out by the noun-phrases occurring in it. That relation is that of *causing*; for purposes of logical form assignment, it does not matter whether we yet say any more about how that relation is to be analysed. It is an open question whether we can give some informative, decompositional analysis of it or whether we must rest with an austere, 'uninformative' axiom for it; and if the latter, it is an open question whether we can provide a useful *gloss*, or useful glosses, upon it. Such a reading of (9) already identifies the *kind* of contribution 'caused' makes to (9), namely the kind found in all two-place predicates. But we also have to consider the *relata*, the question of the *kind* of item picked out by the noun-phrases occurring in it, the kind of item this relation obtains between. An obvious enough thought is: events. What else could those noun-phrases refer to, and what else could be a more natural understanding of causes and effects? Lacking argument, we are, of course, vulnerable to the overlooked possibility; but until alternatives are spelt out, and provided with adequate identity and individuation conditions, this need hardly concern us.

The presence of the definite articles in (9) suggests that the noun-phrases pick out particular events. Since the descriptions of the events picked out are far from complete, we cannot use Russell's treatment of definite descriptions in handling those phrases (cf. pp. 152–5). My earlier discussion suggests that we should, somehow, invoke demonstratives in handling them. However, I shall now follow Davidson, for heuristic purposes, in handling those noun-phrases in a different way. Let us introduce a primitive operator, the Fregean description operator, which forms a uniquely referring description out of a predicate or set of predicates. Thus '$(\imath e)$ (short-circuit (e))' is a noun-phrase equivalent to 'The one and only short-circuit'. The precise semantics of this operator is of considerable importance, but, for present purposes, need not delay us (see Barry Taylor in Evans and McDowell, *Truth and Meaning*). Using this operator, (9) becomes

(9*) $(\imath e)$ (Short-circuit (e)) caused$(\imath e)$ (fire (e)).

Some sentences, similar to (9), are, to different degrees of obviousness, to be treated rather differently because of their *general* character. For example,

(11) A short-circuit caused a fire

is to be

(11*) $(\exists e)$ $(\exists e')$ (Short-circuit (e) & Fire (e') & e caused e').

We thus immediately validate the inference from (11) to

(12) A short-circuit caused something

and to

(13) Something caused a fire

by dropping either the middle or the first conjunct in (11*). By analogy with the treatment of adverbs, we also validate the inference from

(14) A short-circuit at midnight caused a fire in the greenhouse

to (11) by treating (14) as

(14*) $(\exists e)$ $(\exists e')$ (Short-circuit (e) & AT(midnight, e) & Fire (e') & IN (the greenhouse, e') & e caused e').

An example of a less obviously general, but still general, sentence is

(15) Jack fell down which caused it to be the case that Jack broke his crown.

For, once it is pointed out, it is quite clear that (15) can be true in virtue of any number of fallings of Jack and consequent breakings of Jack's crown; as before, only a failure to distinguish what (15) means from what speakers standardly mean by its utterance could mask this point. Sentences like (15), even with a more complete (perhaps sufficient to guarantee uniqueness) specification of the pairs of events, are general, existentially quantified sentences.

The logical form of singular causal statements does not include a sentential connective, conditional or otherwise; rather, they are relational sentences. There is therefore no question of conditional relations of necessity and sufficiency obtaining between causes and effects illuminating that logical form. But it does not follow that questions about necessity and sufficiency relations do not arise; nor does it follow that traditional discussions in terms of necessary and sufficient conditions have no role to play in an understanding of singular causal statements.

Causes and effects are events. Events are identified in terms of their causal ancestry and causal consequences. Given these (non-trivial) claims, it (trivially) follows that the cause, as a particular event, is both necessary and sufficient for the effect as a particular event. If the cause-event had *not* produced the effect-event, it would not have been the event it was. Likewise, given that *that* event (the effect) occurred, then *that* (the cause) event must have occurred (and must have caused the effect-event), since otherwise the effect-event would have been a different event. Thus the identity-conditions for events introduce into our understanding *of* those events, of the designations of the referring expressions, the notion of a necessary and sufficient condition; but that does not show that a singular causal statement itself involves a conditional connective in its logical form.

If the initial line of thought that led us to replace the relation of a necessary and sufficient condition by that of an INUS-condition is construed as denying this, it must be mistaken. It is not difficult to see how, *so construed*, the mistakes occur. The US-element was prompted by the thought that, for example, the fire referred to in

(9) The short-circuit caused the fire

could have been caused in some other way. But the nature of events, as embodied in their identity-conditions, shows that this very fire could not have been caused in some other way, even if a qualitatively indistinguishable fire could have been. The IN-element was prompted by the thought that much else, besides the occurrence of the short-circuit, had to be the case before the fire would occur. But the event picked out by the description used – 'the short-circuit' – *is* the event it is in virtue of its causal consequences; these consequences do indeed depend upon the *other* conditions adduced – the presence of oxygen, and so forth; but *that* is to say that this event, the cause, is the event it is *in virtue of* these other conditions. We need not, and usually do not, mention all these other conditions in our specification of the cause-event. But to *reduce* the *description* of that event, or to add to it, is still to talk about that same event – the event that occurred in the presence of oxygen, and so forth. Just as, to reduce, or to add to, the description of a particular material object is still to talk about the *same* material object. Events are not linguistically dependent entities, and their identity-conditions do not hang upon, and change with, the description used to pick them out. To pick them out is not just to *pick* them out: it is also to pick *them* out.

This rejoinder to the argument for the INUS-analysis misses the point of that argument, however, by mislocating it. And this location of the notion of a necessary and sufficient condition is a mislocation given the aims of those who have wished to invoke it in accounting for our understanding of singular causal statements. For conditions theorists have always had a distinct, epistemological question in mind.

4 Singular Causal Statements: Logical Form and Epistemology

One minor anxiety about the preceding is this. The claim is made that there is a great deal of *latitude* open to us in the description of cause and effect; but nothing has yet been said as to what determines the particular descriptions of cause and effect used upon a particular occasion of utterance. Why do we pick out the cause-event referred to in

(9) The short-circuit caused the fire

by 'the short-circuit' rather than by 'the presence of oxygen' or 'the absence of fire-extinguishing equipment'? The answer is that this depends upon our interests and beliefs. If we are concerned with the ascription of responsibility, in some quasi-moral sense, we shall often be concerned with, and shall be inclined to pick out the cause-event by reference to, any *unexpected* aspect stemming from human agency (cf. Mackie, 'Responsibility and Language'). If we are theoretical scientists, we shall be concerned with the most general explanatory factors. If we are practical engineers, we shall focus upon the most *controllable* elements. And so on. The claim that there is this latitude in choice of event-description, if true, is of semantic importance; but the further question of how we choose within that range is not of evident *semantic* importance. Semanticists need not be insurance investigators.

There is a much more substantial worry about the preceding discussion. The claim that the cause-event is both necessary and sufficient for the effect-event is a simple consequence of Davidson's account of event-identity. But there are epistemological questions left unresolved by this formal answer. The account so far given does not enable us to *detect* causal relations between events. Suppose events e_1 and e_2 occur in succession. Suppose, further, that e_1 causes e_2. Then the preceding tells us this: if this causal relation between e_1 and e_2 did not obtain, then, so to speak, e_1 and e_2 would have been different events; but it is consistent with the foregoing to say that *qualitatively indistinguishable* events e'_1 and e'_2 could have occurred in succession without standing in this causal relation to one another, assuming that the causal ancestries and causal consequences of events are not, in this context, to figure as *qualities* of events. So given that e_1, qualitatively identified, occurred and given that e_2, qualitatively identified, occurred, we cannot *know* that e_1 caused e_2; for all we know, it was not e_1 and e_2 but e'_1 and e'_2. Likewise, given that e_1 occurs, we cannot yet predict that *because* of that, e_2 will occur; for all we know, it was not e_1 but e'_1 that we observed. It clearly will not help, in this context, to extend the notion of the qualities of an event to include its causal ancestry and causal consequences; for these are precisely what we are attempting to discover.

There is everything to be said for sharply distinguishing semantic from epistemological problems. But there is also everything to be said for holding that any *final* account of our understanding of a class of sentences will include an account of how we understand them *as* true or *as* false. In the present case, this requires some *further* explanation of how we detect that causal relations do, or do not, obtain between events. No explicit answer has yet been given to this request.

This additional epistemological problem has a partial reflection in a *lacuna* so far present in Davidson's proposal. We have said nothing yet about how the relation 'causes' is to be analysed. We thus have not distinguished it from *other* relations occurring between events; in particular, nothing has been said to distinguish it from a possible component in any decompositional analysis of it, the relation of temporal succession. So part of the difficulty here can be expressed like this: how do we distinguish e_1 *causing* e_2 from e_1 merely being *followed* by e_2?

The problem of distinguishing temporal and causal sequences is not new; indeed, there is a recurrent, almost standard, solution proposed to it. Suppose that we have a sequence of events, first, e_1 occurring, and second, e_2 occurring. What more must be known for it to be known (or believed) that e_1 caused e_2? The standard suggestion is this: given a statement that e_1 occurred, it must be known (or believed) that there is a *covering causal law* which combines with that statement to imply a statement that e_2 occurs, and to imply that e_1 caused e_2. A singular sequence of events is a causal sequence in virtue of being an instance of some covering causal lawlike sequence.

It is remarkable that, prior to Davidson's work upon this, nobody had taken sufficiently seriously the matter of the *logic* involved in this. The idea was repeatedly voiced that a true singular causal statement would be an *instance* of a true covering causal law without any attempt being made to give the logical structure of both singular causal statement and covering causal law which would make such a claim precise and substantial.

What, then, are Davidson's proposals designed to make such claims substantial? First, there are two auxiliary claims. The first is that all that can be required is that there be *descriptions* of the events e_1 and e_2 which combine with the covering law in the required way; these descriptions need not be those we customarily employ. We say that the short-circuit caused the fire, that the striking of the match caused the explosion; but whether or not there are exceptionless covering-laws employing these descriptions is an open, empirical question. It may well be that we have to shift the descriptions of the events – even, say, to the level of molecular or atomic physics – before we obtain an appropriate exceptionless covering-law. The second claim is this: if we know (or believe) a singular causal statement to be true, then we have to know (or believe) that there is *some* covering causal law in virtue of being an instance of which (perhaps under redescription) the singular causal statement is itself true. We need not know (or have beliefs about) *which* causal law is the appropriate one; we need not even know (or have beliefs about) what is the appropriate *description* for use in the application of the covering-law model.

With these auxiliary claims before us, we can now state Davidson's proposals. Suppose we have as a premiss the statement that the 'causing' event occurs at a certain time (though *not* under that description): say, an *F*-event, where '*F*' is the appropriate kind of description to figure in covering laws. We have, that is,

(P) $(\exists!e)\,(Fe \;\&\; t(e) = 3)$

asserting the existence of a *unique* (!) *F*-event at time *3*. Using (P) and a covering law, we want to prove that

(C) $(\imath e)\,(Fe \;\&\; t(e) = 3)$ caused $(\imath e)\,(Ge \;\&\; t(e) = 3 + \varepsilon)$.

That is, we want to prove that the unique *F*-event at time *3* caused a unique *G*-event an increment of time, ε, later. Then, Davidson suggests, the format of the requisite covering law is this conjunction:

(S) $(e)(\eta)(\,(Fe \;\&\; t(e)=\eta) \to (\exists!f)\,(Gf \;\&\; t(f)=\eta+\varepsilon \;\&\; C(e,f)\,))$

and

(N) $(e)(\eta)(\,(Ge \;\&\; t(e)=\eta+\varepsilon) \to (\exists!f)\,(Ff \;\&\; t(f)=\eta \;\&\; C(f,e)\,)\,)$.

Both parts of this law – (S) *and* (N) – are needed to prove (C) from (P), just as they are both needed to make the reverse move – to prove from a statement that the effect occurred the statement that the cause caused that effect (though not under *those* descriptions!).

The significance of '(S)' and '(N)' is obvious: (S) concerns the *sufficiency* of the cause for the effect, (N) its *necessity*. On this covering-law model, a cause is both necessary and sufficient for its effect in a sense additional to that deriving from the favoured criterion of event-identity: namely, there exist descriptions of cause and effect such that, given the requisite covering law, a statement asserting the existence of the one is logically implied by a statement asserting the existence of the other. Conditionals do not enter into the logical form of singular causal statements; but if we adopt Davidson's covering-law model, it is clear that the truth of *some* conditional statements must be presumed in the process of *establishing* the truth of a singular causal statement. If we assert a singular causal statement like

(9) The short-circuit caused the fire

then we are committed, on this model, to there being true conditional statements, in which cause and effect may well be redescribed, to the effect that if the cause-event did not occur, the effect-event did not occur, and to the effect that if the effect-event did not occur, the cause-event did not occur. This epistemological role of conditionality, introduced by the covering-law solution to the more general problem of distinguishing causal from merely temporal relations, is quite compatible with treating singular causal statements as relational, non-conditional statements. And, of course, it is utterly unclear that those who stressed the role of conditionals were making claims about the logical form of singular causal statements.

The conditional relations so introduced are straightforward necessity and sufficiency. But if we concentrate upon the *descriptions* actually used in singular causal statements like (9), we can begin to see how the INUS-condition analysis re-enters at a yet more concrete epistemological level. We often, perhaps usually, do not know the redescriptions that issue in the full exhibition of the cause as necessary and sufficient for the effect. Working with the descriptions we have, and wishing to detect causal, as opposed to merely temporal, relations, in asserting a singular causal statement we shall be committed to conditional statements, conditional statements that we are in a position to express concretely, of the form suggested by the INUS-conditional account. Asserting (9) commits us to the truth of the (complex) conditional that *if* the short-circuit did not occur in the circumstances under which it did occur, and *if* no other fire-producing circumstances did obtain (as they did not), *then* the fire did not occur. This, with appropriate elaborations upon the accompanying circumstances, is a far more specific statement than that to the effect that under some redescriptions it can be shown that if the effect-event did not occur, the cause-event did not occur. At the level of explaining how we are led to assert singular causal statements, and of explaining quite what specific commitments accompany such assertion, the INUS-conditional account will have a crucial role to play. And, as before, it is fairly clear that that was the *kind* of problem that prompted the INUS-condition analysis; to construe it as a logical form proposal is simply to misconstrue it.

5 Some Epistemological Worries

One anxiety about Davidson's proposal is this. It need not matter, for the purely semantically motivated account of the logical form of singular causal statements, that the causal relation so revealed is left unanalysed. This is a matter of the priority of questions of logical form over questions of analysis; and there would anyway be nothing as yet to suggest that an austere axiom for that relation – reproducing the structure of designation and use – would be unacceptable. However, that same relation occurs in the schema for lawlike statements, (L), which is introduced to resolve a further, distinct epistemological problem. This epistemologically motivated proposal will be satisfactory *as* an epistemological proposal only if we are given some interpretation for the causal relation as it occurs in such lawlike statements. Is it to be analysed in some quasi-Humean way in terms of constant conjunction and contiguity?[6] If not, how is it to be understood? The central difficulty here is this. Suppose we try to rest with an austere analysis of that causal relation in both singular and lawlike statements. Then what reason have we for preferring the covering-law model, whereby our beliefs about singular causal statements are founded on our beliefs about the existence of covering causal laws, to one whereby the causal relation occurring in a singular causal statement is a primitive relation for *epistemological* purposes? That is, why not just say that we detect instances of that relation in independence of forming *any* beliefs about covering causal laws? We can just *tell* the difference between causal and merely temporal sequences: nothing is gained by the excursion into covering causal laws when they include the same, austerely analysed, predicate. This, of course, squares with the familiar point that we have much more confidence in the truth of *singular* causal statements than we have in the truth of any given covering causal law; it also squares with the blissful disregard we pre-philosophically feel about whether there is any such covering causal law when asserting singular causal statements. (Not that these facts are inconsistent with Davidson's proposal.) This would doubtless be a happier position if some informal *gloss* could be given upon the austerely analysed predicate (cf. Mackie, *The Cement of the Universe,* pp. 29–58); but until some interpretation has been given of the causal relation occurring in the covering law, an interpretation which supports the view that in detecting singular instances of that relation we are committed to there being such a law, the covering-law theorist is in no position to trade upon our unhappiness.

A second difficulty, acknowledged by Davidson, is posed by a class of causal statements that resurrect the idea of an apparently non-truth-functional sentential connective in singular causal statements. Examples of different kinds are: 'The collapse was caused, not by the fact that the bolt gave way, but by the fact that it gave way so quickly'; 'The fact that she was there when he returned caused his anger'; and 'The absence of an early-warning system caused the disaster'. In all these cases, it is difficult to discern the ontology of events; it is also difficult to avoid the view that the descriptions offered are crucial, with there being little of the latitude in description claimed to obtain for other, straightforward singular causal statements. All we need note now is Davidson's acknowledgment that

[6] The Humean idea would be, presumably, to view *C* in laws like (S) and (N) as tantamount to temporal succession.

in such cases there *is* some sentential connective involved – say, 'causally explains'; this combines with the familiar thought that explanations are linguistic, are concerned with the relations between sentences, not things, to explain the peculiarities of these cases. Although, again, it would be reassuring to have a detailed, general characterisation of such cases that goes beyond 'Those to which the original account does not apply'.

Perhaps the gravest difficulty facing Davidson's proposal remains. Consider, for example, the possibility of there being a law component of the form of Davidson's (S):

$$(e)(\eta)(\,(Fe \,\&\, t(e)=\eta) \rightarrow (\exists !f)\,(Gf \,\&\, t(f)=\eta+\epsilon \,\&\, C\,(e,f)\,)\,).$$

Such a component would enable us to *predict* from the occurrence of an *F*-event now the occurrence of a *G*-event, caused by that *F*-event, at some point in the future, however close to the present. But how could such a prediction be made? Something could always intervene to *prevent* the occurrence of the *G*-event; as an extreme case, some holocaust could obliterate the universe. If there is to be a lawlike component of the form of (S) whose truth we could reasonably be assured of, that component must be described in such a way as to rule out, or to be immune to, the possibilities of such intervention. But the only way of rendering it immune is to tag on 'unless something goes wrong': '*F*-events always cause *G*-events unless they do not'. That makes such laws vacuous, leaving them ill-equipped for any epistemological role. While if we try, informatively, to rule out the possibility of intervention, what is finally required is a law that includes a complete description of the universe, fixing the properties and positions of all items so as to rule out the possibility of intervention. Until that is done, we are in no position to assert (S)-type statements, and so in no position to ground our assertion of singular causal statements upon our acceptance of the existence of some (S)-type statements. But even if the idea of such a total description of the universe makes sense, it would be of infinite length, and so something we could never write down and could never know. Can our usage of singular causal statements be founded upon such an idea? Upon our faith in the existence of such a description ruling out any possibility of intervention?

Nor does (N) escape this worry. It is true that while (S)-type statements move from the present to the future, (N)-statements move from the present to the past; and the past is *fixed*, so that no unexpected intervention could occur. But the statement that, say, an F-event did *not* occur at an earlier time combines with an (N)-statement and with the law of *modus tollens* to imply that a *G*-event does not occur at a later time. But a *G*-event could have occurred, for something else could have intervened to bring a *G*-event about.

(S) and (N) do not correspond to prediction and retrodiction; each licenses both.

Until we have some informative account of the causal relation as it occurs in causal laws, we lack reason to adopt the covering-law epistemological account; and there is anyway reason to doubt whether exceptionless covering laws of the required kind could possibly underlie our employment of singular causal statements. If this is correct, Davidson's account of the logical form of causal laws, (L), must be mistaken, as must be his account of the role of those laws in solving our epistemological problem about causality. It does *not* follow that Davidson's proposal about the form of (relational) singular causal statements is incorrect; not does it follow that we cannot rest with an austere account of the causal relation so detected in singular causal statements.

Still, the claim that the causal relation is a primitive one, which we distinguish from that of temporal succession in a quite inexplicable manner, might seem uncomfortable; it seems open, for example, to Russell's challenge that the existence of such a distinct relation is a myth (Russell, *Mysticism and Logic,* pp. 132–51). What is required is *either* an informative decompositional analysis of the causal relation *or* some more informal *gloss* upon it which serves to give sufficient *feel* for the notion to distinguish it from, for example, that of temporal succession.[7] I know of no, even remotely plausible, decompositional analysis of the relation; but there are at least two possible (non-exclusive) informal sets of ruminations that might at least begin to suggest a distinctive notion, even though the question remains open whether there is any *objective* content to that notion.

The first set of ruminations is found in Miss Anscombe's Inaugural Lecture, from which the third of the above objections to Davidson's proposals has been taken (Anscombe in Sosa, *Causation and Conditionals,* pp. 63–81). Miss Anscombe points out that we acquire causal concepts long before we explicitly acquire the term 'cause'. Perhaps it is, in part, this abstracted, general nature of the notion of cause that precludes all but the austere analysis of it; also, those who wish us to reject as myth that notion must presumably wish to reject as myth these other, more specific but causal, notions. Miss Anscombe gives a list of these other concepts: scrape, push, wet, carry, eat, burn, knock over, keep off, squash, make, hurt. Now a striking thing about this list is that each of the concepts involved has two distinct areas of usage: in application to human beings (who can do all these things), and in application to inanimate things (whose interactions can be described in all these terms). Miss

---

[7] Or, perhaps, an informal gloss upon *them*; the need for austerity may reflect the (unsurprising) truth that there are many different kinds of causal relation, bound together by 'family resemblances'.

Anscombe concludes her lecture by saying: 'The most neglected of the key topics in this subject are: interference and prevention.' Again, these notions have the two distinct areas of application.

The thought here might roughly be put like this: the primary notion of causation is acquired through *agency*, through action. The notion of mechanical causation – as it were, *push-pull* causation – is derivative. Causation is an *anthropomorphic* notion in its primary occurrence. Any satisfactory development of this would need to consider a number of questions. Is this primary notion one that obtains between our bodily actions and their external effects or is it one that obtains between, say, my deciding to perform some bodily action and my performing it? In either case, could the covering law have a role to play in distinguishing agency causation from temporal succession? Is there in either case any general epistemological problem of this form, don't we just *know* which occurred? Quite how is the extension from agency causation to inanimate, push-pull causation to be represented? Can it be represented in such a way that it is reasonable to eschew any further (covering-law) account of how we distinguish mechanical causation from temporal succession?

Another set of ruminations, quite compatible with the above, is found in Mackie's *The Cement of the Universe*. What underlies our employment of a singular causal statement, without being part of its logical form, is the thought that if the cause had not occurred in the circumstances in which it did occur, then the effect would not have occurred. We now shift from this (sophisticated) reliance upon conditionals to a simple picture: a picture of a world like ours except, initially, for the absence of the cause; as we trace that picture through time, we see that the effect does not occur either. Thus even the primitive, lacking the sophistication of conditionals, can have a grasp upon the notion of causation. And this picture can be applied to – and perhaps has initially to be applied to – agency causation.

I do not know whether either, or both, of these ideas can be developed in sufficiently intelligible terms to exhibit the distinctiveness of the (semantically primitive) idea of causation and to rebut the Russellian charge that such an idea has no objective reality. My concern has been, not to settle that question, but to illustrate the ways in which logical form proposals, in one concrete case, connect with more traditional philosophical discussions; in particular, I have tried both to distinguish the epistemologically (perhaps ill-) motivated parts of Davidson's discussion of causation from the semantically motivated component, and to dispel the illusion that that semantic component is in wholesale conflict with most other recent discussion of causation.

Part Three

Language and Reality

Chapter IX

Understanding and Reality

1 Understanding and Paradox

Language use is unreflective; linguistic competence is an unreflective practical skill. People say things without, generally, working out how to say them. People understand when others say things without, in general, working out what was said. The manifestation of that understanding is their appropriate response, linguistic or non-linguistic. You ask me to shut the door; I show my understanding by doing so (and, on occasion, by not doing so). You ask me the time of the last train to London; I show my understanding by answering, or by fetching my Bradshaw's.

But there is a recurrent temptation to think of there being *something* about my inner, mental life, some further, non-behavioural component of my understanding, which explains these successful performances. One question is whether there is such a further component, and, if so, quite what it is. The answer to this question, the picture of understanding finally embraced, is of crucial importance. The meaning of an expression, we want to say, is what grounds a competent speaker's understanding of that expression; and the general form of the theory of meaning must be adequate to ground the general form of linguistic understanding. Deficiencies in a proposed general form of a theory of meaning can be illuminated by showing the ill-fittedness of that general conception of meaning to ground an acceptable, general account of understanding.

One, intuitively persuasive, remarkably persistent, and highly abstract thought about the notion of meaning is this: the meaning of an expression is given by a *rule* which determines that expression's correct usage. A companion thought, of comparable persuasion and persistence is this: a sufficient condition of understanding an expression is explicit propositional knowledge of that rule. These two companions yield the following: for any meaningful expression,

217

there is a rule governing its usage knowledge of which would suffice for understanding, for mastery, of that expression. Reason to reject this idea would be a matter of major semantic importance: either we should have to reject the claim that knowledge of the rule governing the meaning of the expression suffices for understanding that expression, which would leave us dangerously close to the divorce of meaning from understanding; or we should have to reject the pervasive conception of meaning as rule-governed.

There is a family of paradoxes, of ancient standing, which are peculiarly problematic: they seem, demonically, to become less and less within one's clear perception and within one's control the more one puzzles at them. But their importance in the present context is that it has recently been argued by Crispin Wright that the depth of these paradoxes has long been overlooked (Wright in Evans and McDowell, *Truth and Meaning,* pp. 223–47). Specifically, Wright argues that these paradoxes require the rejection of the conceptions of meaning and understanding just sketched.

First, then, the paradoxes; and the first, and most ancient, of these is that of the heap. A slightly modified version of this is the following:

(1) One grain of sand is not a heap.
(2) If n grains of sand are not a heap, nor are $n+1$ grains of sand.
∴(3) No number of grains of sand is a heap.

The first premiss, (1), is deemed self-evident; the second is prompted by the intuitive thought that merely one additional grain cannot make the difference between not being a heap and being a heap; the conclusion, (3), follows by mathematical induction.

The second paradox is Wang's, and goes as follows:

(4) A one-ounce elephant is a small elephant.
(5) If an n-ounce elephant is a small elephant, so is an $n+1$ ounce elephant.
∴(6) All elephants are small elephants.

The rationale for the premises and the method of obtaining the conclusion are as for the paradox of the heap.

Third, there is a paradox of colours, discussed by Wright, which has a slightly different format:

(7) A red patch is a red patch. (Or: *this* is a red patch.)
(8) If a patch of colour is not discriminable from a red patch, it is itself a red patch.
(9) Between any two *just* discriminable patches of colour, there is a third patch discriminable from neither.
(10) Between a red patch and an orange (or yellow or green or

blue or . . .) patch there is a series of *just* discriminable colour patches.

∴(11) An orange (or yellow or green or blue or . . .) patch is a red patch.

Premiss (7) is deemed self-evident. Premiss (8) is deemed to be a consequence of the *observationality* of colour-predicates; an observational predicate simply is one satisfying the format of (8). (9) and (10) appear to be empirical truths. The conclusion (11) follows by repeated steps of *modus ponens*.

Finally, a concocted paradox of pictures:

(12) This arrangement of black dots on a white card is a picture of a face.
(13) If a certain arrangement of black dots on a white card is a picture of a face, so is the same arrangement with one dot slightly moved (or removed).
∴(14) All arrangements of black dots on a white card (including an 'arrangement' with no black dots) are pictures of a face.

Premiss (12), with an appropriate reference of the demonstrative, is deemed, if not self-evident, at least obviously true. (13) is meant to be an obvious empirical truth; the conclusion follows again by *modus ponens*.

There are crucial differences between these paradoxes; but for the moment I shall ignore them. The paradox of the heap and Wang's paradox were presented as resting upon mathematical induction. It would, of course, be a matter of importance – though not obviously of semantic importance – if the use of mathematical induction in cases involving *vague* expressions (like 'is a heap') or *vague attributive* expressions (like 'is a small elephant') was demonstrably unsound. But this would not avoid the paradoxes since, as the parallel with the other two paradoxes shows, all that is needed to generate the first two paradoxes is repeated steps of *modus ponens*. Again, it would be interesting if the paradoxes could only be generated by an *infinite* number of steps of *modus ponens*; but this is not so, since heaps of sand need not contain an infinity of grains nor need large elephants be made up of an infinity of ounces.

Any desire to live with the truth of the paradoxical conclusions should be eliminated by seeing the following companion paradoxes to Wang's paradox:

(15) A zillion-ounce elephant is a large elephant.
(16) If an n-ounce elephant is a large elephant, so is an $n-1$ ounce elephant.
∴(17) All elephants are large elephants.

and

(18) An *a*-ounce elephant is neither a large nor a small elephant.

(19) If an *n*-ounce elephant is neither a large nor a small elephant, then an $n+1$ ounce elephant (or an $n-1$ ounce elephant) is neither a large nor a small elephant.

∴(20) All elephants are neither large nor small.

(*a* is, roughly, the weight of the average or typical elephant; not all elephants need be large or small, many, perhaps, being neither.) The rationale for the premises and the method of obtaining the conclusion are as for Wang's paradox. So now all elephants are small, are large, and are neither large nor small. I take that to scotch any lingering desire to buy the conclusions of the paradoxes.

2 Vagueness and Rules

Apparently true premises leading by apparently sound arguments to apparently insane conclusions always represent an intellectual challenge. Such arguments need not be matters of much importance; but since, in the present cases, it is clear that comparable paradoxes could be generated for any *vague* expression, and given the size of the class of vague expressions, some importance must attach to the dissolution of these paradoxes.

I take it that the desire to accept the conclusions of the paradoxes, or to question the validity of the arguments, has been eliminated for the time being. There seem, then, only two options left open to us. The radical one is to accept the paradoxes as demonstrating the *incoherence* of vague expressions, and therefore to conclude that the language should be purified of them. But, first, this is counter-intuitive, since such expressions apparently have a clear role to play in our talk of the world, and apparently fulfil that role quite success-fully. Second, as instanced by the paradox of the colours, elimination (if need be, elimination by redefinition) of all vague expressions from the language will require the elimination of all vague observa-tional expressions. For the moment, we can follow Wright in defining an observational expression as one whose application to an object can be determined just by looking at it, listening to it, and so on. All such observational expressions appear to be vague, they appear to exhibit what Wright calls *tolerance*: an expression *F* (e.g. 'is red') is tolerant with respect to ϕ (e.g. colour) 'if there is . . . some positive degree of change in respect of ϕ insufficient ever to affect the justice with which *F* applies to a particular case'. As Wright has shown, it is not that elimination of this tolerance from observational predicates will of necessity eliminate observationality altogether, will of necessity divorce the language from the empirical

220

world; it is rather that such a revision, if it is not to be open to further paradoxes of the same general form, will produce a language the circumstances of whose use are cumbersome to the point of the comic.

The only other option remaining is to deny the truth of at least one of the premisses generating each paradox. In some cases there are other candidates for doubt, but in both the paradox of the heap and in Wang's paradox the only plausible possibility appears to be the denial of the second, conditional premiss. But if we reject that premiss, for whatever reason, we have also to reject anything which implies it. This brings us to Wright's central point.

The persuasive orthodoxy with which we began is this:

(A) The meaning of an expression is given by a *rule* which determines that expression's correct usage, knowledge of that rule sufficing for mastery of the correct usage of that expression.

Wright's auxiliary claim is this:

(B) Any such rule for a vague expression will imply the truth of a conditional or inductive premiss, of the form of (2), in each of our examples.

Accepting (A) and (B), we shall be committed to the truth of the premiss we otherwise wish to deny; the paradoxes will thus be generated, and the expressions concerned revealed to be incoherent. But they are not incoherent, and are eliminable only at excessive cost. So one of (A) and (B) must be rejected. Wright, holding (B) to be true, draws the radical conclusion that (A) is false: the picture of meaning as *rule*-governed, with knowledge of the rule sufficing for understanding, has to be rejected. We understand vague expressions perfectly well, as shown by our everyday success in their employment; but their meanings cannot be rule-governed except at the price of incoherence; so that understanding of vague expressions *could not be* grounded in knowledge of rules governing their successful employment.

The reply to Wright is that (B) is false: there are rules giving the meanings of vague expressions, knowledge of which would suffice for mastery of the expressions, but which do not imply the truth of the relevant conditional premisses. Nor do they imply their falsity, but that does not now matter.

The rule governing the meaning of 'is red' is simply given:

Something satisfies 'is red' if and only if it is red.

The appropriate rule for 'is a heap' will depend upon whether we consider it, as I suspect is the case, to include an element of attributivity, such that the most perspicuous use of it is of the form 'a heap of ϕ' (e.g. a heap of sand). The appropriate rule for 'is a small elephant' will clearly depend upon our treatment of attributive adjectives, while that for 'is a picture of a face' must wait upon an account of the semantic structure of that expression. But the case of 'is red' illustrates the general point about the treatment of all these cases: for vague expressions, the threat of generating paradoxes requires that we rest with austere, non-decompositional analyses. For example, if Wheeler's treatment of the positive form of attributive adjectives is favoured, whereby some two-place relation something like '. . . is small for . . .' is detected in all occurrences as a positive attributive of 'small', then we should *not* attempt any further, decompositional analysis of that expression, resting content instead with an austere axiom for it reproducing the structure of designation and use found in that just given for 'is red'. The picture example is more complicated yet, since here there is both scope and need for some decompositional analysis. But all that is required to defuse Wright's anxiety is that whatever account is given of that expression, it does not make reference to black dot arrangements on white cards *in such a way* as to imply the conditional second premiss. Wright's argument, as Evans and McDowell point out, is as easily construed as an argument against semantic decomposition of a kind that licenses the appropriate conditional premiss as it is as an argument against the pervasive conception of meaning embodied in (A) (Evans and McDowell, *Truth and Meaning*, p. xi).[1] And as the cases both of attributive adjectives and of the expression 'is a picture of a face' show (as, perhaps, would the heap-expressions in a final treatment), this is quite compatible with deserting as *austere* an axiom as is given for 'is red'.

So far this is little more than an *assertion* that (B) is false. Things become a little clearer, as well as a little more substantial, if we ask, first, what *argument* there is for resting with non-decompositional analyses, other than the apparently *ad hoc* need to avoid the paradoxes, and, second, whether such austere rules are indeed adequate to the role they are required to play by (A).

Consider the concocted fourth paradox about pictures of faces. There are two important truths about the relation between the arrangement of the black dots on the white card and there being a face there to be seen. The first is that it is only *because* there is a certain arrangement of the dots, describable in terms completely free of picture vocabulary (say, by some grid system), that there is a face pictured there to be seen. Much else is needed, of course, most notably conventions of pictorial representation; but the dot arrange-

---

[1] Such non-decompositional rules are not, however, *governing* rules in that they could not *guide* behaviour.

ment is necessary too. But, second, we do not see the face by *attending* to that arrangement *so described*, described in terms free of face vocabulary. Indeed, the more we so attend, the less likely we are to see the face pictured. Our *seeing* the face is not an *inference* from our seeing the dot arrangement so neutrally described.

These two truths are perfectly compatible; the first is worth mentioning in this context only to draw attention to its compatibility with the second. It is the second one that matters now. We do not *infer* the judgment that there is a face pictured from the judgment that the dots are arranged thus-and-so, where 'thus-and-so' is a description of the arrangement of the black dots on the white card free of picture vocabulary. What this shows is that our *mastery* of the expression 'is a picture of a face' is not grounded in our mastery of any predicates, free of picture vocabulary, which characterise dot-arrangements. Our *understanding*, our practical understanding, that issues in application of the expression 'is a picture of a face' is not grounded in our understanding, our practical understanding, of any dot-arrangement characterising predicates free of picture and face vocabulary.

Any semantic rule which implied the truth of the second, conditional premiss of the picture paradox would be a rule relating the application-conditions of the predicate 'is a picture of a face' to the application-conditions of, as it were, *pure* dot-arrangement predicates, predicates concerned solely with abstractly characterised spatial locations of dots. Any such rule would therefore *falsify* our understanding, as evinced by our methods of application, of the predicate 'is a picture of a face'. While any acceptable treatment of that predicate will reveal logical structure within it, it will not, so to speak, atomise it, reductively, to pure dot-language.

To put the point at its simplest: a speaker could have a perfectly secure grasp upon the predicate 'is a picture of a face' while having no grasp upon the pure dot-vocabulary. He need not realise even that the pictures (constitutively) *are* arrangements of black dots on a white card. Think of newspaper photographs. The conditional second premiss of the picture paradox is utterly *irrelevant* to our understanding of the predicate 'is a picture of a face'.

This line of thought – that the semantic unanalysability of an expression ϕ with respect to an expression ψ follows from the irrelevance of ψ-judgments, their lack of inferential role, in making ϕ-judgments – vastly reduces the scope for analysis of expressions. This unanalysability relates, not just to the difficulty of finding adequate decompositional analyses of many expressions (e.g. all 'family resemblance' terms), nor just to the need to avoid immediate entrapment in the paradoxes (i.e. all vague expressions), nor just to the impossibility of such analyses for the primitive expressions in the language, but also to the 'brute phenomenological fact' of the irrelevance of such analyses to our practical application of many expressions, the application which manifests our understanding of them.

It is not clear whether this same moral, quite unmodified, can be correctly carried over to the pairs of expressions occurring in the paradox of the heap and Wang's paradox. Is it true to say that our grasp upon expressions relating to quantities of grains of sand (or quantities of ounces) is utterly irrelevant to our grasp upon the application of 'is a heap of sand' (or 'is a small elephant')? While a speaker could indeed have an adequate grasp upon 'is a heap of sand' without having (without having a grasp upon) the expression 'is a grain of sand', it seems difficult to deny that his application of 'is a heap of sand' must, in some way, be determined by his *perception* of grains of sand and their quantities. But what seems not to be the case is that this competence in the use of the expression 'is a heap of sand' is determined by perception of *exact* numbers of grains of sand. Rather, our application of 'is a heap of sand' is grounded in our detection of *quantities* of grains, and that of 'is a small elephant' is grounded in our detection of *quantities* of ounces; but the quantities whose detection is so operative are not *precise*, but are rather along the lines of 'many', 'too many', 'sufficiently many', 'few', 'too few', 'sufficiently few', and so forth. While these vague quantifiers attach to the very predicates ('grains of sand', 'ounces') which figure in the crucial, second, conditional premiss, it is unclear as yet how appropriately *vague* decompositional analyses along these lines of the expressions 'is a heap of sand', 'is a small elephant', could possibly reveal these premisses, containing exact numerical predicates, to be true. In this difference between the treatment of the expressions occurring in the picture paradox, on the one hand, and Wang's and the heap paradoxes on the other, we see the deficiency in Wright's *general* definition of tolerance given earlier.

The further extension of this treatment to the colour paradox is problematic. For, in that case, we are tempted to say that, far from the paired predicate ('is (visually) indistinguishable from') being *irrelevant* to the application of the predicate 'is red', its application is precisely what grounds that predicate's application. This is a question I shall return to in a moment.

3 Rules and Observationality

Our language is essentially realistic. The manifestation of part of that realism is the non-inferential character of much of its application; the theoretical embodiment of part of that realism is the austere, non-decompositional analysis of many of its expressions.[2] Thus does realism avoid immediate entrapment in the paradoxes.

It still has to be shown, however, that such a semantics is adequate. In particular, we have to show that austere rules such as

(S) Something satisfies 'is red' if and only if it is red

can indeed describe our *understanding* of the expressions designated in them. Would knowledge of this rule suffice for mastery of the expression there designated?

People have wanted to say two things about such rules (and some, somewhat puzzlingly, have wanted to say both). One claim is that they are trivial, and are therefore insufficient to describe understanding. The other claim is that they embody, in a quite strange and inexplicable manner, a deep and profound mystery. Thus while they would be *formally* sufficient to describe understanding, their silence upon the mystery would render reliance upon them unacceptably non-explanatory.

First, the charge of triviality. As Evans and McDowell point out, (S)-sentences, in virtue of the shift from *designation* of an expression to use of that same expression, record a contingent, learnable, forgettable fact about the English language. In the case of unanalysable, because primitive, expressions, there is no other way of giving their meaning when the object-language is part of the meta-language. What is perhaps surprising is the range of cases, as just argued, that must be treated as primitive; but the surprising extent of austere (S)-sentences cannot render them objectionable.

One way of trying to demonstrate the triviality of (S)-sentences is to point out that they are unsuitable, because of their austerity, for imparting mastery of the expression designated to one who does not understand it. If I do not understand the expression 'is red' antecedently, it is no use giving me the rule (S) in an attempt to bring me to understand it. But the (tacit) requirement that a theoretical representation of the sense of an expression be suitable for initiating the uninitiated is unargued for; as a general requirement it is also incoherent. Another way of suggesting the *comparative* triviality of (S)-sentences is to point out that, for example, in the case of 'is red' they overlook the fact that *visual indistinguishability* grounds our application of that expression. Again, we shall return to this thought.

Nobody, by now, should confuse (S)-sentences with any of the following, taking the example of 'is red'.

(S*1) Something satisfies 'is red' if and only if it satisfies 'is red'.

[2] *Part of* because it is (importantly) unclear that austerity implies the full realistic conception developed in this and the following chapter. All that is needed (for present purposes) is the *suitability* of austerity for that conception.

(S*2) 'Something satisfies "is red" if and only if it is red' expresses
a truth.

(S*3) 'Something satisfies "is red" if and only if it satisfies "is
red"' ' expresses a truth.

What might be asked is when we are entitled to embed (S)-sentences
within the '*A* knows that . . .' construction rather than one of the
(S*)-sentences. If (S) and all the (S*)-sentences were trivial, this
would be the request to discern between trivialities. But it is not a
trivial request, for (S)-sentences are not trivial. There is therefore
a substantial question about when knowledge of them can be
attributed to a speaker. Our claim has to be that, because (S)-
sentences are adequate semantic axioms for the terms occurring in
them, knowledge of an (S)-sentence suffices for *understanding* of the
expression designated and used in it. The question is whether this
claim is correct; and the initial challenge is to state when such
knowledge should be attributed to a speaker.

The answer to this brings us to the mysterious and the profound.
Knowledge of (S) can be attributed to a speaker if linguistic actions
of his are redescribable, using the combined theories of sense and
force, as actions which are about the 'redness' of things *in virtue
of* the occurrence in his utterance (prior to redescription) of the
expression 'is red'. That is how he demonstrates his competence in
the *usage* of 'is red'; which is what it is for him to *understand* 'is
red'.

The mystery now is that there seems to be no *explanation* of that
competence. (S)-sentences are silent upon the (supposedly) crucial
question of *how* a symbol *latches on to* the world. An austere axiom
for a proper name gives no explanation of *how* that name *connects*
with the object it names; an austere axiom for a predicate (of the
form (S)) gives no explanation of *how* that predicate *connects* with
the class of individuals satisfying it. Such axioms are silent upon
this because they give us no *route* from symbol to extra-linguistic
counterpart; they simply *pair* them. It follows, then, that when
understanding is represented as knowledge of such a rule, no
explanation is given of how the (competent) speaker's usage of an
expression *connects* with the extra-linguistic world. There is therefore a failure of explanation of that competence.[3]

For example, attribution to a speaker of knowledge of the (S)-
sentence for 'is red' does nothing to explain his competence in the
usage of 'is red'. What *would* begin to explain it, the thought is,
would be his knowledge that *indiscriminability* grounds the application of 'is red'. Only if he has that additional knowledge does he have
an explicable mastery of 'is red'; for that is *part* of the mastery of

[3] See, again, the footnote on p. 222.

'is red'. It must therefore be part of the *meaning* of 'is red', contrary to the suggestion that the (S)-sentence is an adequate specification of that meaning, if knowledge of meaning is to suffice for mastery.

The attraction of this series of thoughts is at least reduced by the following series of reflections. First, the requirement of a route to the reference, which must be known by the competent speaker, is one that there may, in many cases, be reason to reject. In some cases (e.g. proper names), such routes as speakers possess can vary from speaker to speaker, so bringing the requirement of a route into conflict with the fundamental requirement of the intersubjectivity of sense. In some cases (proper names again), such route as there is need not be possessed by the speaker, but only by the semantic theorist; such a route therefore need not be known by the competent speaker, and cannot be part of the meaning of the expression. In some cases (e.g. scientific primitive expressions) such a route cannot be provided. In some cases (e.g. vague expressions) the introduction of such a route inevitably distorts the application-conditions, and competent speakers' understanding, of the expressions.

Second, the demand for non-austere axioms, for a route from designated expression to reference, may be founded upon a mis-apprehension as to the role of the theory of sense. We begin with the observed (uninterpreted) facts of linguistic usage; we then proceed to construct the abstracted theories of force and sense in such a way as to make the initially observed facts intelligible. The abstracted theory of sense plays its role, and its axioms pull their weight, solely by yielding (in conjunction with the theory of force) intelligible redescriptions of linguistic actions – intelligible in the light of the propositional attitude ascriptions they license. If, in a particular case, we attribute to a speaker (say, our now bilingual semantic theorist) explicit propositional knowledge of the axioms of the theory of sense, then the import of our doing so is given by the two ways in which he can *manifest* that knowledge: by *stating* the axioms or by *using* the expressions designated in the axioms in utterances of the language of identifiable mode. But the first way of manifesting that knowledge is, for us as semantic theorists of the speaker, derivative from the second. The primary import of attri-buting knowledge of the axioms to a speaker is that such attribution renders intelligible his ability (both reflectively and unreflectively) to produce linguistic actions which, in the context of that knowledge ascription, are intelligible.

The claim is that no further *semantic* explanation of that com-petence is needed other than that provided by the (posited) know-ledge of the austere axioms. Other *kinds* of explanation of the speaker's action may be available to us. For example, if a speaker observes a red patch and utters the sentence 'That's red', there will

227

doubtless be some (tortuous) physical story that could be told, about the ways in which earlier observations of patches reflecting that wavelength of light have been causally connected with various neural states of the speaker in such a way that this present observation prompts the appropriate larynx-movements. But that explanation is not a semantic one. And, doubtless, many of the observed facts about how speakers (psychologically) detect the application-conditions for a predicate may have an important role to play in determining *when* a propositional attitude ascription (and so a prior linguistic redescription of one of their utterances) is plausible. But that does not require that such observed facts be somehow (often *per impossibile*) incorporated within the theory of sense. The role of the theory of sense leaves the neglect, *within that component of the overall theory of linguistic behaviour*, of these further matters of application-conditions quite unobjectionable; and the attribution to a speaker of knowledge of the resultant austere theory of sense is sufficient, *given the role of that theory*, to describe the speaker's understanding of the expressions designated and used within that theory. What makes a theory of sense acceptable, and the attribution of propositional knowledge of it to a given speaker in part acceptable, is that the theory combines with a theory of force to issue in plausible redescriptions of his actions; what makes the redescriptions plausible is that the propositional attitude ascriptions so licensed be themselves plausible. What makes these ascriptions plausible can be a mass of observed facts about speakers' behaviour, including the ways in which they *detected* the applicability of the expressions involved in their utterances; but this does not require that these methods of detection themselves be somehow incorporated into the relevant axioms of the theory of sense.

A third worry about the argument against austerity, the argument designed to show that within the theory of sense itself a *route* must be provided to the reference of the RHS of (S)-sentences, is that such arguments often reflect, not just a (doubtful) requirement of *explanation* – for these come to an end somewhere – but also a distinctive requirement of *justification*. For example, I think a dominant motivation behind the indefensible classical description theories of proper names was the thought that descriptions are, as it were, *epistemologically primary*: the only possible *justification* for applying a proper name to an individual is the belief that that individual satisfies some set of descriptions. But we should at least be clear when such a supposition is operative in our thinking; we should be clear about the difficulties (those just adduced) attendant upon this supposition; and we should be clear about the irrelevance, at the first stage of semantic analysis, of such an epistemological concern. As we shall see later, there may be *general* arguments designed to support the epistemological presumptions involved in this challenge; but we should be clear about the difference between holding that an account of meaning, and so of understanding, is in commonplace terms inadequate and holding it inadequate in the light of some highly general, abstract argument.

The only mundane version of such an argument – the only version meant to be in commonplace terms – is this: if we rest content with knowledge of austere axioms as sufficient for understanding, then how can we know of someone to whom such knowledge is attributed that he will *continue* to use the expression correctly? One possibility motivating the question is irrelevant: if the question amounts to 'How do we know that he won't cease to understand the expression correctly?', the answer is that we know, and can know, no such thing. Attributing to the speaker knowledge of some non-austere, route-providing rule would not secure this either, since he could, of course, lose that knowledge as well. But the real point behind the question, I take it, is this: might it not be that he has thus far failed to understand the expression, it being a matter of *chance* that he has thus far applied it correctly? Whereas if the axiom were not austere – if it included, for example, reference to *procedures* whereby the applicability of the expression is to be determined – then we could observe whether he had *followed* those procedures; of course, it could still be *chance* that he had done so, but the scope for gratuitous success would be much reduced.

This, of course, does nothing to defuse the previous worries about the attempt to incorporate any such procedures into the theory of sense. And it anyway ignores the point that, upon the present austere theory, these further clues as to whether we have chance success or not, are not neglected but relocated. They are located at the point where we consider the plausibility of the propositional attitude ascription that the redescription of the linguistic action standardly licenses. Whatever observations would show to the non-austere theorist that the speaker has merely been lucky – that he does not really know the non-austere rule – will show to us that the redescription of his action licensed by our austere theory of sense is implausible.

The main points of the preceding emerge if we turn now to the problem, previously put aside, of colour predicates. We have encountered the thoughts, first, that indistinguishability from a red patch is a sufficient condition for being a red patch; second, that knowledge that this is so is required for *understanding* the expression 'is red', so that this indistinguishability claim must somehow be incorporated into a (non-austere) semantic axiom for 'is red'; but, third, that doing so reveals the second premiss of the colour paradox to be true, and so reveals 'is red' to be an incoherent expression.

My concern is only with the first two of these claims; but what I say about them includes the beginnings of a defusion of that paradox.

Vague predicates, of which colour predicates are an example, obtain to *degrees*. This is not to countenance degrees of truth, merely the sensefulness of the comparative form. It is not a novel thought to suggest that it is of the essence of the mastery of such vague expressions that there are clear, exemplary cases of them, even if these cases only exist in the imagination (cf. Slobin, *Psycholinguistics*, pp. 124–5). We grasp the use of a vague predicate at least in part through a grasp of paradigm-exemplars of them – a one-ounce elephant, a vast elephant, a grain of sand, a pile of sand, an elegant crimson cushion, an unripe apple. Our extended application of these predicates is indeed generated by perceived discriminabilities and indiscriminabilities: we would not notice the extra grain of sand, the extra ounce, the slightly moved dot. Hence both the evident truth of the first premiss in each of the paradoxes (the paradigm-exemplar) together with the appearance of truth of the second (founded upon indiscriminabilities).

But that appearance is misleading, for the role of indiscriminability in determining the *truth* of application of colour-predicates to objects is too crudely characterised. Likewise, in the case of colour-predicates, the notion of *observationality* needs to be refined. Instead of focusing upon

(8) If a patch of colour is not discriminable from a red patch, it is itself a red patch

we need to consider three distinct claims that (8) runs together:

(8′) If a patch of colour is not discriminable from a paradigm red patch, it is itself a paradigm of red.

(8″) If a patch of colour is not discriminable from a paradigm red patch, it is itself an instance of red.

(8‴) If a patch of colour is not discriminable from an instance of red, it is itself an instance of red.

What the paradoxes show is that (8′) is false: that indiscriminability from a paradigm of red does not of necessity mean that we have *another* paradigm of red. Our grasp upon colour-words (like all vague expressions) is paradigm-based; but these expressions are coherent, and their coherence is possible because claims of the form of (8′) are false. (8″) is true, and provides a sufficient (though not necessary) condition of being red; but the truth of (8″) cannot generate the paradoxes. It is the truth of (8″), as one reading of (8), which leads us to see the ambiguous (8) as true. (8‴) is false, since, again, paradoxes would be generated by its truth. What might mask the falsity from us (and the same point applies to (8′)) is this: indiscriminability from an instance of red justifies us, *other things being equal*, in saying that an item is red. But to be justified in saying is not the same as to say the true; we can be justified in saying the false, and (8″) is an example of how. The *other things being equal* clause is meant to be operative in the following kind of case. Starting from a paradigm of red, each day I show you an indiscriminable patch, destroying the original after doing so. Going on like this day after day, and excluding your memory of *other* colours, you will be justified in calling *all* of the series of patches 'red'. But when I finally show you what you know to be a clear exemplar of orange, and you find it indistinguishable from the remaining 'red' patch, you will no longer be justified in calling the patch 'red'; but prior to my placing that orange patch alongside, and assuming your failure of memory, you were justified in saying that it was red. This same moral applies to all the tendentious second, conditional premisses in vagueness paradoxes.

The observationality of colour-predicates amounts to this: there is an observationally determinable sufficient condition of the application of a colour-predicate – viz. indiscriminability from a paradigm. (This condition certainly does not need to be explicitly known by every competent speaker.) But there is no *further* 'informative' sufficient condition, observational or otherwise, and there is no 'informative' necessary condition, observational or otherwise. For generally statable necessary and sufficient *satisfaction*-conditions (not, justification-conditions), we have to rest with austerity.

There is no non-austere necessary and sufficient route (observational or otherwise) to the reference of a vague predicate; but this is compatible with its being observational in one sense. There is thus no such route which has to be known by the competent speaker. A speaker manifests his understanding of a vague predicate by producing utterances which our (austere) theory of sense, in conjunction with the theory of force, plausibly redescribes as ascribing the property concerned in virtue of the occurrence in that utterance of that vague predicate. The plausibility of the redescription can be influenced by observation of how he was led to make that utterance – for example, by perceiving indiscriminability relations. But these prompting clues need have no part to play in the theory of sense.

4 Understanding and Knowledge

A sufficient condition for understanding an expression in a language is explicit propositional knowledge of the axiom in the theory of sense describing the use of that expression. Such knowledge could be possessed, of course, only along with knowledge of the senses of at least many other expressions in the language. But is the stated condition also a necessary condition of understanding?

An affirmative answer would be obviously absurd. Lacking, as we all do, a complete truth-theory for English, we can still understand English perfectly well. We manifest that understanding by our practical, unreflective, successful employment, and response to others' employment, of the language. The primary manifestation of the understanding of an expression is the ability to *use* it in saying things in an identifiable mode; any ability we have as native speakers to say things about the semantics of an expression, to mention it in complete utterances of a semantic nature, is a manifestation of an explicit understanding that is both derivative and rare. It is derivative because assertion of an austere axiom does not yet exhibit mastery of the *use* of that expression; it is rare because life is too nasty, brutish and short for many to abandon their unreflective ways for those of the semanticist.

But how, then, does speakers' knowledge connect with our overall theory of linguistic behaviour to *constitute* those speakers' understanding of their language? One persistent move is to talk of *implicit* propositional knowledge of the theory of sense, to suggest that a necessary condition of understanding a language is the possession of implicit knowledge of the axioms, rules, and T-sentences (and even, perhaps, of the derivations of the last-named from the first two) that make up the theory of sense for that language. But this idea is not as pellucid as we might hope. It invites the thought that the native speaker has some quasi-intuitive route to the theory of sense, a route that we, as alien speakers, lack: that once our hard-earned semantic proposals are put to a native speaker (educated, say, in the rudiments of Tarskian truth-theory), he will quickly *see* whether the proposals are correct or not. But this thought has no content, and is immediately in conflict with the uncertainty we, as competent English speakers, feel about the proper semantic treatment of so many English expressions – an uncertainty well exemplified throughout the preceding part of this book. I do not mean to deny that some sense can be given to the notion of implicit propositional knowledge; I merely mean to follow others who have denied that, in the context of the contents of the theory of sense or in similar linguistic contexts, any useful such sense has yet been given to it. (See, e.g. Nagel, 'The Boundaries of Inner Space', and Stich, 'What Every Speaker Knows'.)

It is important to see clearly the motivation behind talk of competent speakers' implicit knowledge of the correct theory of sense for their native language. That theory of sense, the thought must be, is to play an *explanatory* role, in conjunction with the theory of force, in accounting for such speakers' ability to understand an

232

indefinitely large number of novel utterances. But that understanding can itself be represented as propositional knowledge. How could a set of unknown axioms, rules, derivations and consequences explain this propositional knowledge? How could such an explanation work if speakers were in utter ignorance of the contents of the theory of sense?

This motivation is not as secure as it seems. We can accept that native speakers do indeed have the propositional knowledge they are presumed by the argument to have. They can (propositionally) know that so-and-so asserted (or commanded or questioned) that such-and-such. They can manifest that knowledge, and frequently do so, by *saying* it; and even when it is not explicitly said, they can always, under prompting, immediately come up with such an utterance. This may need, in some sense, *explanation*; but it is not clear that any such explanation requires the attribution to speakers of propositional knowledge of all of the abstracted theory of sense.

Here we might be tempted by another possibility, one that anyway does not work, and which yields too much to the demand for cognitive explanation. This is to move from propositional knowledge of the theory of sense to practical knowledge of at least part of it. Starting from an axiom like

(S) Something satisfies 'is red' if and only if it is red

we proceed, not by embedding (S) inside the construction '*A* implicitly knows that . . .', but by saying something of the following form:

(K) *A* knows to say of an object 'It is red' if and only if that object is red.

The general difficulty with this attractive idea is that the move from propositional to practical knowledge loses the connection with *truth*. (K) can be false for many speakers, for the contexts in which they know to say 'It is red' are not exhausted by the *truth* of so saying; politeness, deceit, and a thousand other cases intrude. This is not, I think, just a point about the particular (Glaswegian) idiom I have relied upon in encapsulating talk of practical knowledge. The point is a quite general one: reliance upon propositional knowledge immediately invokes the connection with truth, central to the *literal* understanding of these expressions, whereas the move to practical knowledge threatens the loss of that connection. Various moves might be made to avoid this ('*A* knows truly to say . . .'), but none I think works. Nor is it clear how, in the final stages of the explanation, such practical knowledge is to issue in propositional knowledge of the kind to be explained.

There is, however, another possibility, which is to eschew cognitive relations to (nearly all of) the theory of sense altogether. Suppose that it is an axiom of the truth-theory of a speaker's language that

(S) Something satisfies 'is red' if and only if it is red.

That that is so, that the speaker's linguistic capacities are best described using a theory of sense of which (S) is a part, must mean that the speaker is different from how he would have been if he had spoken a different language – say, one in which 'is red' and 'is green' are interchanged in their usage. But why must that difference be reflected in his having a cognitive relation to an axiom in one theory of sense in one case and a different axiom in a different theory of sense in the other case? *Which* language he speaks will emerge quickly enough in the attempt to construct an overall theory of his linguistic behaviour meeting the condition that it license plausible propositional attitude ascriptions to him. The difference in his understanding of the language he speaks will emerge quickly enough by prompting him (explicitly) to say what he (or others of his speech-community) have said. Why should these differences imply some *cognitive* difference *vis-à-vis* the theory of sense in him? Why could it not be merely a *physical* difference? It is impossible that there be two creatures in identical physical states who speak different languages; creatures speaking different languages will also always be in different cognitive states; but there seems no need, once we move from explicitly manifestable cognitive differences (difference in propositional knowledge of his and others' utterances), to hold that any *further* physical difference must be also a *cognitive* difference.

This might appear to be a bland refusal to give an explanation. But, really, it is a refusal to give an explanation of a particular, somewhat dubious, kind. Suppose we say that competent speakers have knowledge (implicit propositional or pseudo-practical) of all of the theory of sense. We say this to *explain* their customary linguistic competence. The only reason we have for adopting the proffered cognitive claims, the only route we have to their truth, is their utility in providing the required explanation. The postulated cognitive states have no other consequences than the restricted range of facts they purport to explain – except, perhaps, a bogus psychologism and a false optimism about the ease of assessing a semantic proposal. Such an explanation is no explanation at all.

The position is comparable to (though ultimately weaker than) that which attributes to all those competent in arithmetic implicit propositional knowledge of Peano's axioms. These axioms, belying the name, are not self-evident truths to all users of arithmetic when put to them; nor are they in any plausible sense relied upon by all who solve arithmetical problems. Their attribution to numerates as implicit propositional knowledge is therefore detectable only by the very facts they purport to explain – viz. arithmetic competence. The content of such an explanation of arithmetic competence is exhausted by the particular range of facts it purports to explain, and that is no explanation at all. Nothing is gained – not even in answer to the question 'How do you know he'll continue to add up correctly?' – by such a knowledge attribution – except a bogus psychologism and a blindness to the difficulty of the task that Peano set himself. If one person is competent in arithmetic and another not, then there are indeed cognitive differences between them; one knows that seven nines are sixty-three, the other does not. And that difference must reflect some *other* difference between them: but that further difference may be merely a physical one, not a cognitive one. In fact, the arithmetical cognitive claim is in a better position than the semantic cognitive claim: for the theory of sense is yet more of an abstraction, requiring as it does the deliverances of the theory of force before the 'data' to be explained are yielded. Any final cognitive explanation of customary linguistic competence would therefore also need a cognitive account of the relation of a speaker to the theory of force.

Someone whose linguistic behaviour is usefully described as being that of an English speaker speaks a language that is usefully described by a theory of sense including axiom (S). As an ordinary, unreflective English speaker his understanding and knowledge of English is exhausted by his everyday competence in simply saying things in English in an identifiable mode of utterance, and by his appropriate responses to the utterances of others including saying what they have said. The theory of sense plays a crucial role in *describing* that competence in a way that makes it intelligible, but is not itself an object of that speaker's understanding. If more is asked for of quite how that theory of sense *explains* his behaviour – if an explanation is asked for not in terms of the *descriptive constitution* of his overall linguistic practice but in terms of the *causal* origin of particular examples of that practice – then the only possible explanation will be obtained by seeing that his being a speaker of that language, abstractly so characterised, implies that he is in a different physical state from that he would have been in had he not been a speaker of that language so characterised. The further explanation this will issue in of his linguistic competence will be of doubtful worth, both from the viewpoint of prediction and of generality. But the fault lies with the request for that further *kind* of explanation.

The theory of sense in its totality is in no way known by the competent speaker of the language. We should not allow the reflectiveness that our task as semantic theorists requires, nor the

235

lifelong unreflective access as native speakers to the data aiding that reflection which the alien theorist consciously sets out to collect, to blind us to this fact.

It is compatible with the foregoing to hold that the competent speaker knows part of the (homophonic) truth-theory of his language, though not to hold that he knows it *as* part of that truth-theory. What he knows is each of the T-sentences yielded by that truth-theory; and this is a knowledge that he can (and often does) manifest quite explicitly. This is a consequence of the concession made earlier to the propositional knowledge theorist.

Some native speaker produces an utterance – say, of sentence *p*. That same native speaker, or his audience, understands what was said. They can manifest that understanding by saying: 'He (I) asserted that *p*'. The notion of assertion that figures here, if not utterly obscure, entitles us to say of the utterer of this report: 'The reporter knows that the native speaker's utterance of "*p*" is true if and only if *p*'. When we report another's assertion we do so by interpreting his utterance, interpreting it by producing another utterance (of the content-sentence) which is true if and only if his original utterance is true. The ordinary, explicitly manifestable understanding of the assertion of another (or of oneself) reveals knowledge, explicitly manifestable knowledge, of the T-sentence for his utterance.

Competent speakers, then, know, and can explicitly manifest their knowledge of, the T-sentences of the theory of sense for their language. But they do not know them *as* T-sentences of that theory, nor do they know the axioms and rules of the theory of sense which suffice to generate those T-sentences. Understanding as independently manifestable knowledge ceases at the sentential level. Any further request for explanation of speakers' knowledge of the T-sentences, other than that satisfied by a description of the overall theory of linguistic behaviour and the location of that knowledge within that theory is misplaced: it could issue only either in incoherent pseudo-psychological explanations or in irrelevant physical explanations.

5 Language, Reality, and Verification

In interpretative semantics, austerity and realism, while not inseparable, can be, and here have been, made to go hand-in-hand.[4] The conception of semantic theory that has been developed here has been an austerely realistic one. The theory of sense, which is held to describe (cognitively or otherwise) the ordinary speaker's linguistic

[4] See, again, the footnote on p. 225; in this section, the complexities of realism are developed – complexities which reveal the unclarities of its logical connections with austerity.

competence, exhibits a striking disregard for the recognitional procedures employed by speakers. The axioms for proper names make no reference to the ways in which speakers determine that a given object is the referent of some name. The axioms for vague predicates (like colour-words) make no reference to the ways in which speakers detect whether a given object satisfies some predicate. The axioms for quantifiers make no reference to the procedures speakers use in *applying* the terms 'all', 'most', 'many', 'more', and 'some'. The T-sentences for complete indicative sentences make no reference to the procedures speakers adopt in determining the truth-values of those sentences. Thus the theory of sense which, cognitively (T-sentences) or otherwise (all sub-sentential components), is held to describe competent speakers' understanding of the language neglects the ways in which these speakers recognise the applicability of given linguistic forms.

The realistic conception of the theory of sense does not just neglect the recognitional procedures speakers employ; it effectively ignores the limitations of their recognitional capacities. That theory credits speakers with an understanding of sentences, with propositional knowledge of their T-sentences, even when it is beyond their capacities to recognise whether a given sentence is true or false. For example, the theory implies that speakers can produce and understand a sentence in which a vague predicate is attributed to an individual designated by means of a proper name, even though, lacking any effective procedure for either recognising or identifying the bearer of that name and lacking any effective procedure for determining of an object whether it satisfies or does not satisfy that predicate, speakers lack any procedure for determining the truth-value of that sentence. Similarly, the theory implies that speakers can produce and understand quantified sentences even though they lack, and perhaps must lack, any procedure for determining whether the quantified sentence is true or false. A standard example of this is quantification over an infinite domain: our theory of sense will attribute to speakers an understanding of the truth-conditions of the sentence 'A city will never be built here' even though the verification of that sentence is in principle beyond the recognitional capacities of ordinary speakers, even though the recognition of the obtaining of those truth-conditions is in principle beyond them. The same point applies to the recognition of the falsity conditions of the existentially quantified sentence 'Some day a city will be built here'. (Dummett, 'Truth', p. 65).

This consequence of the realistic character of our semantic theory is of the profoundest importance. It embodies a picture of our language reaching out to, connecting with, the external world in ways that are (at least) beyond our present practical comprehension.

It embodies a picture of an independently existing, somewhat recalcitrant world describable by our language in ways that transcend (at least) our present capacities to determine whether those descriptions are true or not. It embodies a picture of our language, and our understanding, grappling with a stubbornly elusive reality. Perhaps, with effort, we can improve our capacities to understand that world, to know that our characterisations of it are true. If we succeed in so doing, we do not bring that world into being, we merely *discover* what was there all along. But that reality will always exceed our capacities: we can struggle to achieve *approximately true* beliefs about that reality, approximately true beliefs about the entities and their characteristics which, independently of us, make up that reality. But we have to rest with the approximate belief, and ultimately to resign ourselves to (non-complacent) ignorance: for the world, austerely characterised by our language, will always outrun our recognitional capacities.

I find this conception of the world profound, sympathetic, and (healthily) depressing. Its profundity would emerge more vividly if we were to consider the possibilities it presents for human knowledge in the areas of science, the arts, and morals were we to attempt to incorporate these areas of discourse within our austerely realistic semantic theory. But the picture, like the realistic truth-based semantics which prompts it, is open to serious challenge. The most direct of these challenges comes from verificationism (cf. McDowell in Evans and McDowell, *Truth and Meaning,* pp. 62–6).

One verificationist objection is misplaced. This objection starts from the thought that language-acquisition proceeds through the acquisition of habits of sensitivity to evidence. We learn expressions by learning sentences containing them; and the crucial element in the learning of a sentence is that of learning when to say it and when not to say it; and the crucial element in that as regards learning its *literal* significance is learning to say it when the *evidence* supports that saying, when the evidence suggests that its truth-conditions obtain. But the austere, truth-based theory of sense expounded ignores this matter of evidence. By thus radically separating our grasp upon the truth-conditions of sentences from the matter of the evidence for their assertion we render that grasp something we could not have acquired in the way that we did in fact acquire language – viz. by establishing habits of sensitivity to evidence.

As said, this objection is misplaced: it assumes that if the role of evidence in the acquisition of language is not acknowledged in the theory of sense, it is not acknowledged at any point in the theory of linguistic behaviour; the theory of sense is thus isolated from evidential considerations. But as our earlier discussion of proper names suggests, this is a simple error.

238

It is true that a theory of sense of the austere, realistic character described makes no reference to matters of evidence; but those matters enter into our overall theory of linguistic behaviour in ways that bear upon the acceptability of a proposed theory of sense. Acceptability in a theory of sense requires that it combine with a theory of force to produce redescriptions of linguistic actions which then license the ascription to speakers of plausible propositional attitudes. The verificationist must accept that central in the attitudes so ascribed are beliefs; he must further accept that beliefs can only be plausibly so ascribed if they can be seen as prompted by, or, at least, potentially sensitive to, evidence for their truth. Thus evidential considerations enter into the theory of linguistic behaviour, not at the theory of sense, but at the point of assessing the plausibility of the propositional attitude ascriptions licensed by that theory in combination with other considerations; but this is sufficient to ensure that considerations of evidential import can determine whether a theory of sense is acceptable or not. So the claimed isolation of that theory from those considerations does not obtain.

There is a second verificationist objection to our realistic, truth-based conception of the theory of sense that is less easily met; but the consequences of accepting the objection would be much more drastic than anything (consciously) accepted by classical verificationists. This objection is that mastery of a language should be represented as consisting *solely* in sensitivity to evidence. In acquiring his mastery of the language, a speaker has *nothing* else to go on than others' encouragement and discouragement of his linguistic actions in given evidential situations, together with the further evidence of the observable linguistic actions of others in given evidential situations. All that this can induce, and so *all* that his mastery can consist in, is a set of dispositions to fit his utterances with the observed evidential circumstances.

But this is incompatible with the realistic truth-based conception of sense that has been expounded. Suppose a speaker produces an assertoric utterance of 'p'; then another speaker, competent in the language, can say of that speaker that he is asserting that p. But, as claimed earlier, if that employment of the notion of assertion is to have any content, then we must be able to say of the comprehending reporter that he *knows* that the sentence the original speaker uttered is true if, and only if, p. Since, on our realistic conception of the theory of sense, speakers can understand assertions of sentences that are undecidable by them, p can be a sentence whose truth-value is undetermined by what is observable evidence. In that case, we credit our comprehending reporter with knowledge of the truth-conditions of sentences which transcend his evidential recognition capacities; we thus credit him with a conception of truth as independent of evidence. But that is a conception of truth, of truth-conditions, that could not have been acquired in the way in which his language was in fact acquired.

If convinced by this objection, we shall need to replace our realistic conception of sentence-sense and of speakers' understanding of such sentence-sense by conceptions which in no way go beyond what is accessible in dispositions to linguistic behaviour in observable circumstances.[5] This will ultimately require a conception of sentence-sense and of understanding which starts from stimulations prompting utterances of sentences, and which finally does not go beyond dispositions to make such utterances in the light of such stimulatory promptings. Such a conception would take us far indeed from the realistic conceptions of language and of understanding, and so would take us far indeed from the realistic conception of the world earlier described. The strangeness of this non-realist conception of the world, both in its view of the present observable world and in its view of the past, is evident, but is no objection to that conception.

Like McDowell, whose presentation of these verificationist objections I have closely followed, I am not at all sure how to defend realism against this second challenge. It would not be enough to show that any intelligible description of linguistic practice requires the employment of the realistic conception of the world that the extreme verificationist shuns; it would not, for example, be enough to show that the verificationist cannot, within his own non-realistic terms, give coherent accounts of *assertion* and of *belief*. For the anti-realist argument remains.

Two of the key notions in any evaluation of this anti-realist argument are those of *explanation* and *reduction*. That argument starts from a conception of the proper form of any explanation of linguistic competence and of specific manifestations of that competence. The idea appears to be that the best such explanation is the quasi-scientific story in terms of induced dispositions to respond verbally to stimulations and exercises of those dispositions prompted by particular stimulations received. This form of explanation is deemed to be better than that, merely 'descriptive', one which sees language-acquisition as the inculcation of dispositions to fit utterances with the (independently existing) real world and which sees particular utterances as prompted by recognition (or misrecognition) of (independent) features of that (independently existing) world because it, so to speak, *fills in the steps* in the story that the realistic account

---

[5] Whether this would require the abandonment of an austere theory of truth meeting Convention T as the theory of sense is unclear; perhaps that *format* could be retained.

ignores.[6] Favouring the step-filling explanation incorporates the (supposed) ideal of *reducing* semantic facts to physical facts. The problem with the realistic picture is that it ignores these further physical facts and so treats semantic facts as autonomous of physical facts in such a way as to allow (senselessly) those semantic facts to *outrun* the physical facts. (See Quine in Davidson and Hintikka, *Words and Objections,* pp. 302–4.)

Thus we start with the realistic idea of symbols attaching to the (independently existing) world. Feeling that there is something unacceptably mysterious about saying that, semantically, this attachment is just a *brute fact*, we proceed to ask for some further semantic *explanation* as to how that attachment comes about and is relied upon on particular occasions of utterance. We then see that the only further explanation available is the quasi-scientific explanation just sketched; so we interpret that further explanation as part of a semantic account. Doing so, we discover the incoherence of realistic conceptions of meaning and understanding, and so of the world.

But the suppositions so revealed behind the anti-realist argument are not beyond dispute. First, the claim of the superiority of the step-filling explanation is not, independently of the concluded anti-realist position, at all clear. That story will be immensely complex, will vary from speaker to speaker, and will vary for the same speaker through time. Its explanatory utility will thus be drastically reduced in point both of predictive capacity and of generality. 'Why did he say that the cushion was red?' Because he believed (or saw) that *it* was *red*, not just because the particular pattern of reflected light waves produced a particular stimulation of his retina which produced a particular stimulation in his visual cortex which prompted a vocalising disposition previously induced by experience of (similar!) cortical stimulations which prompted (similar!) vocalisings which were suitably rewarded. For that second explanation, filled-out in detail, will not apply when next week he makes the same assertion, nor will it apply to another's assertion of the same sentence. Even if the story were made more behavioural and less mechanical, or more stimulatorily recognitional and less behavioural, the same moral would apply. 'How did he acquire mastery of the sentence "That cushion is red"?' By being taught to say *of objects* that they are red (or are cushions) only when he holds it *true of the objects* that they are red (or cushions), not just by virtue of the truth of the tortuous quasi-physical (or quasi-behavioural or quasi-stimulatory)

---

[6] Any suggestion that the anti-realist *goes beyond* the realist is, of course, odd; the final anti-realist view is that the realist goes beyond what is coherent. Still, in terms of pursuing explanations, the anti-realist, as presented here, goes 'further' than the realist.

story of the kind just outlined, a story itself intelligible only in realist terms.[7]

Second, even if we pass over these deficiencies in the further explanation proffered, it remains completely unargued for that this *further* explanation is a further *semantic* explanation. Why must such a fleshing-out of the austere semantic description be itself incorporated into that description? Only that incorporation, with the consequent connection between *understanding* and the (pseudo-evidential) considerations mentioned in that further explanation, can produce the result that the realistic conception falsifies our acquired capacities for understanding. Only an (as yet) unargued for *reductivism* could prompt that incorporation.

It is anyway quite clear which of the realist and anti-realist views produces a false picture of our understanding of our language. And it is equally clear that the best semantic description of our semantic capacities – and, except from the (narrow) viewpoint of the scientific, the best description *tout court* – is that posited by the realistic view of language, its acquisition and mastery. Perhaps we shall need to add to this description some 'innate propensity' to realistic thinking about the world (cf. Mackie, *Problems from Locke,* p. 211); but there would be no great puzzle about how that propensity was induced, since its utility is clear: for the alternative to realism is silence in thought as well as in deed. We must, to counterfeit a Strawsonian coining, rest content with our knowledge (and indefinite ignorance) of the real world; for we lack words to say what it is to be without it.

---

[7] And if the anti-realist rejoinder is 'That's no explanation at all', the realist response is 'Exactly!'.

Chapter X

Moral Reality

1 The Nature of Ethical Realism

This chapter is almost by way of being an epilogue to the foregoing. The term is aptly chosen, since here, even more than elsewhere, the danger of evangelism is great. But no matter. My concern is to determine quite what would be involved in extending the realistic view of language just expounded and defended to include moral discourse and so moral thought. I do not know if this extension can defensibly be made; I am sure that much hangs upon the question.

Two major ethical traditions which can be construed as realistic are the intuitionist and the utilitarian. Some of my reasons for focusing upon the former, as the more plausible tradition, will emerge on the way.

The form of ethical intuitionism I shall consider has three main positive characteristics and two important negative ones. The first positive characteristic is that moral judgments are viewed as *factually cognitive*, as presenting claims about the world which can be assessed (like any other factual belief) as true or false, and whose truth or falsity are as much possible objects of human knowledge as any other factual claims about the world. This amounts in part to the denial of anything in the literal meaning of a moral judgment which compels us to assess those judgments on some dimension other than (or in addition to) that of the true and the false. It thus amounts also to the claim that if a moral judgment is true, it is true in virtue of the (independently existing) real world, and is true in virtue of that alone. This characteristic, or set of characteristics, is shared by utilitarianism.

The second positive characteristic of this form of intuitionism is that, in general, it is *austerely realistic*. Within the theory of sense for the language of which they are a part, particular moral expressions – 'sincerity', 'loyalty', 'honesty', 'prudence', 'courage', 'integrity'

243

– will generally be handled in an austere interpretative manner trading upon the structure of designation and use, whether they be treated as nominatives, adjectives, or adverbs. We may be able to give informal glosses upon some of these expressions, glosses which will help both to exhibit their interrelations (like those between prudence and courage) and to connect with some of the procedures sometimes used in determining their application; but such glosses are not acknowledged within the theory of sense.[1] The motivation behind this is not just to avoid the (usually fruitless) task of producing 'informative' decompositional analyses of these expressions producing truly necessary and sufficient conditions for their application, but also to deny any attempt to *reduce* (obviously) moral claims to (supposedly obviously) non-moral claims. The converse of this is the denial of the claim that moral judgments are *inferences* from non-moral judgments. This pair of denials amounts to a strong version of the claim that moral judgments are *autonomous* of non-moral judgments.

The parallel to exploit in understanding this autonomy is the relation, discussed earlier in another context, between there being a certain arrangement of black dots on a white card and there being a face there pictured to be seen. There is only a face there to be seen because the dot-arrangement is as it is; the dot arrangement *fixes* (subject, perhaps, to existing conventions of pictorial representation) whether or not there is a face there to be seen. Still, we do not *see* the face by *attending* to that dot-arrangement, where that arrangement is characterised in terms free of picture and face-vocabulary – say, by a mathematical grid-system. Indeed, the more we so attend, the less likely we are to see the face that is there pictured. Thus we do not *infer* that the face is there from judgments in this non-pictorial, non-facial vocabulary about the arrangement of the black dots.

This is a dangerous parallel to invoke, both because of the role in such perceptual judgments of conventions of pictorial representation, and, more importantly, because the judgments that finally issue – 'That's a face' – are not *literally* true. Still, it need not lead us astray. The picture it invites in the moral case is this: once all the non-moral facts about a situation are fixed, so are all the moral facts; but we could know everything about those non-moral facts while being in utter ignorance of the moral facts. If we now go on to make moral judgments about the case, we do not do so by

---

[1] In these first two characteristics of moral realism, and in the ensuing discussion of moral relativism in the light of those characteristics, the area in which bridges can be built between austerity and full-blooded realism is approached. In my specification of this second characteristic as *austere realism*, I assume these bridges to have been built.

attending to the non-moral facts, the facts described in vocabulary free of moral import; we do not *infer* the moral facts from the non-moral facts. The more we attend to the non-moral descriptions of the case, the less likely we are to see the moral aspects of that case.[2] But, unlike the picture case, when we make moral judgments about the situation, what we say can be literally true or false; and, again unlike the picture case, there is no question of that truth or falsity being the result of conventions. It is the result of the (independent) world.

This motivation for this conception of autonomy is as coherent (or incoherent) as the contrast between moral and non-moral descriptions, between moral and non-moral facts. (Not that the import, in specific cases, of what has just been said requires adherence to such a general contrast.) Does, for example, the utilitarian deny this autonomy in his attempts to define moral terms using the vocabulary of pleasure, utility, or whatever? If his definitions worked, would this not show merely that the vocabulary of pleasure, utility, or whatever is moral vocabulary? Such definition is as compatible with *elevation* as with reduction. Still, for our purposes it will suffice to construe the (usual) austerity of the treatment of moral vocabulary within the theory of sense as being simply the denial of the possibility of *any* 'informative' definition of the terms so treated. If, subsequently, sense is given to the contrast between moral and non-moral vocabulary; and if, subsequently, sense is given to the claim that a definition is *reductive* rather than *elevatory*; then the motivation just sketched will emerge as a (coherent) consequence of the austerity accorded to moral vocabulary within a realistic, interpretative theory of sense.

Competence in understanding the sayings of others, and of themselves, implies in realistic semantics that speakers can have knowledge of the truth-conditions of sentences that transcend at least their present capacities for determining whether those sentences are true or false. This general consequence of realistic semantics must be accepted in the area of moral vocabulary by anyone wishing to treat such vocabulary realistically. A speaker can know, have a grasp of, the truth-conditions of a moral sentence even if those truth-conditions are beyond his (present) recognitional abilities. I shall return to this consequence of realism in morals a little later.

The third positive aspect of this form of ethical intuitionism is designed to admit, what the utilitarian must deny, the possibility of genuine moral dilemmas, of genuine moral conflicts. In one standard version of ethical intuitionism, the direct object of intuition is The

---

[2] The plausibility of this element of the picture presented is difficult to assess without a much surer grasp than we yet have upon the contrast between moral and non-moral facts. See also the footnote on p. 254.

Good. If that is the direct object of intuition, it is difficult to see how genuine dilemmas can arise: just as for the utilitarian the only problem-case is that in which the utilitarian consequences of, say, two possible actions are more or less indistinguishable, so, for this kind of *monistic* intuitionist, the only problem-case is that in which each of two possible actions shares to the same extent the property of being good. Such cases are not true dilemmas. The version of intuitionism I want to consider does admit of such dilemmas by being *pluralistic*. For this version, there are *many* distinct ethical properties whose occurrence can be detected – sincerity, loyalty, honesty, and so on – and there is no reason *a priori* to assume that they cannot conflict, even, perhaps, in tortuous ways.

Such a pluralism seems to me a desirable feature in any plausible form of intuitionism (or of any other moral theory). First, there seems the brute fact that moral dilemmas do occur, and with rather painful frequency. Only moral laziness or moral blindness could hide this from us. Second, we only think of an action (or attitude or person) in terms of whether it is good or not *either* when we are being lazy *or* as a consequence of having thought about it in terms of other, more specific, terms of moral appraisal, so that *The Good* becomes an *indirect* object of moral judgment. Wittgenstein says that we only call a picture 'beautiful' when we cannot be bothered to think of anything more specific (or interesting) to say about it. The same is true of calling something 'good'. The interesting, basic terms of moral description are things like: 'sincere', 'loyal', 'compassionate', and so on. We have a grasp of each of these ideas independent of (indeed, determining) our grasp of 'good'. There is therefore no *a priori* reason to believe that, in their instantiations, these ideas cannot conflict in deep ways, nor any reason to believe that subsuming them under the (derivative) expression 'good' will dissolve such conflicts. Third, acknowledgment of pluralism with the consequent acknowledgment of genuine moral dilemmas may serve to free us from a naive conception of morality as a decision-procedure. Doubtless, our moral thought about the world is geared, in part, to helping us decide what to do. But there seems no reason to believe that that thought does, or acceptably could, yield a print-out as to what we should do in every situation; there is certainly no reason to believe that there is one kind of decision-procedure, some one golden rule (Do the best!), that will determine, in any given state of affairs, what we should do. Pluralistic intuitionism, unlike utilitarianism, requires the abandonment of the false hope for such a procedure.

The ethical intuitionism that I am considering, then, is cognitively factual, austerely realistic, and pluralistic. Now for what it is not.

246

First, it is no part of this intuitionism to suggest that we detect the moral aspects of a situation by means of some *special faculty* of the mind, the intuition. We detect moral aspects in the same way we detect (nearly all) other aspects: by looking and seeing. Any further claim, like that positing a distinctive faculty of ethical intuition, is a contribution to the unintelligible pseudo-psychology of the faculties of the mind. Second, contrary to a persistent strand in classical intuitionist thought, certainty plays no role in this form of intuitionism. This is a consequence of taking realism seriously. By the process of careful attention to the world, we can improve our moral beliefs about the world, make them more approximately true; by the same process, we can improve our practical understanding, our sensitivity to the presence of instances of the moral concepts that figure in these beliefs. But this process of attention to improve beliefs and understanding will go on without end; there is no reason to believe that we shall ever be justified in being certain that most of our moral beliefs are true, and no reason to believe that we shall ever be justified in being certain that we have now completely understood any of the moral concepts occurring in these beliefs. Our moral language, like all the realistic part of that language, transcends our present practical comprehensions in trying to grapple with an independent, indefinitely complex reality; only ignorance of that realism could prompt the hope for certainty.

2 Relativism and Reason

We have, now, a picture of a realistic ethical intuitionism, together with some of the considerations that prompt its particular form. But is it defensible? More generally, what difficulties does this attempt to embrace moral discourse within semantic realism encounter?

One familiar set of difficulties, which merits a much more detailed discussion than I can give it here, is raised by the moral relativist. He begins by pointing to the 'observed' fact that moral judgments about some particular action, or about some particular kind of action, vary drastically even within a given community, let alone between different communities; he further points to the 'observed' fact that categories of moral assessment can vary drastically between communities. The utilitarian will often give a different moral assessment from that which (we) old-fashioned moralists give. The act of vengeance by the Sicilian may be deemed by us to be wrong, by his native community to be right. It may even be that the Sicilian has moral concepts that we lack, and vice versa, and claims to be able to 'detect' instances of these concepts that we cannot 'detect', and vice versa. Even if we can *roughly* translate the terms he uses in morally describing his action, that translation cannot be a good one, our grasp upon the relevant concept must be lacking, if we cannot see how that characterisation makes that action even *prima facie* morally desirable, let alone morally praiseworthy *tout court*. But there is no way of resolving such moral 'disputes', no way of ensuring that we can first be led to see things as the Sicilian sees them (or that he be led to see them as we see them), and no way of then deciding, *externally* from any such system of moral perception, which is the correct one. Each system is coherent in its own terms, and there is no external standpoint for viewing, for understanding, and deciding between such systems.

In such a situation, the relativist claims, there is no sense to the claim of objective, cognisable truth in moral judgments, and our intuitionist picture of them must be wrong. The nature of those judgments is, perhaps, closer than we realised to the nature of pictorial judgments discussed earlier. Moral judgments, too, are partly the result of conventions which could have been, and in some places are, otherwise. Moral judgments, too, cannot be called literally true or false. We do indeed, from our particular standpoint, *see* moral aspects of situations; but what we see is the result of sets of (perhaps unconscious) conventions, and has no independent objective reality.

The substantial, quite general worries the relativist raises are these: when do differences in judgments imply differences in concepts? And when do differences in judgments (failures of inter-subjective agreement) compel us to abandon the view of the subject-matter of the judgments as objective? Both are familiar questions from the writings of the later Wittgenstein. I wish I had detailed answers to those questions; but even while lacking such answers, I think we can see that the relativist is prone to answer these questions in too simple and hasty a manner. His case is thus not proven.

First, the 'simple fact' of differences of moral judgment does not yet imply the falsity of moral realism. In moral judgments, as in others, people can, and do, make mistakes. What realism requires is that their errors be *explicable* – in realistic terms. It is not, for example, difficult to explain the erroneous moral judgments of many white (and some black) South Africans. Their perceptions are clouded by their desires and fears in just the way that many of our own factual judgments are clouded: *of course* my wife is completely faithful to me, *of course* my son is quite exceptionally academically talented! The popularity of Lamarckian genetic theory in Stalinist Russia, even though that theory is probably false, does not make us doubt the realistic reading of genetic claims, for we can see quite easily what blinded its proponents to its deficiencies; they fell victim to the perpetual human tendency of allowing something other than the evidence as to how things are to affect their beliefs about how things are. For the intuitionistic realist, this same pattern of explanation can be applied to moral errors.

Second, such errors can sometimes be corrected by rational consideration. Many proponents of Lamarckian theory came to see the error of their ways with the passage of time and discussion. Given reflection upon our own experiences and psychological characteristics, we can come to see the error of our moral views; we can come to change our moral views in an intelligibly non-arbitrary manner. We can come to see how that dreadful experience in the potting-shed, or that charismatic personality of the priest, has quite *irrelevantly* influenced our views upon the good and the right. If the errors of others are explicable, our own are discoverable.

Third, moral differences are exactly what a realist should expect. Moral concepts exhibit the characteristic of *semantic depth*. Starting from our grasp upon them through our knowledge of the austere truth-conditions of sentences containing them, we have to struggle to improve our sensitivity to particular instantiations of them. This process proceeds without limit; at no point, for the realist, can we rest content with our present sensitivity in the application of these concepts. So at no point can we rest *secure* in all our present judgments involving these concepts. For the realist, moral language, like all other realistic areas of language, is trying to grapple, in ways which transcend our present practical capacities, with a recalcitrant world. Moral differences are no more surprising (or perturbing) to the kind of realism under discussion than are scientific, or historical, differences.

This leads to a fourth point against too hasty a relativism. The fact that people use different criteria in detecting the presence of an abstractly described moral feature does not yet show that they have literally different concepts. Their central grasp upon that concept is grounded in the austere theory of sense for the term expressing that concept. That austere concept can be the same even if they use different procedures, yielding different results, in detecting instances of that feature. This must be so if genuine moral conflicts are to arise between people, genuine disputes, for example, as to what is a manifestation of generosity. Many of the differences the relativist points to are not differences in the concept of a particular vice or virtue, but differences of quasi-empirical view as to what counts as a manifestation of the virtue, as to how that virtue is to be detected.[3] Perhaps there is no substantial, non-verbal issue here; or perhaps there is a point where differences about the manifestations of a

---

[3] That is, many of the facts which motivate relativism do indeed point to different *conceptions* of a virtue; but this is not yet to show that different *concepts* are involved. 'Different conceptions *of* one thing' implies realism, not relativism.

virtue require us to say that the disputants hold different concepts; but that point, if it exists, is neither as clear nor as quickly reached as the relativist suggests. The *semantic* depth of moral notions is reflected in our austere, realistic treatment of terms expressing them; it leaves quite unclear the (important) question as to *when* different concepts are to be attributed to different speakers. But for the realist, that is a desirable initial lack, not to be remedied in too simplistic a manner.

Fifth, the fact that others apparently lack moral concepts that we possess (or vice versa) no more shows realism to be false in moral matters than the fact that others lack scientific concepts we possess (or vice versa) shows realism in science to be false. What the realist requires is an explanation, in realistic terms, of that lack; and there is usually no shortage of these.

The relativist can, up to a point, concede the foregoing. He is likely to insist upon two points, one incidental, the other central. The incidental point he will insist upon is that no account has yet been given of *how* we can come to understand the (different) moral concepts of others, of how we can come to see things morally as they see them. We have no account, that is, of how we can truly understand different moral schemes of thought in the way that we can understand different scientific, or historical, systems of thought. And the central point he will insist upon is this: that process of comprehension, on any account, will issue in a free choice. Having once come to see things morally as an alien sees them, there is no procedure open to us for deciding which is the *true* way of seeing things. At such a reflective point, we have a *free* choice of adopting (or rejecting) the alien way rather than living with the (usually unthinking) choice originally made for us by those who taught us our initial moral scheme. Incidental as the first point is, it bears closely upon the second: for the anti-realist conceives of the process of understanding others' moral views as comparable to the (perhaps usually *practical*) process of being educated into a different set of *conventional* procedures for seeing things, and so views the state so achieved as itself merely conventional.

Once more, this position is less simple than it seems. Consider, first, the parallel with pictured faces. Having once seen the face, we are convinced that there is (non-literally) a face there to be seen. The failure of others to see that face does not make us doubt its 'presence' as a possible object of detection. And there are, of course, many ways in which we might try to draw another's *attention* to that 'presence'. In so doing, we demonstrate our conviction that there is something there to be seen; we do not attempt merely to encourage hallucinations. But the closer parallel for the realist is, perhaps, that with the detection of an ambiguity in a spatial figure.

Having once seen that ambiguity, we are convinced that there is, literally, an ambiguity there to be seen. The failures of others to see that ambiguity does not make us doubt its presence, and there are many ways in which we might attempt to draw somebody's *attention* to that ambiguity. If we succeed, we succeed in making them see what was all along there to be seen.

This parallel with ambiguous figures is useful since the existence of ambiguities in spatial figures need not be in any clear sense a matter of convention, nor is the process of drawing an ambiguity to someone's attention always correctly represented as a process of educating them into conventions of seeing. Its limitation is, however, clear: there is no sense to the thought that there is *one* correct way of seeing such a figure. Indeed, the best is to be capable of seeing all its ambiguities.

Still, the idea is left available to the realistic intuitionist of accounting for the process of understanding the ways others see things morally, and of explaining to them one's own way of seeing things, as a process of attention being drawn to features previously overlooked or misperceived. There is no guarantee that this will work; but, then, there is no guarantee that any realistic vocabulary can be taught. What the realist has to deny in the moral case to produce the requisite disanalogy to the example of perceiving spatial ambiguities is that in *radical* cases of moral difference the alien way of seeing things can be fully (perceptually) understood alongside one's own. Cases of misperception – of false claims that an action instantiates some virtue we recognise – are no problem for the realist; the important case is that where an alien claims to have a grasp upon a distinctive virtue that we cannot grasp. But, for the realist, if we cannot see it, then (tentatively) it is not there to be seen. People can have empty moral predicates (which they believe to be non-empty), just as they can have empty proper names (which they believe to be non-empty); trivially, no realistic account can be given of such empty moral predicates. Explanations have to be given of their error, as in the case of proper names; but there is no reason to believe that this cannot be realistically done.

The procedure for understanding another's moral view is that of leaving oneself open to his efforts to draw our attention to the (distinctive) features he claims to detect, perhaps by his engaging us in the practices he engages in. Usually, we shall come to see the difference as non-radical, as a difference of conceptions, not of concepts; but if that difference is radical – if we just cannot *see* what he is talking *about* – then the tentative conclusion is that he is in radical error – or that *we* are.[4] While if his efforts are successful, if

---

[4] Thus, in aesthetics we may suppose that we are blind to the point of some alien art form.

we can indeed see things as he sees them, then our original way of seeing them must be rejected. It is an unargued-for dogma that we shall find ourselves in a position comparable to that in the case of spatial ambiguities, an unargued-for dogma that we shall find at least two radically different ways of seeing things with equal (un)reality.

At least two of the worries raised by the relativist can be raised quite independently of that position. The first is the thought that realism leaves no scope for moral discussion and reasoning; the second is that it neglects moral choice and moral responsibility.

The deficiencies in the first thought – that for the intuitionist you either see it or you don't, and that's the end of the matter – have already been partly exhibited. First, for the realistic intuitionist of the kind described, there need be nothing *obvious* about particular moral truths or about specific categories of moral assessment. Discussion with others, like self-reflection, may prompt the *attention* that is needed, both to focus upon particular moral aspects of a given case that would otherwise have been overlooked and to see instantiations of novel moral concepts of which we previously had no grasp. Likewise, discussion and critical reflection may force us to examine our views upon what constitutes a manifestation of a particular virtue, it may force us to think about why we consider various distinctive manifestations to be manifestations of the same (austerely characterised) virtue. Such discussion may induce reflection upon the ways in which manifestations of distinct virtues relate to each other, and so make us see, indirectly, the relations between these virtues. And more concretely, moral discussion may lead us to see the ways in which our moral perceptions have been clouded by the inclusion of irrelevant attitudes. Examples of such considerations would concretise these abstract points; but it is anyway clear that the value of moral exchange is great for the species of intuitionism under consideration.

The second of the worrying thoughts, that about moral choice and moral responsibility, is less clear, and less worrying than it seems, partly because it is often muddled with a (mistaken) objection to moral realism to the effect that it cannot account for the (supposed) desirability of a *plurality* of moral views.

It is indeed a consequence of moral realism of the kind considered here that, in some sense, everybody *should* have the same moral beliefs, just as they should all have the same scientific, or historical, beliefs. But that *should* relates to a world in which we are cognitively more secure than is the actual world. The same considerations in this world favour a plurality of moral views as favour a plurality of scientific views: we are tawdry, inadequate epistemic creatures struggling with an indefinitely complex world, and the dialogue between competing – but *competing* – views may make us attend to features of that world which we would otherwise have overlooked. But what we might overlook are features *of the world*, not fictions of our own imagination. Moral pluralism is desirable, not for liberal-cum-aesthetic reasons, but for *epistemic* ones. Only the mistaken identification of the cognitive element in realism with the indefensible hope of moral *certainty* could blind us to this *consequence* of realism.

The point as regards moral responsibility is simple, and, in the context of this defence of pluralism, forceful: my moral beliefs, like all my other beliefs, are *mine*. When I act, or prompt others to act, upon any of my beliefs – my belief as to the best thing to do, my belief about the last train to London – I have to live with the consequences, and with the consequences for others. When expressing a belief, I present a claim as to *how the world is*; I do that as a tawdry epistemic being, and should do it in the light of that fact; if I have been negligent in attending to evidence, or have allowed considerations other than evidence to intrude, then I am indeed culpable. But that remains true of me for all my realistic beliefs and their expressions; it remains unclear why there should be any further role for a distinctive notion of responsibility for my *moral* beliefs.

Once these points about pluralism and responsibility are seen, it remains unclear what force there is to the demand that moral choice be further acknowledged. Only the assumption that moral judgments reflect desires, or some comparable attitude, together with the assumption that desires, or whatever attitude, are a matter of choice, seems to give any force to that demand. But, then, the realist simply denies the first of these assumptions. Perhaps there are further arguments for that assumption to be met; but the claim for moral choice seems to have no independent ground.

The earlier consideration of the scope for discussion and reason within moral intuitionism leaves one deep problem unresolved, a problem arising from the autonomy *vis-à-vis* non-moral facts accorded by intuitionism to moral judgments. The realistic intuitionist holds that, while non-moral facts fix moral facts such that two circumstances cannot differ in a moral respect while being alike in all non-moral respects, still moral judgments are not analysable (or translatable) into non-moral terms; the making of a moral judgment is not an *inference* from non-moral facts. The problem now is that that picture appears to be in tension with the role usually accorded to non-moral differences in *accounting* for differences of moral judgment, accounting in a *reason*-giving way. If I make different moral judgments about situations that appear indistinguishable to you, then, the thought is, I have to *justify* that

253

difference by pointing to a non-moral difference, I have to give a non-moral *reason* for the difference in moral judgment. Indeed, this non-moral reason giving is the foundation of moral *consistency*: such consistency precisely requires (because is constituted by) the principle that if two situations are non-morally indistinguishable, we have to give the same moral judgment in each case, together with the principle that if a difference in moral judgment is given it has to be justified by a non-moral reason. (Cf. Simon Blackburn in Casey, *Morality and Moral Reasoning,* pp. 101–24.)

As said, the first of these principles is, as stated, quite compatible with realism: it is a simple consequence of the claim that non-moral facts *fix* moral facts. The problem is with the second principle, with accounting for the role of non-moral reasons in justifying differences of moral judgment; for this role seems simply incompatible with the autonomy claimed for moral judgments, seems simply incompatible, for example, with the denial of the claim that moral judgments are *inferences* from non-moral judgments.[5]

Still, two points suggest that this objection is less straightforwardly successful than it seems. First, the proper statement of the thesis of autonomy is in terms of the austere, realistic non-decompositional treatment given to moral terms in our theory of sense for moral language. Further expressions of that thesis, or of theses claimed equivalent to it, in terms of the relations between moral and non-moral facts require that content be given to the *contrast* between moral and non-moral facts. Until that contrast is, independently and defensibly, explicated, it is open to the realist to reply to the argument from moral reasons in a simple way: if the giving of a reason intelligibly accounts for a difference in moral judgment, it is itself a *moral* reason. How could it play that role if it were not? Nor, for the realist, is there anything puzzling about the role of those, as it were, lower level, more concrete moral considerations in justifying moral judgments involving austerely characterised moral concepts. Those austerely characterised moral concepts, like any other austerely characterised concepts, have, in judgments about particular cases, to be *applied* to these cases; it is always a reasonable request to ask what criteria of application we are using. Those are indicated by the reasons we give for our judgments. But the considerations so adduced, if reasons for the application of a moral notion, must themselves be *moral* considerations; they need not, however, be suited for incorporation in non-austere analyses of the abstract moral concepts involved.

---

[5] Although this appearance of incompatibility may only arise from too crude a view of the relations between *reasons* and *inference*. Why cannot we acknowledge the role of non-moral statements as reasons for moral judgments while denying the inferred character of moral judgments?

Second, even if an acceptable content is given to the distinction between moral and non-moral considerations, and even if the thesis of autonomy is then re-expressed in such terms, the force of the objection from moral consistency and moral reasoning remains unclear: for it remains unclear that that notion of consistency and that notion of reasoning have acceptable roles to play. The ideas behind the conceived roles of these notions appear to be these: first, in deciding what moral judgment about a particular situation is correct, we need to consider our judgments about situations encountered in the past; and, second, that what should *ground* our moral judgments about a specific situation is some rule, or set of rules, in which moral and non-moral terms are connected in such a way that the applicability of the latter determines the applicability of the former. But both these ideas are counsels of moral laziness, are counsels of the neglect of the *particular* situation, in all its (non-obvious) complexity, at present before us. In ordinary moral life, the problem is not that of squaring our present judgments with our previous judgments, but that of *attending* to the full, unobvious moral complexity of the present case. In ordinary moral life, determining our moral judgment about a particular case by means of some rule seizing upon non-moral aspects of that case will simply mean that we neglect the full complexity of that particular case.

Doubtless, for the pressing purposes of everyday life, considerations of consistency with previous judgments on the basis of crudely observed similarities and of rules for making specified kinds of judgments in crudely described states of affairs are useful, perhaps indispensable, *rules of thumb*; but for the realist, they are no more than that. In ordinary life, moral situations do not repeat themselves; only insensitivity can suggest that they do. The objection to moral realism starts, not just from the practical exigencies of ordinary moral life, but from a supposed feature of that moral life; but that feature does not exist.

3 Morality and Action

The discussion so far of moral judgments has one curious lack: any consideration of the relation between moral judgments and *action*. Reflection upon that lack prompts a further series of objections to the kind of intuitionistic realism here expounded.

Moral judgments apparently connect with action in two ways: first, a moral judgment always purports to give a *reason for action*; and, second, assessment of the *sincerity* of one who makes a moral judgment is determined by seeing how he *acts*. Both of these points might be thought quite inexplicable upon the intuitionistic view of moral judgments.

The worry about reasons for actions, connecting with the earlier worry about moral choice, is this: any full specification of a reason for action, if it is to be a reason *for the potential agent* for action, must make reference to that agent's *desires*; moral judgments always purport to be (sufficiently) full specifications of at least *prima facie* reasons for the agent to act; so moral judgments must include (perhaps, within the antecedent of a conditional) reference to the potential agent's desires. It is thus misleading to assimilate them to straightforward factual descriptions of the world which make no such references. Whether a moral 'description' of a case is 'true' or not depends upon the desires of the person considering it; those desires are, or admissibly can be, a matter of choice; so, therefore, are the moral 'descriptions' given, there being in consequence no question about those 'descriptions' being objectively true or false.

The crucial premiss in this argument is the claim that any full specification of a reason for an action, if it is to be a reason for the potential agent for action, must make reference to that agent's desires. At first sight, it seems a painful feature of the moral life that this premiss is false. We perform many intentional actions in that life that we apparently do not desire to perform. A better description of such cases appears to be that we perform them because we think them desirable. The difficulty of much of moral life then emerges as a consequence of the apparent fact that desiring something and thinking it desirable are both distinct and independent.

The premiss can, of course, be held true by simply claiming that, when acting because we think something desirable, we do indeed desire it. But this is either phenomenologically false, there being nothing in our inner life corresponding to the posited desire, or utterly vacuous, neither content nor motivation being given to the positing of the desire. Nothing but muddle (and boredom) comes from treating desire as a mental catch-all (cf. Woods, 'Reasons for Actions and Desires').

There is a weaker, more abstract claim, difficult to state in non-metaphorical terms, which perhaps underlies the premiss about desire just discussed, and which is still incompatible with the realist position developed. Miss Anscombe, in her work on intention, has drawn a broad distinction between two *kinds* of mental state, factual belief being the prime exemplar of one kind and desire a prime exemplar of the other (Anscombe, *Intention,* §. 2). The distinction is in terms of the *direction of fit* of mental states with the world. Beliefs aim at the true, and their being true is their fitting the world; falsity is a decisive failing in a belief, and false beliefs should be discarded; beliefs should be changed to fit with the world, not vice versa. Desires aim at realisation, and their realisation is the world fitting with them; the fact that the indicative content of a desire is not realised in the world is not yet a failing *in the desire*, and not yet any reason to discard the desire; the world, crudely, should be changed to fit with our desires, not vice versa. I wish I could substitute a less picturesque idiom for that of *direction of fit*, but I cannot. I wish also I were clearer as to whether there are *any* mental states for which the direction of fit is purely of the second kind; desires seem not to be such a candidate, since all desires appear to involve elements of belief. Still, the picturesque distinction may, for present purposes, suffice; and all these purposes require is a conception of factual belief which is purely of the first kind *vis-à-vis* direction of fit.

The point now is that the realist treats moral judgments as being pure members of the first cognitive category of mental states, and that the anti-realist claims that any full specification of a reason for action must make reference to the (potential) agent's mental states of the second category. If thinking something desirable is to be a reason for doing it, then that notion cannot, contrary to the realist's view, be assimilated to pure factual beliefs. Such an assimilation divorces moral judgments from reasons for action.

The realist has two, ultimately connected, lines of response to this challenge. One focuses upon the fact that the realist's assimilation of moral judgments to purely factual beliefs *vis-à-vis* direction of fit with the world is an assimilation only in point of literal sense. The other line of response is simply to demand argument for the general point about reasons for actions made by the anti-realist. Both lines of response, like the possible anti-realist counter-responses, are indecisive; I cannot yet see how the issue is to be resolved.

When we express mundane factual beliefs, we often, in doing so, also express, as it were indirectly, other mental attitudes of a less cognitive kind; but these other attitudes do not enter into the literal truth-conditions of what is said. It is open to the realist to hold the same to be true of expressions of moral beliefs: such expression is often, perhaps standardly, also an indirect expression of other attitudes or mental states of a less cognitive kind, of moral *sentiments*. But, first, it is not easy to produce a general, plausible, non-vacuous description of these standard accompaniments of moral expression. And, second, even if such a description of the standard role of moral sentiments can be given, they need not enter into the literal truth-conditions of what is said; the realist thought is thus that the appearance of an objectionable element only arises through the neglect of the crucial distinction between the literal sense of an expression and the matter of what is done upon occasions of utterance of it. For the realist, these further elements cannot affect the basic mode of moral utterance, which must remain that of *assertion*; but that does not mean that these further elements have no role to play in a full account of what is *done*, standardly, by the assertoric utterance of a moral sentence.

One trouble with this concessive response is that it incurs an obligation to explain how this *standard* connection with expressions of other non-cognitive attitudes comes about. It does not *seem* very satisfactory to hold that the obtaining of this connection is simply an inexplicable feature of moral discourse, an (otherwise) inexplicable consequence of the *sui generis* importance of moral facts; but nor does it *seem* very satisfactory to withhold the initial concession by claiming that the connection misleadingly labelled 'standard' is simply a chance, contingent fact. That last claim would require, to say the least, a very sophisticated account of the phenomenology of moral language use to dispel the 'illusion' of a critical connection between moral judgments and moral sentiments.

The other line of realist defence is to demand argument for the claim that any full specification of a reason for action must make reference to a mental state of the second, non-cognitive kind *vis-à-vis* direction of fit with the world. Why should it not just be a brute fact about moral facts that, without any such further element entering, their clear perception does provide sufficient grounding for action? Two anti-realist lines of thought lead nowhere. One is that there must be such a further element to *impel* action; but this contribution to a pseudo-psychology grinds, or should grind, to a quick halt. The other is to claim that there must be such a further element because any list of sufficient conditions for an action being intentional must include the attribution to the agent of such a mental state. Here, the halt is much slower, deriving from a simple point: since no one has presented a truly sufficient set of conditions for an action to be intentional, it must remain quite undecided whether any given putatively necessary condition is indeed a necessary condition; it might well be that some *further* condition, anyway required for sufficiency, will reveal the putatively necessary condition to be unnecessary. If it is replied that this could only occur by the new, sufficiency-achieving condition incorporating the previous necessary condition, then the realist has two rejoinders. First, this assumes that *any* set of sufficient conditions for intentional action must include *every* element which within any one set of sufficient conditions is necessary. Doubtless, for *many* kinds of action reference to some 'pro-attitude' or whatever is necessary in giving sufficient conditions for the action being intentional; it does not yet follow that it is a necessary condition in *any* set of sufficient conditions. And second, the realist claims to have a counter-example to the claim that it does follow: viz. the fact that clear moral perceptions are sufficient as reasons for actions. It is utterly unclear how the claim that moral perceptions have this *sui generis* feature is to be settled one way or the other.

These realist manoeuvres are also available when the matter of *sincerity* of moral judgment is raised. The anti-realist thought is that there is a distinctive notion of sincerity involved in expression of moral 'beliefs' since such sincerity is assessed by seeing what the person *does* in a way that is different from the assessment of sincerity in expressions of ordinary factual beliefs.

To this the realist can reply, first, that the *sui generis* feature of moral perceptions just relied upon in meeting the worry about reasons for actions does indeed import the requisite connection between sincerity and action. If a person does indeed see the moral nature of a situation clearly, and does indeed express that perception sincerely, then what he does will, subject to later qualifications, accord with what he says; at least, it will accord with what he says to the degree that such accord is plausibly required in deeming his expression sincere. For that clear moral perception, *ex hypothesi*, presents sufficient reason for him to act (which is not yet to say that he *will* so act). Second, the appearance of a distinctive notion of sincerity in expression of moral judgments may only arise upon a mistaken view of the notion of sincerity in expression of ordinary, factual beliefs. We tend to treat this latter notion as being a more derivative one than it is. Starting from the identification of sincerity with *truthfulness*, we focus upon the notion of *truth* occurring there, and interpret it realistically: we think of there being two, quite independent elements, the inner, private mental states of the person, and what he says *about* those states, as his *expression* of those states; we then think of sincerity, of truthfulness, as being the result of the latter *fitting* the former. There is then no question of what the person does as opposed to what he *says* determining his sincerity. But there is another way of seeing the elements so described. Starting from what he says *and* does, we invoke the (non-derivative) notion of sincerity in 'constructing' his inner, private life, we gain access to that life by seeing what he says *sincerely* and what he does *sincerely*, where this notion of *doing sincerely* cannot *ex hypothesi* be grounded in the way the first picture suggests. How, if at all, it can be 'informatively' grounded is another question; and how, if at all, he is in a superior position to us in his access to his inner life is another question too. But what is clear is that the notion of sincerity we have acquired has its core, and must have its core, in the second, not the first, picture. And what is also clear is that in this alternative picture what a person does can affect our view of his sincerity in the expression of his ordinary, factual beliefs. Of course, there may still be differences between the factors that guide our construction

259

of the inner mundanely factual beliefs and those that guide our construction of the inner moral beliefs, as there may be differences in the analysis of an intentional action in which the one plays a part and in the analysis of an intentional action in which the other plays a part. But the appearance of radically different notions of sincerity – radically different in focusing on or shunning non-verbal actions – is not obviously correct.

It is anyway very difficult to state in a plausible form the connection between sincerity of moral expression and action. One idea is that such expression is sincere if, and only if, in a suitable circumstance the moral agent concerned acts accordingly. But this is far too strong. While lying on a beach, we see a young child playing in the sea; suddenly, we notice a swarm of sharks approaching; heroically, you plunge into the sea to save the child, risking death in the process. I describe your action in the most flattering moral terms. The next day, on the beach when alone, I see a similar incident happening; being less heroic, I do not plunge into the sea. Does that show that I was *insincere* the previous day when expressing my moral beliefs about your action? Of course not – and not because (or not just because) the notion of moral consistency phrased in terms of similar circumstances is sufficiently vague to leave me with sufficient logical leeway to escape the charge, but because (or also because) whatever the relation is between moral sincerity and action, it does not imply that I avoid the charge of insincerity only by being *heroic* (cf. Urmson, 'Saints and Heroes'). It is no part of the moral life that insincerity is avoided only by being saintly or heroic; our notion of sincerity is far more realistically connected with our view of *what people are like*. Here there is a substantial problem for *any* ethical theory in accounting for the relations between sincerity and action; but it is not a problem specific to the ethical realist, and there is no reason to believe that he is less well equipped to solve it than any other theorist.

There are two further, importantly distinct questions about the realist view of the relation between moral judgment and action. One is this: when will an agent act upon his moral judgments? It is a mistake to say: when, and only when, those judgments are sincere expressions of what he believes to be clear moral perceptions. The important mistake is not the neglect of actions based on (knowingly) cloudy perceptions, nor the naivety of the assumptions about the saintly and the heroic built into this answer, but is rather the belief that there is *any* useful answer to this question. Agents act upon their judgments when, and only when, they act upon them; beyond that, nothing useful can be said. Saying that they act upon their judgments only when they decide to act upon them, or when they *will* that they act upon them, is either vacuous or false. The question in the philosophy of action should not be: when does an agent act upon his judgments? It should rather be: when he has acted intentionally upon his judgments, what is the correct analysis of his having done so? An answer to the latter question will not give the *kind* of pseudo-predictive answer the first question requires; for there is no such answer.

But there is a second, more substantial question. How can the realist position, as developed here, account for the possibility of weakness of will? That is, how, on this account, is it possible for an agent knowingly to perform an intentional action against his best moral judgment? This is quite different from a question tantamount to the first, namely, how is it possible for an agent not to act in accordance with his best moral judgment?

The puzzle about weakness of the will, so-called, is this. Aside from genuine moral dilemmas, clear perception of the moral character of a situation gives, we have said, sufficient reason for action – which is not yet to say that action will ensue. The distinctive feature of clear moral perception is that it gives us a *compelling* reason to act. There are many reasons why action might not follow; but the puzzle misdescribed (for the realist) as weakness of will is how it can be that intentional action does follow, action done for a reason, which conflicts with the action suggested by that *compelling* moral perception. What could 'compelling' mean here if not that if the agent does *any* intentional action, he will do that action?

Two connected peripheral matters should first be mentioned to be put aside. First, it need not be relevant in this context to ask why moral considerations are overriding, if they are. The case to focus upon is that in which the akratic action performed is one which has no very substantial non-moral reason behind it. Second, cases where strong passions are involved are not the most puzzling ones; for in such cases, it is plausible to say that at the moment of action passion clouds the agent's perception. He simply does not see at the point of action the relevant moral aspects. The really puzzling case would satisfy the following description: in a cool, detached frame of mind the agent performs an action with no great point that does not accord with his clear moral perception of the situation.

One might question whether there are such cases, whether this could ever be a correct description of a case, but I shall not now consider this. Instead, I shall suggest that the *semantic depth* of moral concepts is the key to the dissolution of this puzzle.

Moral concepts have a kind of semantic depth. Starting from our austere grasp upon these concepts, together perhaps with some practical grasp upon the conditions of their application, we can proceed to investigate, to experience, the features of the real world answering to these concepts.[6] Precisely because of the realistic account given of these concepts and of our grasp upon them – precisely because they are designed to pick out features of the world of indefinite complexity in ways that transcend our practical understanding – this process of investigation through experience can, and should, proceed without end. Our grasp upon what, say, *courage* is can, and should, improve without limit; we must rest content with the thought that at death *approximate* understanding is all that we can hope for. But all along we have a grasp of what the concept is, as manifested by our grasp upon austere T-sentences involving it; and, perhaps, all along we have a grasp upon some *gloss*, some *dictionary definition*, of the term picking out that concept. But for the realist this austere grasp, that knowledge of the dictionary, is the beginning of understanding, not the end; there is, for us, no end, yet that starting point is far indeed from it.[7] Just the same could be said, by the realist, about scientific concepts.

This invites the following picture of the most puzzling kind of akratic action – *only* a picture, but that is a persistent feature in this area. At least at the moment of action, the akratic's perception is not *cloudy* but shallow: the concept he is then employing in his moral perception is the skeleton, austere concept, the shallow, dictionary defined concept, not the concept fleshed out by years of experience. He regresses to an earlier point in his conceptual development – *if* he ever moved beyond that point. He regresses to a *formal, non-experiential* understanding of the moral notions involved. He becomes like a Martian who translates our dictionary but has had no *experience* of our moral world. For a moment, he is morally blind: he has to be, for if he saw the moral reality through an experientially enriched concept, he could not act as he does. He has forgotten all that experience has taught him, all that gives moral concepts life; he is like the man whose perception of beauty has been jaded to the point of mere encyclopaedic knowledge. He sees but he does not feel; and he does not feel because he does not *see* sufficiently. Morality, for him, is a dead language.

Such thoughts prompt another challenge to realism, the challenge of undue optimism. The manner in which akrasia is made intelligible apparently makes genuine evil unintelligible. A genuinely evil action, on this anti-realist view, is one done in full, vivid, deep knowledge of its evil character. The genuinely evil man is not the nihilist, with

---

[6] These, and the ensuing remarks, are meant as preliminary ruminations about the theory of moral language implicit in Miss Murdoch's brilliantly thought-provoking *The Sovereignty of Good*; the detailed development of that theory of language seems to me a matter of great importance.
[7] Experience can enrich our conception of what, say, courage is; our concept can meanwhile remain the same.

only dictionary knowledge of moral concepts (if that), nor the man who allows non-moral considerations to *override* the moral, nor the man who makes errors of moral judgment: it is the man who knowingly does the evil precisely *because* it is evil, and whose knowledge of its evil character is as deep as ours. It is just that he *chooses* to be evil. For the realist, this is simply not possible.

It is not, however, obvious that the realist is wrong in denying this possibility. First, most such cases as readily fit some other description – the nihilist, the shallow, the overrider, the erroneous – as they do the anti-realist's description. And, second, this is supported by the ways in which we make the evil actions of others intelligible to ourselves. We see them as seduced by the trappings of evil (the devil has a monopoly of elegance); we see them as desiring to shock, to present an (excessively) rakish image to the world; we see them as insanely unintelligible. We do not pretend to see how the fact that an action is evil is ever a *prima facie* reason for doing it: we hunt for one, intelligible reason, and when the hunt fails, we plead incomprehension – and invite the agent to plead insanity.

'I did it because it was the loyal thing to do' may seem erroneous both in detail and in principle, but is at least intelligible. 'I did it because it was the disloyal thing to do' is unintelligible until *further* reasons are adduced. This linguistic point reflects a fact of moral reality: that seeing the good compels action (without ensuring it), while seeing the bad repels it (without preventing it). The final substantial challenge to moral realism comes in the form of a demand for an explanation of this posited fact; I am unclear what explanation can be given of it.

'Human language is like a cracked kettle on which we beat out tunes for bears to dance to, when all the time we are longing to move the stars to pity.' Flaubert's thought is not a novel one, but is as profound as any utterance of a philosopher. In this chapter, I have tried to show how the view of language previously sketched will lead us, finally, from the fixation with kettles to wonder at the stars. I have tried to show one way in which all the technicalities earlier discussed can bring us closer to an understanding of the profound questions that contemporary philosophy of language so often appears to neglect. I do not know whether the way considered, the way of realism, will ultimately lead to a true understanding of those questions; I do think that that way is deeply attractive and of the very greatest importance.

Bibliography

Anscombe, G. E. M., *Intention*, Oxford, 1963.

Austin, J. L., *Philosophical Papers*, Oxford, 1961.

Austin, J. L., *How To Do Things With Words*, Oxford, 1962.

Ayer, A. J., *The Concept of a Person*, London, 1963.

Bar-Hillel, Yehoshua (ed.), *Logic, Methodology, and Philosophy of Science*, Amsterdam, 1965.

Burge, Tyler, 'Reference and Proper Names', *Journal of Philosophy*, LXX (1973), pp. 425–39.

Burge, Tyler, 'Demonstrative Constructions, Reference, and Truth', *Journal of Philosophy*, LXXI (1974), pp. 205–23.

Carnap, Rudolf, *Meaning and Necessity*, Chicago, 1947.

Casey, John (ed.), *Morality and Moral Reasoning*, London, 1971.

Chomsky, Noam, *Cartesian Linguistics*, New York, 1966.

Chomsky, Noam, *Language and Mind*, New York, 1968.

Davidson, Donald, 'Theories of Meaning and Learnable Languages' in Bar-Hillel (ed.), pp. 383–94.

Davidson, Donald, 'The Logical Form of Action Sentences' in Rescher, *The Logic of Decision and Action*, pp. 81–120.

Davidson, Donald, 'Truth and Meaning', *Synthese*, VII (1967), pp. 304–23; page references to Davis, J. W. *et al.* (eds.), *Philosophical Logic*, Hingham, Mass., 1969, pp. 1–20.

Davidson, Donald, 'Causal Relations', *Journal of Philosophy*, LXIV (1967), pp. 691–703; and in Sosa (ed.), pp. 82–94.

Davidson, Donald, 'True to the Facts', *Journal of Philosophy*, LXVI (1969), pp. 158–74.

Davidson, Donald, 'On Saying That' in Davidson and Hintikka, *Words and Objections*, pp. 158–74.

Davidson, Donald, 'The Individuation of Events' in Rescher, *Essays in Honor of Carl Hempel*, pp. 216–34.

Davidson, Donald, 'In Defense of Convention T' in Leblanc, *Truth, Syntax and Modality*, pp. 76–85.

Davidson, Donald, 'Radical Interpretation', *Dialectica*, 27 (1973), pp. 313–28.

265

Bibliography

Davidson, Donald, 'Belief and the Basis of Meaning', *Synthese*, 27 (1974), pp. 309–23.

Davidson, Donald, and Harman, Gilbert (eds.), *Semantics of Natural Languages*, Atlantic Highlands, NJ, 1972.

Davidson, Donald, and Harman, Gilbert (eds.), *The Logic of Grammar*, Encino, Cal., 1975.

Davidson, Donald, and Hintikka, Jaakko (eds.), *Words and Objections: Essays on the Work of W. V. Quine*, Hingham, Mass., 1969.

Donnellan, Keith, 'Reference and Definite Descriptions', *Philosophical Review*, LXXV (1966), pp. 281–304; also in Steinberg and Jakobovits, *Semantics*, pp. 100–114, to which page references are made.

Dummett, Michael, 'Truth', *Proceedings of the Aristotelian Society*, 59 (1958–9), pp. 141–62; also in Strawson, *Philosophical Logic*, pp. 49–68, to which page references are made.

Dummett, Michael, *Frege: Philosophy of Language*, London, 1973.

Dummett, Michael, 'What is a Theory of Meaning?' in Guttenplan, *Mind and Language*, pp. 97–138.

Dummett, Michael, 'What is a Theory of Meaning? (II)' in Evans and McDowell, *Truth and Meaning*, pp. 67–137.

Evans, Gareth, and McDowell, John (eds.), *Truth and Meaning*, Oxford, 1976.

Feinberg, Joel, *Moral Concepts*, Oxford, 1969.

Frege, Gottlob, *The Basic Laws of Arithmetic*, trans. Montgomery Furth, California, 1964.

Frege, Gottlob, *Philosophical Writings*, trans. Geach and Black, Oxford, 1970.

Grice, H. P., 'Meaning', *Philosophical Review*, LXVI (1957), pp. 377–88; also in Strawson, *Philosophical Logic*, pp. 39–48.

Grice, H. P., 'The Causal Theory of Perception', *Proceedings of the Aristotelian Society*, Supp. Vol. 35 (1961), pp. 121–68.

Grice, H. P., 'Utterer's Meaning and Intentions', *Philosophical Review*, LXXVIII (1969), pp. 147–77.

Guttenplan, Samuel (ed.), *Mind and Language*, Oxford, 1975.

Haack, Susan, *Deviant Logic*, Cambridge, 1974.

Harman, Gilbert, 'Three Levels of Meaning', *Journal of Philosophy*, LXV (1968), pp. 590–602; also in Steinberg and Jakobovits, *Semantics*, pp. 66–75.

Keenan, Edward (ed.), *Formal Semantics of Natural Languages*, Cambridge, 1975.

Kripke, Saul, 'Naming and Necessity', in Davidson and Harman, *Semantics of Natural Languages*, pp. 253–355 and pp. 763–9.

Kripke, Saul, 'Outline of a Theory of Truth', *Journal of Philosophy*, LXXII (1975), pp. 690–716.

Lakoff, George, 'Hedges: A Study of Meaning Criteria and the Logic of Fuzzy Concepts', *Chicago Linguistics Studies*, 8 (1972), pp. 183–228.

Langford, C. H., 'The Notion of Analysis in Moore's Philosophy', in P. A. Schilpp (ed.), *The Philosophy of G. E. Moore*, LaSalle, Illinois, 1942, pp. 321–42.

Leblanc, H. (ed.), *Truth, Syntax, and Modality*, North Holland, 1973.

Lewis, David K., *Convention,* Cambridge, Mass., 1969.

Mackie, J. L., 'Responsibility and Language', *Australasian Journal of Philosophy,* XXXIII (1955), pp. 143–59.

Mackie, J. L., *The Cement of the Universe,* Oxford, 1974.

Mackie, J. L., *Problems from Locke,* Oxford, 1976.

McDowell, John, 'On the Sense and Reference of a Proper Name', *Mind,* LXXXVI (1977), pp. 159–85.

McFetridge, I. G., 'Propositions and Davidson's Account of Indirect Discourse', *Proceedings of the Aristotelian Society,* LXXVI (1975–6), pp. 131–45.

McGinn, Colin, 'Semantics for Nonindicative Sentences', *Philosophical Studies,* 32 (1977), pp. 301–11.

Mendelson, Elliott, *Introduction to Mathematical Logic,* New York, 1964.

Montague, Richard, *Formal Philosophy,* New Haven, Conn., 1974.

Murdoch, Iris, *The Sovereignty of Good,* London, 1970.

Nagel, Thomas, 'The Boundaries of Inner Space', *Journal of Philosophy,* LXVI (1969), pp. 452–8.

Pitcher, George (ed.), *Truth,* New York, 1964.

Putnam, Hilary, *Mind, Language, and Reality,* Cambridge, 1975.

Putnam, Hilary, *Meaning and the Moral Sciences,* London, 1978.

Quine, W. V., *Word and Object,* Cambridge, Mass., 1960.

Quine, W. V., *From a Logical Point of View,* (2nd edn), Cambridge, Mass., 1961.

Quine, W. V., *The Ways of Paradox,* (2nd edn.), Cambridge, Mass., 1976.

Reichenbach, Hans, *Elements of Symbolic Logic,* London, 1974.

Rescher, Nicholas, 'Plurality-quantification', *Journal of Symbolic Logic,* 27, 3 (1962), pp. 373–4.

Rescher, Nicholas (ed.), *The Logic of Decision and Action,* Pittsburgh, 1967.

Rescher, Nicholas (ed.), *Essays in Honor of Carl Hempel,* Hingham, Mass., 1970.

Russell, Bertrand, *Mysticism and Logic,* Harmondsworth, 1953.

Schoenman, R. (ed.), *Bertrand Russell, Philosopher of the Century,* London, 1967.

Searle, John, 'What is a Speech Act?' in Searle (ed.), *The Philosophy of Language,* Oxford, 1971, pp. 39–53.

Slobin, Dan I., *Psycholinguistics,* Glenview, Ill., 1971.

Sosa, Ernest (ed.), *Causation and Conditionals,* Oxford, 1975.

Steinberg, Danny D., and Jacobovits, Leon A. (eds.), *Semantics,* Cambridge, 1971.

Stich, Stephen P., 'What Every Speaker Knows', *Philosophical Review,* LXXX (1971), pp. 476–96.

Strawson, P. F., *The Bounds of Sense,* London, 1966.

Strawson, P. F., *Logico-Linguistic Papers,* London, 1971.

Strawson, P. F., *Freedom and Resentment,* London, 1974.

Strawson, P. F. (ed.), *Philosophical Logic,* Oxford, 1967.

Tarski, Alfred, *Introduction to Logic and to the Methodology of the Deductive Sciences,* Oxford, 1941.

Tarski, Alfred, *Logic, Semantics, Metamathematics,* Oxford, 1956.

Urmson, J. O., 'Saints and Heroes' in Feinberg, *Moral Concepts,* pp. 60–73.

Bibliography

Wallace, John, 'Positive, Comparative, Superlative', *Journal of Philosophy,* LXIX (1972), pp. 773–82.

Wheeler, Samuel C., 'Attributives and their Modifiers', *Noûs VI* (1972), pp. 310–34.

Wiggins, David, *Identity and Spatio-temporal Continuity*, Oxford, 1967.

Wittgenstein, L., *Prototractatus,* London, 1971.

Wittgenstein, L., *Tractatus Logico-Philosophicus*, trans., Pears and McGuinness, London, 1961.

Wittgenstein, L., *Philosophical Investigations,* Oxford, 1953.

Woods, M. J., 'Reasons for Actions and Desires', *Proceedings of the Aristotelian Society*, Supp. Vol. 46 (1972), pp. 189–201.

Ziff, Paul, 'On H. P. Grice's Account of Meaning', *Analysis,* 28 (1967), pp. 1–8.

Index

269

Index

271

Index

272